HUMANIZING MEDICINE

MAKING HEALTH TANGIBLE

MEMOIRS OF ENGAGEMENT WITH
A GLOBAL DEVELOPMENT AGENCY

AZIM H. JIWANI MD

◆ FriesenPress

Suite 300 - 990 Fort St
Victoria, BC, V8V 3K2
Canada

www.friesenpress.com

ISBN
978-1-03-910907-0 (Hardcover)
978-1-03-910906-3 (Paperback)
978-1-03-910908-7 (eBook)

1. Biography & Autobiography, Personal Memoirs

Distributed to the trade by The Ingram Book Company

DEDICATION

In memory of my beloved parents, to whom I owe everything.

Acknowledgments

The impulse to write this memoir was born almost a decade ago, when some friends and colleagues strongly encouraged me to record conditions, experiences, events, and challenges of my work in global health development, particularly as it related to my work with an international university and development network deeply engaged in striving to improve the quality of life of people in some parts of the developing world.

I balked at the effort required to chronicle these times, more because I could not convince myself that I had something worthwhile to share. Mahmoud Mitha, an old friend, several years ago gifted me a portable recording device to record memories and moments as they occurred to me, knowing my penchant for procrastination. Sadly, Mahmoud departed this world far too early; my gratitude to him for his friendship and encouragement and faith remains undiminished.

Doreen Littlejohn, likewise, gave me fountain pens, diaries, and sticky notes to remind me to jot down my memories that I occasionally shared with her and close friends. She understood my moods when I railed against the state of the world – the disorder, the narcissism, the narrow interests, the lack of appreciation and gratitude for having all that it considered its rightful entitlement. I cannot thank Doreen enough for her affection, friendship, and encouragement that eventually stirred me into using the enforced periods of lockdown from the COVID-19 pandemic to finally muster the energy and the will to dig deep into memories of times and places and events, but also to reconstruct thoughts, ideas, and passions that shaped my life and worldview. This reconstruction, of course, is a process fraught with risks, traps, illusions, and blind alleys of the mind, especially when viewed retrospectively and in manifestly altered times globally.

One constant, however, that runs through the period of the narrative is the steadying presence of my wife, Nilu, who bears witness to the unfolding of the period and time covered in the book. It is her patience, her gentle forbearance, her love and constancy in times of my shifting moods and occasionally flagging determination, I am convinced, that enabled me to plod though periods of blankness, doubt, and frustration while working on the chronicle. She was always there to hear me think aloud, to find a document relating to an idea or work I was referring to, and the first to read the bare early draft of chapters as they took form.

I am most grateful to Khairunessa Ahmed for her meticulous work in ploughing through hundreds of pages of old documents, lectures, memos, letters, and other odds and ends that underpinned the content of the book. She cheerfully and assiduously organized and collated information from my old files, which I needed to refer to from time to time. Khairunessa had worked as a senior secretary at the Aga Khan University and in the Office of Continuing Medical Education that I directed. I was most fortunate to find her in Vancouver, just when I needed someone who could make sense of hundreds of old documents in my files. I am also grateful to her nephew Kashif, who helped sort out some technical glitches in my computer and helped organize my book.

Many of the documents that I referred to were systematized by my secretary in Dar-es-Salaam, Fatma Mawji, who, on her own accord, downloaded onto a memory stick papers I had written while in Africa, consisting of a treasure trove of lectures, communications, memos, and other useful pieces that proved critical for the constitution of the book. I cannot thank Fatma enough for her initiative, her support, her foresight, and her faith in me.

I have gratefully received support and encouragement from many other well-wishers, who are in my thoughts as I write this book.

In the final analysis, it is a tribute to the people from all walks of life: some I have named, and others I have referred to in my encounters and anecdotes, most without their express consent or knowledge. It is my hope they will forgive the liberty I have taken in using their stories and their part in shaping my narrative. Ultimately, it is also a tribute to the countless number of players who work diligently to improve the health, well-being, and quality of life of people in developing parts of the world, individually or as members of various organizations and institutions whose mission it is to make the world more equitable and humane. The Aga Khan Development Network and its constituent agencies is one such notable organization.

TABLE OF CONTENTS

PREFACE

A number of global trends in the internal and external environments of societies worldwide are making it necessary for national and international health care organizations to change the way they operate and underscore the importance of establishing responsive services to meet the needs of populations they serve. The health status of large segments of populations in many parts of the world are not improving, and indeed, past gains in some instances are reversing. The burden of disease, changing patterns of disease, the emergence of new diseases, the aging of the population, migration, globalization, consumerism, and advances of new clinical technologies all have implications for health care organizations, and we need to anticipate how the world might change and its implications for the future. Most national health systems are trailing behind in these developments. Never have so many had such broad and advanced access to sophisticated care, but never have so many been denied access to even basic health care.

At the time this chronicle is being written, the world is in the grip of a global pandemic resulting from a new deadly pathogen, declared by the World Health Organization (WHO) to be the worst global health crisis of the century. A novel coronavirus, a strand of RNA thought to have jumped the species barrier – presumably from bats to humans – has spread rapidly and buffeted most countries and regions of the world, ravaging human health, straining inefficient health systems, and devastating economies. Previous *zoonoses*, as diseases caused by these infective particles are called, echo the history on a much smaller scale, including outbreaks such as those resulting from SARS, MERS, Ebola, the Marburg virus, and many others. But this global pandemic, while not entirely unpredicted, caught the world utterly unprepared for the resulting onslaught.

More than a century ago, the world was struck by one of the most catastrophic events in history. The 1918 influenza pandemic is estimated to have killed between twenty and fifty million people worldwide. It overlapped the end of World War I.

Called the Spanish flu – although it is not believed to have started in Spain, but Spain first reported its outbreaks – it echoes many of the public health, political, and geopolitical rhetoric of today.

At the time this book is written, more than 130 million people worldwide have been affected, with more than two million deaths reported. According to the WHO, virtually every national health care system in the world has revealed systemic weaknesses at multiple levels – some glaring, some in a state of near collapse, few sufficiently responsive or prepared. The strain is experienced by countries both of the developed North and low-income countries of the South, as well as by rapidly transitioning, industrializing, and developing countries such as Brazil and India.

To add to the complex issues relating to the organization and delivery of effective health care, the world is, at present, bedevilled by heightened levels of psychological, economic, and geopolitical anxieties. Sharp ideological divides at the time of an epoch-defining global health crisis manifest themselves in diverse ways: by an increasingly tense global trade relationship, diminished knowledge sharing, more muscular military posturing, and intensifying curtailment of human rights and dignity. A decided turn towards authoritarianism to offset popular dissent is arguably becoming a defining feature of politics in Asia, the Middle East, South America, and, indeed, the democratic West.

Health at both the individual and population level is impacted and interconnected with the multiplicity of indirect factors, such as poverty, quality and availability of education, climate change, environmental degradation, loss of biodiversity and habitat, and global trade and travel. Compounding the current crisis are geopolitical tensions and a rise of nationalism, populism, and obscurantism. While there is increasing recognition of the environmental crisis and its effects on human health through the displacement of populations, forced migration, and pollution of land and water resources, there are few manifest signs of progress towards global cooperation or coordination for combating its inexorable toll on the quality of life, especially for those most vulnerable.

The cleavage of the world into rich nations and poor ones divides care in sickness quite as sharply as it does any other aspect of the human condition. These facts determine the nature of the entire practice of medicine in developing countries and show how wide the disparity is. Something must be said about what is meant by the terms *medical care* or *health care*; a distinction can be made between finding out fundamental knowledge in the first place and finding out how best it can be applied to the community. Health sciences is the study of how the fundamental knowledge embodied in medicine and public health can best be applied to the benefit of the community and society. In this respect, medical care in developing countries differs significantly from medical care in industrialized countries. The main determinant of this divide is poverty rather than geography.

There are individuals, civil society groups, governmental and non-governmental organizations (NGOs), and institutions at local, national, regional, and international levels that are dedicated to striving for equity, quality, access, affordability, and context in human health, despite complexities, policy inertia, and economic and socio-cultural obstacles stacked against their mission and aspirations.

Thus, it is timely to reflect back to the decades of efforts in strengthening global health practices and systems, the successes and setbacks of national, international, and institutional efforts through policy actions, education, and material and human resources development and commitments. Much has been achieved globally, yet much more remains to be achieved; significant inequalities in access, quality of care, and disparities in national and global wealth distribution have widened.

This book reflects upon one individual's modest efforts and many roles undertaken over many years under the aegis of the Aga Khan Development Network (AKDN), a non-profit, international development network of repute. It narrates a story of personal search and growth and engagement. It focuses largely on challenges and experiences lived at various times and places – principally in the health and education domains – and efforts to strengthen institutional capacity, to foster internal and external linkages, and to strive towards fostering replicable models of quality medical care and health sciences education in parts of Asia and Africa. It attempts to narrate a journey of personal growth through joyful and professionally fulfilling engagements and an enterprise in global health improvement in some of the most challenging settings in the developing world. It recounts some stories, encounters, experiences, ideas, initiatives, and efforts during a period essentially between 1985 and 2010. And it reflects upon the impediments, complexities, setbacks, and failures observed and experienced in my work, and equally, the hopes, aspirations, dreams, and potentialities of the human spirit and its resilience.

An interregnum of approximately twelve years occurred between 1990 and 2002, during which time I was engaged in more regular clinical and academic work in Canada, taking the opportunity to acquire further competencies and invaluable experiences in clinical medicine, medical administration, and strategic planning. All the while I maintained a close interest in and relationship with the Aga Khan Development Network and its expanding range of programs and projects, and I continued to offer voluntary advisory and consulting services. This informal association continued after I formally retired from Aga Khan University (AKU) in 2010.

Much has changed since 1985 and the subsequent 35-year time period this account chronicles. The climate crisis is reaching a crescendo pitch with its manifold sequelae more apparent; income disparities in most regions of the world are more stark; abject poverty and marginalization are on the rise in some parts of the world; and mindless consumerism and materialism are reaching a fever pitch, encouraged by the widely prevalent economic model of disposable goods and services. It is said that we live in the *Anthropocene era*, a set of conditions developed as a result of human activities that cause deleterious effects on our physical and natural environment, and hence our own health. At the same time, societal and individual moral underpinnings and traditional foundations of ethics and values have loosened and become increasingly submerged under the ethos of uncritical *modernism*.

The journey for me has been highly intellectually and spiritually enriching and transformative; my conviction in common humanity and common ultimate destiny has deepened; diversity within a cosmopolitan ethic is more fully embedded in my consciousness; and the value and purpose I find in intellect, education, and knowledge are more ethically attuned. It has also engendered in me a sense of personal and intellectual humility and a deepened respect for the innate wisdom, grace, and traditions of the "common people" – more in tune with their own environment, communal needs, and local solutions. Above all, it has opened new horizons of contacts and interactions with innumerable people from all walks of life who have generously shared their experience, their wisdom, their insight, and their example, whether they be international or institutional leaders, staff, faculty, junior or senior doctors, nurses, public officials, administrators, or planners of public services. Particularly, it has been a privilege and pleasure working with countless patients, students, and other learners, who have taught me as much as they have learned, and who have shared their joys as much as their pain.

The mind is a capricious construct, subject to the vagaries of mood and temperament. With the passage of time, memory dims and is less clear and definitive; the past gets blurred and elusive. As one tries to mentally re-enact the memories of days gone by, the sweet and poignant memories surface more readily; the less vivid memories submerge into deeper layers of consciousness. Not being a committed diarist, to claim perfect recollection or fidelity of names, events, and times would be more than a little disingenuous. Hence, in chronicling a memoir relating to several decades in the past from the time of its writing, I can only say that I have sedulously endeavoured to reconstitute a complex and variegated career as accurately as possible, drawing from what scant sources of reference are available. Errors and inaccuracies are my responsibility only. The effort to write this limited memoir, as it comports with my personal views, perspectives, observations, sentiments, expressions, and interpretation of events and times, is bound to be imperfect and incomplete. As it has been stated:

> *Not all that exists is destined for everyone, and not everyone can see what is destined for him, nor can one know all that one sees, nor can one express (in speech) all one knows, and not everyone can write all that he can express.*

> *Nasir al-Din al-Tusi, Persian polymath,*
> *philosopher, astronomer, scholar*

The recording of this history does not imply that I held positions of great authority or power within the complex of the Aga Khan Development Network, particularly Aga Khan University and Aga Khan Health Services, with which I was most closely affiliated; nor do I claim their imprimatur. The concerned institutions did, however, give me considerable intellectual space to imagine lofty goals and ideals, the resources to search for creative solutions, the freedom and encouragement to be daring. Its history, philosophy, ethos, vision, and multi-sector engagements provided a smorgasbord of opportunities to conceive, innovate, plan, lead, coordinate, and manage a host of initiatives and programs in the wide sphere of human development internationally. That is the privilege that allowed me to make the small contribution that I express.

The thoughts and opinions expressed are offered, for what they are worth, with the hope that they represent one person's well-meaning longitudinal perspective on the history, issues, challenges, development, and trajectory of a unique institution operating in highly complex and challenging conditions. The immense good fortune that allowed an odyssey of wide-ranging forays into the domains of medicine, global health, medical education, and human development enables me to draw upon both personal experiences and times, obtained during periods of formal affiliation and, in the later years, more informal association.

The goals of Aga Khan University, as expressed by its founders, were ambitious and far-reaching. It was to serve as a model for higher education standards, knowledge, competencies, values, and ethics that serve the needs of both Muslim and non-Muslim societies in developing countries. Its vision is to develop the intellectual capital and knowledge societies of tomorrow by promoting an ethos of excellence, eclecticism, and social justice, always to develop competent and caring leaders in all aspects of social, economic, scientific, and professional endeavours. The shifting sands of the environmental, demographic, socio-economic, technological, and geopolitical conditions, coupled with the ambitious expansion of the university's geographical and academic programs, appear to strain the institution's ability to respond adequately and consistently. The external countercurrents posed by the times and place – of poor governance, weak civil society institutions, lax ethical and legal frameworks, corruption, public policy deficits – can pose powerful headwinds to even a well-intentioned institution's ability to maintain true fidelity to its values, vision, and purpose.

Much has changed over the last few decades in the work of Aga Khan University and other agencies of the Aga Khan Development Network. This is characterized by remarkable growth in its programs and its reach, particularly in Asia and Africa, and in its progress towards its ultimate goals of fostering and catalyzing pluralistic, more inclusive civil societies wherever it is engaged. It continues to assist governments, NGOs, and civil society organizations in upgrading their performance by fostering a more enabling environment for a more humanistic and inclusive society, poverty reduction, and marginalization underpinned by a cosmopolitan ethic and shared values.

The only thing constant in life is that nothing is permanent; everything is in perpetual motion. As it applies to the world at large – to environments, to nations, to societies, to fashions and cultures – it also applies to the lives of individuals and their changing needs. However, values that ensure a sustainable human future endure, values such as compassion, sharing, justice, acceptance of the other, basic rights, and dignity. These values for a shared "common humanity" could be termed *cosmopolitan ethics*, and it is my conviction in the validity and primacy of this ethic and the providential and gratifying conflation with the institutional ethos of the Aga Khan Development Network that resulted in the narrative that follows.

> *Life is a great and noble calling, not a mean and groveling thing to be shuffled through as best as we can, but a lofty and exalted destiny.*
>
> Sir Sultan Mohamed Shah, Aga Khan III

CHAPTER 1

THE EARLY YEARS: FOUNDATIONS OF AN
ECLECTIC MEDICAL EDUCATION

In the midst of winter, I found there was within me, an invincible summer.

Albert Camus

As the train approached the small desultory station, I could not help feeling some trepidation, wondering if anyone would meet me in this strange little town.

The train ride from Oslo had been quite fascinating, with flashing vistas of wide expanses of pine forests interspersed with deciduous woodlands and dotted with tidy little wooden cottages and villages. For a young man from hot, tropical Africa, setting off for the first time to learn the wonders of modern Western medicine in one of the most developed countries in the world, Norway, it looked like a world of pristine fairy-tale fantasy of children's literature, tantalizing yet somehow unreal. The small town of Tonsberg was smaller and more sparse than I had expected, although it had been a capital city in the times of the Vikings and the centre of the whaling industry in its heyday. It is generally regarded as the oldest city in Norway, founded by the Vikings in the ninth century.

I need not have worried because at the station stood an elderly gentleman, bearded and capped, holding up a sign with my name displayed in bold letters. As I got off the train, he smiled and came forward with an extended arm to take my one large suitcase. I held a bulging briefcase in my other arm. We were soon on our way to Tonsberg Hospital in an old Saab, driving down a narrow winding road that ended at the broad, arched doorway of an old, slightly grimy two-storey stone building and a cluster of other facilities. An attendant from the hospital's entrance came towards me. I told him that I was a visiting medical student to meet with Dr. Magnus Koppang, who was expecting me. He led me up a wide, granite stairway to the second floor, knocked on an office door, and gestured for me to enter. I entered a warm, little, wood-panelled office.

I was met by a diminutive, smiling, middle-aged lady who came from behind her desk with her hand held out. She welcomed me cheerfully and said that she was Dr. Koppang's wife and his secretary, that she was delighted that I had made it to the hospital, and that Dr. Koppang was very much looking forward to meeting with me as soon as he finished his ward rounds. She pointed me to a leather chair and asked if I would like coffee. As she rang for coffee, she asked me about my trip, how Dr. Christensen and his family were, and whether this was my first time in Scandinavia in a rapid succession of questions and comforting chatter. She mentioned the letter that Dr. Christensen had written to Dr. Koppang, how he had written about my supposed talent and potential in medicine and requested if he would host my visit to Norway for an elective study period. Evidently, Dr. Koppang had gladly agreed to do so.

It had started several months earlier in the cafeteria of the Mulago Hospital in Kampala, Uganda, in 1970. Dr. Christian Christensen was a visiting radiologist at the Makerere University Medical School on a sponsorship from the Norwegian government under its development aid program. He was a charming and cheery person who enjoyed sitting down with the medical students in the cafeteria, engaging in small talk, and taking a deep interest in their background and interests. We had somehow become quite friendly and would often share a table over coffee or lunch. In our fourth year at medical school, we were encouraged to broaden our learning over the more than three months' elective period set aside between the fourth and fifth year of school. Dr. Christensen had suggested I consider going to Norway for my elective, to a hospital that was headed by a friend of his, Dr. Koppang, who was a renowned neurologist and a well-loved teacher. He said he expected he could arrange free boarding and lodging for me at the hospital, but I would need to make my own way to Tonsberg.

While many of my friends and fellow students found placements at various hospitals and clinics in eastern Africa, I was excited at the prospect of travelling to Europe and seeing first-hand the practice of advanced clinical medicine for diseases rarely encountered in sub-Saharan Africa, such as coronary heart disease, neurodegenerative diseases, and other non-communicable diseases that we only learnt from textbooks. There was a markedly different disease spectrum and epidemiology between wealthy countries of the industrialized West and developing countries of sub-Saharan Africa, where life expectancy was much shorter and disease pattern was generally characterized by infections and communicable diseases, malnutrition, complications of pregnancy and childbirth, trauma, and late presentations of common conditions. Conditions such as measles, chickenpox, tetanus, meningitis, typhoid, severe protein-calorie malnutrition, and failure to thrive were amongst our daily clinical grist in the overcrowded clinics and in-patient hospital beds. Underlying poverty, lack of environmental sanitation, and poor or overcrowded housing were contributing factors to much suffering, ill health, and disability in Africa.

My parents were naturally somewhat apprehensive at my travelling to a cold and friendless, foreign, northern country for an extended sojourn, even though I tried telling them what a marvelous opportunity this was to learn and observe advanced and sophisticated medical diagnostics and treatments that at home we could only read about. They eventually saw the merit in my arguments, although I suspect their real concern was of the threat of my being closeted with blue-eyed, blonde, Nordic, liberated women popularized in movies. While my father took me to a sartorial artist of some local fame to be measured for smart-cut suits and custom-made leather shoes, my mother set about preparing and packing some savory snacks she was sure I would crave after weeks of subsisting on bland "European" food.

Back in Tonsberg, about half an hour later, in walked an erect, impressive-looking elderly man in a white coat with a head of unruly white hair, who upon seeing me sitting in a chair came forward and firmly shook my hand. He had a surprisingly firm grip and kindly twinkling blue eyes. He spent a few minutes talking to his wife, then led me to his inner book-lined office to a desk strewn with numerous documents and medical journals. He inquired about my trip, asked some questions about his friend Dr. Christensen, and probed about my interests and expectations. He said they were delighted to host me at the hospital and had made arrangements for me to stay in the staff nursing block adjacent to the hospital. He said I was free to use all the hospital facilities, join in his and other consultants' ward rounds, teaching seminars, and use the hospital medical staff room. He was heading down to the medical staff room for lunch and asked me to join him so he could introduce me to the hospital medical staff.

We walked into a large, well-lit room, like a drawing room, which was furnished with several chairs and stuffed sofas and a table that held a buffet of cold meats, breads, and cheeses. There were several men of varying ages and two or three women in the room. They greeted Dr. Koppang, who introduced me to several of them, stating that I was a medical student from East Africa who would be spending a few weeks or months with us on an elective. There was one doctor, a rather striking, blond, tall man in a white coat, who introduced himself to me at the buffet table, said his name was Dr. Lars Strom, and said he was the head of the Department of Medicine. He said he would be pleased to have me join his ward rounds and clinics, and then pointed out a variety of meat cuts and cheeses I should try, particularly a type of goat cheese famous in that area.

I was later shown to my room on the second floor of the nurses' hostel, where a housekeeper who was just finishing cleaning the corridor led me to my room. It was rather sparsely but adequately furnished. My luggage was already in the room. She showed me the common bathroom, which held an old bathtub and warm ceramic fittings. As we stepped out of the bathroom, two young women walked by along the corridor, walked towards their room up the corridor, glanced at me, giggled lightly, and entered their room. I knew this was going to be an interesting stay, and I was set to learn a lot during my time here.

The next few weeks were highly educative; the ward rounds gave many opportunities to engage in discussions around a range of cases. Surprisingly, my opinion was freely sought and appreciated. It was rewarding to feel that the thorough, systematic clinical examination and assessment skills that we were stringently taught and practised at my medical school stood me in excellent stead in holding my own with respect to the junior doctors and the medical staff.

Over the coming few weeks, I saw many diagnostic pieces of equipment in use, as well as the use of drugs and surgical treatments less familiar to me. I thoroughly enjoyed the ward rounds, where several doctors and nurses accompanied the consultant. I came across cases that stood out for their poignancy and clinical content. Dr. Koppang often demonstrated useful clinical signs and occasionally asked me to examine patients.

One day on our ward round, I remember entering a small private room where I saw a little, skeletal woman in her mid-fifties sitting in a chair. She had ashen, waxen skin, a sunken, expressionless face, and emaciated arms. Dr. Koppang glanced at her medical chart and talked to her gently in Norwegian; she said nothing beyond giving him a blank stare. There was not any teaching or discussion around this case, and we started to move on. I asked a junior doctor on our team what her problem was. He said she had a brain tumour spread from her lung. It had involved areas of her brain that affected her eating, sleep, cognition, and mental state. There was nothing more they could offer her beyond palliation and supportive care. It struck me that even in advanced countries, they were powerless to change the course of many clinical conditions they frequently encountered.

The medical and nursing staff were unfailingly courteous and generous to me, and I was soon making new friends and receiving invitations to dinners and home visits from several staff members, where I tasted cuisine entirely foreign to me: eel, salmon, cold cuts, and, I am told, shark steak, amongst other delicacies. I appreciated the long drives along country roads through alpine forests of pine, spruce, aspen, and birch along fjord-hugging roads and small hamlets where some of the staff lived. I marvelled at the neatness and orderliness of the place, quite a change from the dusty, noisy bustle and clutter of Kampala and Nairobi that I was so used to.

The relaxed mood of my hosts during these visits gave me a better insight into their quality of life, their foibles, and their seemingly minor hassles of work and life. They were proud and magnanimous people, proud of their history, culture, and traditions, who lived in a liberal democracy and a just and egalitarian society. Their main "beef" seemed to be their perceptions of their more assertive neighbour, Sweden.

One particular friend I remember fondly was an occupational therapist named Annelise Thorbensen. In my very early days in Tonsberg, she had befriended me in the hospital cafeteria, and on more than one occasion, she had saved me from making embarrassing gastronomic blunders when presented with unfamiliar delicacies and regional cuisine. She had spent a few years in the United States and spoke excellent English. I spent a few wonderful days with her and her family, who lived in Oslo. They took me to their country cottage on an island in a fjord, to which we travelled by hovercraft. Annelise, an affectionate, blue-eyed blonde, was exactly what my parents had feared. She did a lot to make my life in the frosty autumn and winter in Scandinavia comfortable and pleasant.

One afternoon in early November, while stepping out of the hospital front door, I suddenly somersaulted backwards and landed on my backside. I soon learnt that the leather soles of my finely handcrafted shoes were not made for the wintery conditions five thousand miles to the north of where they were lovingly crafted. It had snowed quite hard over the previous hours while we were busily closeted in the heated hospital interior, and the ground was covered with several inches of fine, glistening snow. Laughing, Annelise held out her arm to help me get up, which I did, my ego considerably more bruised than my bottom. She insisted we get to the market right away so I could be fitted with footwear more suited for the approaching chilly weather and more snow. She saw me fitted out in a warm pullover, a warm woollen coat, a scarf, and gloves. My introduction to the white stuff was going to remain memorable. With her, I experienced the joys of cross-country skiing – battered and bruised, but essentially intact. She had the temerity to send a picture of me flat on my back to my family back home, who, understandably, were considerably perturbed about my well-being!

My education of the country continued with visits to Bergen, the birthplace and home of the famous composer Edvard Grieg, where my former high school biology teacher in Nairobi, Mr. Georg Lonoy, lived and had very warmly invited me to spend a few days with him and his wife. They fondly remembered their time spent in Kenya on an exchange program sponsored by the Norwegian government. He was now a director of a fisheries institute and delighted in showing me the local cultural sites, and I got insight into the life and culture of the region. I visited several other towns and cities in Norway, including the place of birth of great explorers like Roald Amundsen, who led the famous Antarctic expedition in 1911, and Thor Heyerdahl, an ethnographer and adventurer who sailed the South Pacific on a raft and later in another vessel called the *Ra II*. Annelise had proudly taken me to the museum that housed the *Kon-Tiki* and the raft *Ra*.

Broadening Horizons: A New World Experience

I decided I needed to move on to broaden my knowledge of Western health care and culture. One day, I mentioned this to Dr. Koppang, who wrote to a friend who worked at the famed Karolinska Institute in Stockholm, a world-renowned hospital and research centre.

I was well received at Karolinska and saw some advanced medical and surgical techniques. On one occasion, I was taken into an operating room where the neurosurgeon was using a stereotactic operating frame to remove a brain tumour. This was not a technique I had heard of in Africa. I was peering into the world of advanced medical technologies, which in years to come stood me in good stead in my career.

In my discussions with doctors and others, I tried to understand socialized medical care's intricacies and its challenges. I was generally impressed by the societal cohesion and discipline in Scandinavia, although this facet of health care and society was not something I had given much thought to at home.

Soon I developed itchy feet again, and a hospital-recommended travel agent booked an extensive train travel package for me. I travelled to Copenhagen and then Helsinki, staying a few days, and continued onwards covering a number of countries in Western Europe, including passing through divided Berlin. I remember well the communist East German security officers boarding the train in the middle of the night, scrutinizing the passports and documents carefully. I had no trouble crossing the tense divide.

I travelled as frugally as possible, often travelling at night in order to save on the cost of lodging, staying in student hostels, and finding fresh fruit in the markets as my main source of nourishment. I was very short on funds but managed to obtain an interesting cultural experience creatively. I reached Paris, where, while waiting at Gare du Nord to catch a train to Calais and onwards to London, I was very artfully separated from my heavy suitcase, which I had put down for a moment to study the timetables. Fortunately, I had held on to my briefcase, which held my passport, my tickets, and other essentials. That, too, was education, which I believe I took cheerfully in stride.

~ ❧ ~

I reached London uneventfully, from where I had started my European travels several months prior, having passed through more than half a dozen European countries. A few months earlier, I had taken a ferry from Newcastle in England to Stavanger in Norway, meeting interesting people on the route. I remember two sociable girls from Zurich – Helen and Françoise – and a university lad from Malaysia on the overnight ferry trip, out on his first solo foreign foray like me.

In London, I had the opportunity to visit and hear lectures and attend grand rounds at some renowned medical institutions, such as the Great Ormond Street Hospital for Children and the Queens Square Institute of Neurology, as well as visit famous museums, such as the Museum of Anatomy at the Royal College of Surgeons in Lincoln's Inn Field. The London School of Hygiene and Tropical Medicine, founded in 1899 by Sir Patrick Manson, after a donation by the Indian

Parsi philanthropist Banerjee Dinshaw Petit, is one on the most prestigious institutions in the field of public health and infectious diseases and lived up to its august reputation. Dr. Patrick Manson, a physician in Asia, where he correctly deduced the cause of a widespread tropical parasitic disease – filariasis – also mentored Ronald Ross, who discovered the cause of malaria in 1897, winning the Nobel Prize for his efforts. A visit to the Wellcome Trust, a charitable foundation that funds urgent health challenges facing human health, enhanced my understanding of global interconnections, health, and well-being.

First Love: Enduring Passion

My interest in and love for medicine had started early in my life. In my early teens, after having passed through the usual childhood dreams of future career plans – soon discarded – to become an airplane pilot or a big game hunter, I settled in my unwavering determination to become a doctor with a single-mindedness that surprised a lot of people. At around fourteen or fifteen, I pestered my father to buy several lots of old medical books from an auction house, put to auction by some retiring or returning British doctors on their way back to the home country after Kenya got its independence from Britain in 1963. These big fat volumes, over thirty of them, included some well-known titles such as *Samson Wright's Physiology*; several volumes of anatomy dissection manuals; outdated books on surgery, biochemistry, and bacteriology; *Synopsis of Medicine* by Sir Henry L. Tidy, the consulting physician to the royal household; W.A.D. Anderson's *Synopsis of Pathology*; and at least ten volumes of an old edition of the classical *British Encyclopedia of Medical Practice*. I derived great joy from browsing through these books at odd times, even in bed at night, neglecting to pay sufficient attention to my school homework, which before long caught my father's attention and got me a well-deserved ticking off. My mother picked up these heavy tomes lying around the house. Finally, she insisted that I get a proper bookshelf and pick up my own books after myself. The fascination with the complex inner structures of the human body, healthy and diseased – microbes with long names; constituents of human blood and urine; the structure of tissues under magnification of a high-power microscope – never left me and was not an infrequent source of aggravation and puzzlement to my regular schoolteachers, whom I pestered with questions on the minutiae of human anatomy and physiology.

Venerable Heritage: Germs and Germination

Upon my return to Kampala, I felt somehow more edified, more worldly, certainly more confident, and perhaps a bit cockier. But I had also acquired a new appreciation of my medical school and its environs of the very high prevalence of disease, advanced and diverse pathologies, limited resources, a severe shortage of qualified health care staff, and its valiant struggle to serve and educate growing populations.

Makerere University was established in 1922 as a humble technical school and became one of the oldest and most prestigious English universities in Africa. HRH the Duke of Gloucester cut the first sod of the foundation grounds in 1923. New courses were soon established, including medicine, agriculture, veterinary science, engineering, and education. It became one of the most admired colleges in British Colonial Africa.

Makerere University Medical School was founded in 1924. In 1949, Makerere was brought into a special relationship with the University of London and became one of the University Colleges of East Africa, offering courses leading to the general degrees of the University of London. With the independence of the countries of East Africa, the University Colleges of Dar-es-Salaam, Nairobi, and Makerere were made constituent colleges of the newly formed University of East Africa, which was established in 1963. It became the new guarantor of standards and the apex of the East African systems of education. The special relationship with the University of London came to an end, and degrees of the University of East Africa began to be awarded. Before long, there were some tensions, with differences in the development interests of the three African countries and the three university colleges. In July 1970, the University of East Africa gave way to the three independent Universities of Makerere, Nairobi, and Dar-es-Salaam.

Over its almost a century of existence, Makerere has hosted many eminent visitors, including the Crown Prince and later the Sultan of Zanzibar; the Prince of Wales Edward VIII; Her Majesty Queen Elizabeth; the presidents of Kenya, Tanganyika, and Zambia; and many other prominent figures. It developed numerous international collaborations and partnerships over the years, as it expanded its range of educational offerings and research.

In my early years, I had little appreciation of the complex nature and challenges of higher education, especially in a resource-constrained environment of newly decolonized countries and their delicate political and diplomatic dance with their former colonial overlords and in the milieu of the competing dogmas of the

Cold War. Little did I realize that my subconscious assimilation of the comparative psychologies and paradigms of the advanced industrialized societies and those of developing societies – which had little experience of governance and political leadership during the period of the last few decades of the twentieth century – would lead me later in my career to better appreciate the imprints of history, culture, the legacy of colonialism, and the multidimensional nature of development.

In the 1960s and 1970s, Makerere University Medical School was staffed by a wonderful assemblage of an international faculty, visiting faculty, and researchers. I fondly recall that the head of surgery was a cricket-loving Scotsman, Sir Ian McAdam; the head of medicine was Professor Parsons, an American endocrinologist; and pathology Professor Michael Hutt was a gentle and cultured Englishman, who would occasionally offer rides to the students on sultry days in his little Morris Minor.

My first memory of the first day of medical school is that of an elderly man in a short-sleeved white shirt and with a head of balding, shocking, unruly, grizzled hair, who walked into the anatomy lecture hall and got right into introducing cadaver dissection by illustrating the anatomical position, saying, "This is the anatomical position." This remarkable man was Professor Wheeler Haines, a renowned anatomist and embryologist. He had wonderful stories to tell about his younger days as a student of anatomy and surgery, where he had made significant contributions to human and primate anatomy. There was Dr. Walker, a visiting anthropologist and anatomist doing research in comparative primate anatomy and paleoanthropology, a scientific study of the origins of humans.

One of the most fascinating lecturers and demonstrators in anatomy was Dr. John Church, who we later learnt was a winner of the Gold Medal in Anatomy from the Royal College of Surgeons of England. Our pathology teacher, Dr. Sandy Templeton, brought arcane concepts to life with his humour and artful cartoon illustrations on the blackboard, and his packed daily lunchtime tutorial sessions included post-mortem displays of freshly harvested body parts laid out on the pathology dissection table, which gave it the appearance of a grisly marketplace. Slicing through lungs oozing tuberculous pus, hardened cirrhotic liver, or slices of brain inflamed and congested with findings of acute meningitis, he made pathology come "alive" – this while we sat at the elevated side benches quickly munching our sandwich lunches and sipping hot coffee, at the same time trying to answer questions he fired our way.

Later, these pathology demonstration classes were taken over by Dr. John Owor, a brilliant Ugandan pathologist, who in later years became a dean in the Faculty of Medicine. Many memorable teachers come to mind, amongst them Dr. Buck, an American physiologist who kept a hippo in a large swimming pool–like pit outside the physiology labs; his research interest was the respiratory physiology of hippos and other animals. Dr. Dutt, an Indian gastrointestinal physiologist, created gastric pouches in dogs to study digestive processes, and Dr. Itiaba, a Canadian renal physiologist, made us collect our urine to test its specific gravity under different conditions. The department was headed by Professor Wright, a quiet and elegant Englishman with a special interest in neurophysiology, from whom we learnt about the innate reflexes of the nervous system of felines – from cats to lions!

The clinical departments also had a very multinational mix of clinical and teaching staff, with, over time, an increasing number of local faculty joining the junior ranks and advancing up the totem pole of seniority. Senior faculty included Professor Trussell, the head of obstetrics and gynecology, an expert gynecological surgeon who demonstrated to us the technique for the repair of the all-too-common and highly debilitating and distressing vaginal fistula, literary a hole in the wall of the vagina resulting from the extreme trauma of unattended childbirth labour and delivery. Professor Krishna Sommers, a highly dedicated mentor and a renowned cardiologist, obtained his early training in South Africa and was well aware of the far-reaching effects of apartheid practices and colonial history on local development of institutions of higher learning in Africa and elsewhere. He was soon joined by Dr. Paul d'Arbela, an outstanding Ugandan physician and cardiologist, who set high standards, demanded much from his students, and brooked no nonsense or delays. He later was also appointed dean of postgraduate medical education at Makerere. Dr. Anil Patel, an irascible but brilliant chest physician doing world-class research on tuberculosis, was the in-charge consultant of the large TB ward, which he watched over like a mother hen.

Surgery had Professor Huckstep, an indefatigable orthopedic and trauma surgeon, whose little handy reference manual we used to carry in the side pockets of our white coats; Dr. Dixon, a pediatric surgeon who had a visible surgical scar on his upper lip from childhood repair of cleft lip; Dr. Loeffler, a German surgeon who loved teaching and loved Africa in equal measure; and Mr. Ogondo, a Ugandan general surgeon who was also later appointed dean of the medical faculty.

Professor Olav Erickson, a Norwegian eye specialist, headed the Ophthalmology

Department. Dr. Kim, a Korean neurosurgeon, taught us how to observe clinical signs and drill burr holes into the skull to relieve increased pressure on the brain from the all-too-frequent head injury patients presenting to the hospital in the days before modern technologies like the CT scans were available. Always cool and elegantly dressed Professor German, a sophisticated Englishman, headed the Psychiatry Department; his finely pressed suits seemed a bit out of place in Uganda's hot and sweltering environment, although we never saw him sweat.

Dr. John Bennett headed the Preventive Medicine Department for many years. There was also a smattering of clinicians and staff from countries such as Yugoslavia, Czechoslovakia, and the United States in various departments. This virtual United Nations of faculty enriched our exposure and learning immeasurably, and more than just about medicine and surgery. A number of them were on short-term teaching and research programs, others on longer-term contracts sponsored by bilateral or multilateral arrangements with countries and institutions. If there was a hint of paternalism in their work, it was usually accepted as part of their goodwill towards their less materially endowed brethren. Invariably, it seemed to me they loved what they were doing and had an affinity for all things African; some chose to commit their entire lives to the uplift of resource-poor societies.

The main teaching hospital, the Mulago National Hospital, was really two hospitals: a new one-thousand-bed, six-floor multispecialty hospital, and the old Mulago Hospital, which was a cluster of low buildings that later housed special units such as the tuberculosis ward, children's malnutrition treatment unit, burns unit, lymphoma research unit, and amputee and rehabilitation units. Old Mulago Hospital was founded in 1913 by Albert Cook, a medical missionary, and the new Mulago National Hospital was commissioned in 1963. It now has a capacity of approximately two thousand beds and includes various special units and services, such as the Infectious Diseases Institute. The hospital initially started as a treatment centre for venereal diseases and sleeping sickness.

The medical school library was also founded by Dr. Albert Cook, later Sir Albert Cook, in 1924, and it houses his original handwritten patient notes dating back to 1900. He was known for his efforts to train Africans to become skilled medical workers, and he also founded another hospital in Kampala, namely Mengo Hospital.

Early in its history, renowned teachers, clinicians, and Christian missionaries, driven by their calling and innate curiosity, had brought many to this part of the world. They were awed by the verdant countryside and the rich canvas of diseases and pathologies all around them, and they embarked on field studies and observations that proved to be classics of medical research, opening up new channels of inquiry into fundamental questions of the nature of many diseases. A number of them were evangelical missionary doctors such as Dennis Burkitt, a British surgeon, who had made observations on environmental factors, such as the effects of altitude on the distribution of malaria and its effects on the prevalence of tumours in children, later called Burkitt's lymphoma. He had observed children with swellings on their jaws that were associated with tumours at unusual sites. He kept copious notes and made brilliant clinical deductions.

In another ground-breaking study, by sheer obstinance and perseverance, Dr. Burkitt measured the fecal output of Africans and Europeans and concluded that the refined European diet had a bearing on the prevalence of many diseases found in the European populations but rarely seen in the African people, who had deviated little from their traditional way of life. He linked conditions like diverticulosis, gallbladder disease, hemorrhoids, appendicitis, obesity, varicose veins, heart disease, and certain cancers to a low-fibre diet. Professor Hutt and other observers hypothesized on the relationship between exposure to mosquitoes and other insects to common local conditions such as tumours and big spleen disease.

A relatively common presentation at the Mulago Teaching Hospital was a condition of *Kaposi's sarcoma*, a tumour of lymph nodes, blood vessels, and skin caused by a virus. It was much later linked to the human immunodeficiency virus (HIV), which causes AIDS. Davis first described *tropical endomyocardial fibrosis* in Uganda in 1948, which was relatively prevalent in low-income countries of Africa, Asia, and South America. Dr. John Stanfield and others made important contributions to the study of diseases of malnutrition such as *kwashiorkor* and *marasmus*.

The power of clinical and epidemiological observation, deduction, and intelligent application of basic pathophysiological sciences was essentially the cornerstone of clinical practice and research in those days. Laboratory and high-tech imaging and other laboratory research modalities were limited. There was certainly no dearth of living clinical learning material. There was, however, an early model of an electron microscope in the Anatomy Department, being used by some American scientists.

Apart from the main teaching hospital, our learning and teaching were conducted at various sites and in the field, including visits to villages, farms, factories, rural health facilities, and specialized institutes, such as the Virus Research Center in Entebbe and the Butabika Psychiatric Hospital.

One day, our student group was driven to visit a leprosarium, a leprosy hospital, centre, and village in an outlying district of Uganda. Leprosy was endemic in Uganda, as in many tropical and subtropical countries of Asia and Africa. Pioneers like Dr. J.A. Kinnear Brown had made outstanding contributions to the treatment of leprosy in Uganda and in 1932 had developed the Uzuakoli Settlement for leprosy patients and inaugurated a mass treatment campaign throughout Uganda. He also tested the use of the BCG vaccine, used for prevention of tuberculosis, in the prevention of leprosy, a disease caused by a similar bacterium to the tuberculosis bacillus.

The damning impact of leprosy – on individuals, their families, and society – is as old as human history. The many images and connotations that have accumulated throughout history and its metaphoric resonance gives it more significance than it should. Not uncommonly, persons afflicted with leprosy were inhumanely isolated, forcibly detained, and shunned. They were abandoned or isolated in leprosy colonies and neglected. Yet, this affliction does not deserve the fear and the myths surrounding it. Also called Hansen's disease, it is a slow-growing bacterial infection that can affect the nerves, skin, eyes, and lining of the nose. It does not spread easily, and treatment is very effective. However, left untreated, the nerve damage can result in the crippling of hands and feet and its signature deformities. It is not easily transmissible and requires prolonged close contact with someone who has a form of the disease that is untreated.

The centre we were taken to consisted of a single-storey hospital, an outpatient clinic, a rehabilitation workshop, and a workshop for the production of splints and prostheses for leprosy patients. The tranquil, well-cared-for grounds had small gardens and tracts of land brought under cultivation. There was an adjoining village and a school and playing fields. It was staffed by two or three medical assistants, nurses, physiotherapists, a leprosy dresser, and the resident medical officers.

The hospital and centre were under the supervision of a German physician and surgeon, a formidable middle-aged woman of great dedication, tenacity, faith, and medical capability. She gave us an overview of the work of the leprosarium, one of several in Uganda at that time, with great emphasis on countering stigma and fallacious beliefs about the disease; she was a fervent proponent of re-integrating patients and their families into productive lives. She reviewed advances in the early diagnosis and drug treatment of leprosy, as well as rehabilitation programs of the centre. We got to understand the remarkable surgical correction on limbs and diseased tissues of the sufferer. The small operating theatre where she operated seemed quite inadequate in comparison to the bold initiatives and ambitions that were taken by the voluntary organizations and the Department of Health of Uganda.

⟡

I remember one day when a group of us were driven in a Land Rover to the idyllic countryside and its small rural health centre. After spending some time listening to the health officer explaining to us their work and procedures, we were all getting hungry and restless to explore the surrounding lush countryside. My friends dared me to "borrow" the Land Rover (like a Jeep) for us to take a joyride into the country. The driver, a trusting fellow, called Omari, had left the vehicle key on its dashboard while enjoying a cup of chai with his friends, the Askaris and other drivers.

The temptation of the joyride and the dare was too much; I jumped into the driver's seat, while my friends piled up into the heavy vehicle. The car responded instantly, and off we set to enjoy the rough red dirt roads in the lush countryside, the sturdy vehicle picking up speed as we shot down a small valley into a neighbouring little village, with several food stalls by the side of the road. We stopped by one open stall displaying posters of local models in traditional dresses, the ubiquitous anti-malaria pills, and the Ministry of Health poster depicting family planning virtues, though the thing that caught our attention was a pile of local pastries and stacked crates of soft drinks. We piled out of the car and ordered plate-fuls of local pastries. I ordered local "pies," which turned out to be the tastiest pie I had ever eaten. I found out it was made out of local soya beans, fried in a pastry of local ground flour. I also learned from the stall owner that the protein-rich recipe was suggested to him by one of our public health faculty members as a recipe to counter the effects of protein malnutrition, very common in children and women. It was proving to be a best seller amongst the local population, who had tinkered with the recipe until they got just the right mix of taste, nutrition, and acceptability to the local palate. High levels of poverty meant that people largely subsisted on cooked banana, maize, and groundnuts, and rarely could afford animal protein sources. We discovered the value of itinerant education, and better appreciated the value of the outreach of the university enterprises in promoting public health by other means.

Upon our return to the health centre, we found Omari naturally somewhat anxious and unsure how to react to our unsanctioned "borrowing" of the vehicle that he was responsible for. But he was gracious in forgiving our youthful prank since all was well upon our returning the vehicle in good repair. And sharing some pastries and a good laugh seemed to put him in a forgiving mood.

These germs of subliminal education had not yet crystallized into a definite form in my mind, but the cumulative effects were to have a significant bearing on my future perspectives. Makerere University freely offered opportunity to attend a wide range of academic debates and invited speaker programs to its students and the public on a broad range of political, social, cultural, developmental, and global issues particularly as it applied to Africa and Africans.

A leading and highly admired academic, well loved and applauded by students of all faculties, was Professor Ali Mazrui, the professor and head of political science at Makerere, whose trenchant analysis of issues and fiery discourses of development issues always resulted in standing-room only attendance whenever he was on stage. He also directed the World Order Models Project in the Department of Political Science, a project that brought together political scientists from across the world to discuss what an international route to lasting peace might be. Born in Mombasa, Kenya, he had obtained his doctorate from Oxford University, published several books, was a prolific writer and public speaker, and in later years taught at several prestigious American universities. Amongst his many distinctions in later years, he was recognised as Top 100 Public Intellectuals in 2005.

There were other forums for broadening the mind and perspectives. One I recall well was an evening university forum soon after Dr. Christiaan Barnard, the South African heart surgeon, performed the world's first human-to-human heart transplant in December 1967 in Cape Town. There was a thrill of excitement as we were drawn into pondering questions of scientific advances, ethics, and resource allocation.

The final year at Makerere taken upon my return from Europe was more summative and, I believe, somehow more keenly syncretic. It aroused in me an appreciation of a broader compass of global medicine and health care.

The graduation convocation itself was noteworthy because it presaged a period of transition from a relatively peaceful and harmonious society to one of brutality, dislocation, disruption, and tribal warfare in Uganda under the rule of Idi Amin Dada, the self-proclaimed "President for Life." He administered the rites of passage marking our graduation by personally handing us our degree certificates. But few could have believed these were portents of stresses and degradations for years to come. We were not to know at that stage the impending upheaval in the lives of millions, a breakdown in the structure and processes of public services such as health care and education, which had taken decades of sacrifice, hard work, and commitment to construct. There was also wide-spread suppression and incarceration of the local intelligentsia.

This was, sadly, not an uncommon pattern of the rule in parts of Africa in the post-colonial period, and its setbacks and impact on the quality of life of millions often depended on the degree of kleptocracy, autocracy, and egocentricity of the head of state at that time. So, we celebrated our graduation in the usual way with our family and friends, little realizing we were witnessing an end of an era of pluralism and traditional egalitarianism of the African culture in Uganda and its far-reaching effects on its neighbouring countries, which had to deal with its spin-off effects. This marked the end of my first formal training program in medicine, and we were let loose to seek further training and career choices. It also marked the end of the halcyon days of youth.

Maturing Outlook: Career Progression

Upon returning home to Nairobi with a newly minted degree in medicine with honours, the requirements were to proceed with at least a year of internship in order to be registered as a medical practitioner. There were exciting choices; having experienced a taste of foreign culture, I briefly considered a post at the Queen Elizabeth Hospital in Hong Kong as another potentially exciting adventure. However, I settled on going to the U.K. where most opportunities existed for further training, and it was a track well-trodden by many earlier graduates from many parts of the world, especially from the Commonwealth countries. This marked the beginning of the next phase of my educational development.

Following a period of the basic assessment of medical knowledge, undertaken at a charming small hospital in Pontefract, Yorkshire, I soon landed an interview for a "house surgeon's" (intern) post at a hospital in North London. A minimum of one-year rotations as a house physician and surgeon was required to be fully registered with the General Medical Council of the United Kingdom.

On presentation for the interview, I found myself as one of about six or seven young graduates, both local and from several other countries, waiting nervously in a small waiting room, vying for the one opening offered at the hospital. When my name was called, I walked into a room and faced a panel of about five or six people sitting behind a long desk, amongst them two consultant surgeons, two surgical registrars, and the head nurse of the surgical service for the hospital. The interview seemed fairly desultory, centred largely around background and interests, and a few questions on the basic management of surgical issues.

I seemed to have satisfied them, since a few hours later, I was called in and congratulated. I was told I would be a house surgeon on Mr. Hendry's firm. He was one of the surgeons who had interviewed me, with piercing blue eyes peering over the edge of his steel-rimmed reading glasses. On my way out, I ran into Mr. Hendry's outgoing surgical registrar. He had just completed two years of training under Mr. Hendry. He quickly deflated my enthusiasm for the job by informing me I was going to be working for one of the toughest, most obnoxious, most demanding, impossible to please so and so, and that he felt sorry for me and good luck to me!

With that happy thought in mind, I decided to be well prepared psychologically for the toil and sleepless nights expected in a house surgeon's life. I showed up early Monday morning a week later and presented myself at the two-storey impressive brick building with a tall, peaked clock tower, the Administration Building of the Highlands General Hospital. I was met by a kindly, cheerful, middle-aged lady at a desk. She was expecting me and took me to various desks and places, where I was provided two white coats and a pager; shown the hospital dining room, where I was expected to take my meals; and shown a corner room on the second floor of the staff residence that was to be my home for the next six months. It was a small but pleasant room, with a dormer window, a bed, chairs, a desk, and a wall-mounted bookshelf.

Located on World's End Lane in Winchmore Hill in North London, at first sight, I had been struck by the unusual design and layout and striking appearance of this rambling hospital complex. It was laid out on a fifty-three-acre site and was made up of around eighteen separate L-shaped two-storey pavilions or villas, constructed of yellow brick and red brick dressings in the Queen Anne revival style. They resembled large domestic houses. I later learnt that it had started its career in 1885 as a convalescent hospital, called the Northern Convalescent Fever Hospital, in order to cater to the care of patients with infectious diseases such as typhoid, scarlet fever, and diphtheria.

Later, Fever and Convalescent were dropped from the name of the hospital. It later was used to treat patients with advanced tuberculosis. They were treated with heliotherapy (sunlight treatment), a popular form of treatment before the advent of anti-tuberculous drugs. A special unit for children was later added, to look after children who survived *encephalitis lethargica* – a residual Parkinson's-like brain damage disorder from the Spanish influenza epidemic – who needed long-term care. Various pavilions were later closed and boarded up, and others were upgraded to serve as an acute care facility, in concert with the neighbouring Chase Farm Hospital.

Regrettably, this beautiful hospital closed its doors in 1993, and the site was sold to property developers. My memories are quite vivid of long walks, often in the middle of the night, from one pavilion to another where the patients were located, or to the *Casualty*, as the Emergency Department was called. Equally tantalizing are memories of late-night trysts in the little side ward kitchens, where the night nurses, sympathetic to the stressful life of a houseman, would offer coffee and buns and a generous hug in the dimmed lights of the ward.

With some trepidation I showed up for my first full day of work, in my new white coat, pager clipped in the top pocket, armed with a new copy of the "House Surgeon's Survival Guide" in the side pocket of the lab coat. The rest of the medical paraphernalia loaded onboard the many pockets of the doctor's white coat included a stethoscope discreetly protruding in the other side pocket; a reflex hammer; a miniature pocket version of the otoscope and an ophthalmoscope for the examination of eyes, throat, and ears; and a penlight for examining eyes and various dark orifices. Newly qualified I might be, but I was armed to the teeth to take on human sufferings from inflamed gallbladders to hemorrhoids.

That day was the surgical outpatients' day, and the waiting room soon filled up with men and women of all ages in various states of wear and tear, some clutching letters from their general practitioners (GPs) in their hands. The charge nurse showed me a desk where I was to collect referral notes, enter some preliminary information and histories in the patient files, and then assist the consultant and the registrar, who would be doing most of the heavy lifting in caring for the patients.

Soon I was joined by a man also in a white coat, who came over and introduced himself to me. He was Mr. Akuma Akuma, FRCS, who had joined a few days prior as the new registrar in Mr. Hendry's surgical firm. He was from Ghana but had lived for many years in England and obtained his basic surgical training mostly in Scotland. He seemed quite pleasant and helpful. He showed me the paperwork that would be required to enter the patients onto the surgical list; the list I found extended well into the following year. He walked into his consulting room and started seeing patients ushered into his room by a nurse.

And then came Mr. W. Garden Hendry, FRCS. Middle-aged, slightly on the heavy side, but erect, looking sharp in a well-worn blue pinstripe suit, he clearly had an aura of authority around him. He would brook no nonsense, and everyone, including the hospital administration it seemed, was well aware of this. He welcomed me curtly but politely, nodded at the charge nurse, and entered his consulting room. Soon patients started streaming into the examination rooms, and I noted it was exactly nine o'clock. Names were added for prostate surgery, gallbladder removal, varicose vein strips, stomach ulcer surgery, hernias, and many other surgical procedures to be performed.

But it was the following day, which was Mr. Hendry's operating day, that I was baptized by fire into the world of medicine; I soon learnt what was expected of me. Little had been told to me of my precise duties; it was assumed I would soon learn and show the necessary initiative. I showed up a little before eight to the surgeons' changing room of the operating suite and found both Mr. Hendry and Akuma already attired in their green surgical scrubs. Mr. Hendry was reading the *Times* newspaper, with his trademark reading glasses perched low on his nose. He said, "Good morning, Azim. Did you sleep well?"

"Yes, very well, thank you, sir," I said, embarrassed at showing up later than what I supposed was normally expected of the most junior member of the surgical team.

Akuma showed me a locker that I could use to change into the surgical scrubs and operating room boots, which were two sizes too big for me. He asked me if I had seen the surgical list for the day. I said I hadn't. A theatre nurse popped her head into the doorway of the room at that moment and said, "We're ready for you, Mr. Hendry."

Akuma and I followed Mr. Hendry into the theatre scrubbing area, and after a thorough scrubbing of hands and arms up to the elbows, we were helped into our green operating gowns and gloves. The patient was already anesthetized and lying on the operating table, the anesthetist holding a face mask on the patient's face and twiddling the dials of his anesthetic machine, the patient's vital signs bleeping on a raised oscilloscope. The large, bright operating room was full of gleaming surgical instruments; a table by the side of the patient held an extensive array of stainless-steel surgical instruments, and a nurse, garbed in a green surgical gown, cap, and mask, was setting things in order on the trolley. Two more nurses were floating around the theatre in quick, silent, sure-footed movements as they expertly drew more instruments from their sterile packaging and autoclaves.

The first case of the day was a cholecystectomy, removal of a diseased gall-bladder; the patient was a middle-aged woman. Mr. Hendry and Akuma parked themselves across the operating table from each other, adjusted the huge ceiling-mounted operating light, started to cleanse the abdomen with two different surgical disinfectants, and draped the patient in green sheets, leaving a portion of the upper abdomen on the right side bare. Mr. Hendry asked me to stand by his left side. Then, almost as an afterthought, he said, "Oh, this is Dr. Azim Jiwani, my new house surgeon. He is from beautiful Kenya." The people in the operating room nodded and made some vague sounds of welcome.

"Scalpel," he called out, and smartly the scrub nurse slapped into his hand a surgical scalpel. He immediately made a deep, bold, clean incision on the patient's abdomen just below the ribcage, and multiple tiny rivulets of blood soon filled the incision site. Calmly, he clipped the "bleeders" with small artery forceps and tied them off within seconds. The nurse handed me a pair of scissors with which I shortened the ends of the surgical catgut. He quickly proceeded to open the layers of the abdominal wall. Within less than ten minutes, he was reaching his hand into the patient's abdominal cavity to reach the distended gallbladder, quickly identifying the blood vessels below the liver and the anatomical markers in the tight space, while I was dutifully retracting the open wound with a curved retractor, which I had been handed tactfully by the nurse, all the while craning my neck to get a better view into the open surgical site. The rest of the operation proceeded smoothly, and a few minutes later, the whole turgid gallbladder was removed. The nurse handed Mr. Hendry a kidney dish in which he placed the gallbladder. He incised the gallbladder open with a surgical knife and out poured dark viscous liquid bile, and a large number of gallstones tinkled into the metallic dish.

In the meantime, Akuma had been attending to the liver bed where the gall-bladder had been attached to check for any bleeding or injury to the liver and the blood vessels and ducts. There was a faint buzzing sound and small puffs of acrid smoke as he cauterized tiny bleeding points with a diathermy tip – an electric current to stop the tiny bleeding points. Soon the abdominal wall was closed in layers; I had the honour of snipping the sutures that Mr. Hendry and Akuma applied with amazing speed and precision. The whole procedure had lasted about an hour, but it was one of the slickest and cleanest operations I had ever seen.

The day continued with a series of cases until about four in the afternoon – a string of operations for enlarged prostates, stomach ulcers, resections of colon cancer. By the end of the day, I was feeling exhausted but oddly elated at my first contact with real patients since graduating. I soon got into the swing of quickly verifying the identity of the patients, their histories, ensuring their latest blood tests were clearly posted in the chart, requisitioned units of blood were on hold from the blood bank, and preoperative antibiotics had been administered. Between patients, Mr. Hendry read his newspaper and occasionally had a cup of tea, Akuma wrote long operative notes, while I frantically tried to not again be caught off guard regarding a patient's history or other essential information.

Soon I got into the rhythm of what was expected of a good house surgeon, and I tried to keep a step ahead. I boned up on house surgeon's manuals, which were full of survival tips of new junior medical staff: efficient clerking of patients, obtaining and chasing the necessary tests, booking units of blood from the blood banks, dropping into the pathology labs to obtain and understand the pathology reports, ensuring consent forms were properly understood and signed, highlighting any known allergies, informing patients and their families of the care plan and surgical procedures, and countless other chores.

We had two or three full operating days a week and at least two days of ward rounds. The ward rounds were almost sacredly ceremonial. The wards were squeaky clean, the patients lying in their beds in the open male and female or children's wards. An assemblage of ward staff – most of the nurses, from nursing students, the junior to the most senior nurses – often joined the ward rounds, with the ward head nurse ensuring that everyone was presentable. The house surgeon, sometimes a senior house officer, and the registrar made up the medical vanguard. A ward trolley holding all the patient records clipped into a metallic clipboard awaited the consultant's arrival. The other consultant, Mr. Farley, had his own surgical team, but they rounded on different days, and their rounds tended to be much less formal.

Upon arrival, usually attired in his usual blue pinstripe suit and different ties, Mr. Hendry was received by the head nurse and the ward round began. These were usually patients who had had their operations, a few admitted preoperatively for diagnostic tests or being treated before they were fit enough for surgery. As we walked to each patient's bedside, I would be expected to give a brief summary of the progress of that patient. Mr. Hendry would often ask what his postoperative hemoglobin level was, how much blood the patient had been transfused with, his or her temperature, the pathology report. All this was expected to be recited without recourse to the patient's file. After a few blunders, I soon learnt the value of making late-night rounds the day before or very early morning on the day of the round, quickly going through the file of each patient and trying to not mix up the critical data of different patients. The patients who had undergone prostatectomy – surgical removal of an enlarged or cancerous prostate gland by an open bloody operation – or those who had portions of the stomach or bowels excised often required the most blood and careful monitoring after their operation.

The nurses were a treasure; they often saved my bacon, particularly in the early weeks and months into my job. They would sometimes slip me a note with the patient's latest numbers jotted on it or mime a figure behind Mr. Hendry's back whenever I got stuck or forgot a vital piece of information. I suspect Mr. Hendry was aware of this favour conferred upon me by these angels of mercy, and I suspect there was a glint of mischief in his eyes behind his gruff manner. He would briefly examine the patient and ask them how they felt. The patients seem to hold him in God-like awe. He would then step aside and dictate a ward round note into his portable Dictaphone.

At the end of the rounds, there was a visible sigh of relief if everything had gone satisfactorily. He would walk into the staff nurses' little office, be offered tea and biscuits, and seem quite human again. Sometimes, the registrar and I would join in to partake in the tea routine before rushing off to attend to countless chores that had arisen from the ward round. I began to realize how much I was learning about medicine and surgery, but more importantly about people. Marion, the attractive young surgical head nurse, was sharp as a tack, understood Mr. Hendry's moods, and was always aware of patient issues. To my great fortune, both she and her assistant Linda were favourably and warmly disposed towards me, thus greatly easing an inexperienced house surgeon's bumbling engagement with life-and-death situations in real life.

One morning, while doing my morning round after a weekend off, I found Mr. Anderson in a side bed. He had been admitted over the weekend under our service because of vomiting and abdominal pain. The admitting house doctor from the other surgical service had written a brief admitting history and ordered some preliminary tests and medications. I introduced myself to Mr. Anderson, who was about fifty-five years old, still in the prime of life, but looking tired. He had a slightly distended abdomen and appeared in some discomfort. He had a tube through his nose into his stomach that was draining brownish fluid into a glass bottle. I looked through his notes and laboratory tests and then examined him. His abdomen was tense, and I could feel some hardness in his upper abdomen and liver area. He had ascites, fluid in the abdominal cavity, usually a sinister finding. I found out that he was a greengrocer, but had found it difficult to continue work because of increasing fatigue and weakness over the last few months. His wife had insisted he see a doctor, who had promptly referred him to the hospital.

I discussed the case with Akuma and Mr. Hendry, who asked for several more X-rays and tests. The following morning, I put a needle into his abdominal cavity and drew out a large quantity of light brown fluid, which was sent to the laboratory for analysis. From all the test results and examinations, we concluded he had an advanced form of cancer of the stomach and liver. It was too late for curative surgical treatment. Mr. Hendry gently explained the situation to him and his wife and the advanced nature of the disease. His wife was quite shaken by the news, but Mr. Anderson put his hand on her shoulder and comforted her. Mr. Hendry suggested that we could try a new technique of delivering drugs directly into his cancer areas by putting a cannula (a plastic tube) into the main artery supplying blood to his liver and the stomach. In the operating theatre, Mr. Hendry expertly cannulated the arteries in question. He asked me to inject the anti-cancer drugs through the opening of the cannula at the required intervals on the ward.

Every day, after I completed my ward rounds, I would come over to Mr. Anderson, and inject the drugs into the cannula. I did this for a couple of weeks; his lab tests were showing no improvement and were in fact deteriorating. His discomfort and pain were more obvious. I started visiting him several times a day, adjusting his pain and other medications. We got to be talking about many things; he was quite interested in my work, and my life, family, and Africa, which he said he would have loved to visit to see the big game in the wild. Occasionally, if I was on the ward to see another patient in the ward to change an intravenous drip or attend to or admit a patient from the Casualty, I would stop by his bed to check and see how he was. Although he appeared asleep, he always seemed to know I had visited to check on him in the night, and the following day he would ask me if I got any sleep at night.

Over the next week or two, his condition was deteriorating. One afternoon I was adjusting his IV line, and he said, "Doctor, you worry too much about me. You've tried everything. You know I am dying, and I know also. There isn't much more to be done. I'm OK with that. I am completely at peace with that, but I would like you to look after yourself. You're very young; go and enjoy your free time. Stop worrying about me. I want to thank you for everything you've done." With that, he took my hand, shook it, and closed his eyes, a slight smile on his shrunken face.

I hurried out of the ward, a slight tremble going through my body. The next morning, I entered the ward and started going through the patient records. The head nurse, Marion, joined me and gently said, "You know, Mr. Anderson passed away in the night."

I said, "What? At what time? Why didn't anyone call me?"

"There didn't seem to be any point in waking you. He died at about four in the morning. You can sign his death certificate. It's attached to his chart."

I walked into the mortuary, lifted the cover, and looked at his face reposed in peace. I proceeded to sign the death certificate. Later in the afternoon, I received a call from the Accounts office, asking me to pick up my envelope. I asked what it was for. She sounded surprised at the question, "It's your fee for the death certificate." I didn't go to the Accounts office for a few days, but later I found a separate envelope along with my regular paycheque. It contained four one-pound notes. This was a quaint custom of the time; for most house staff, it meant a treat in the nearby pub with friends.

The following few months were filled with alternating moments of terror, exhilaration, friendships, midnight calls, and exhausting ninety- to one-hundred-hour weeks. We were allowed alternate weekends off and counted the moments until Friday at five o'clock in the evening, when you were allowed to be considered relieved. By the time you finished handing over your caseload to the house surgeon of the other surgical firm, it was usually at least six o'clock when you dashed off to catch the bus and subway to your weekend plans.

One Friday, at about four in the afternoon of my weekend off, I received a call from the Casualty officer to see and admit a patient to the surgical service. I walked briskly along the long path interspersed with trees and few disused villas to the Casualty. I saw a thin, haggard, unshaven man lying in the bed. He looked like a half-starved vagrant who had been brought in by well-meaning neighbours. The Casualty officer briefly said he thought this gentleman seemed to be suffering from *cachexia* (wasting) and malnutrition, probably from an underlying malignant disease. He had ordered a few basic tests and left the rest to the surgical service. I briefly examined the patient, thought him dehydrated, with dry tongue, sunken cheeks, flat non-tender abdomen, and clear chest and heart examinations. He was conscious and cooperative but taciturn, denied feeling any discomfort, and could not say much about his medical history. With one eye on the clock, I ordered some more tests and a chest X-ray, and started intravenous fluids at low flow and wrote an admission note. I called the senior house officer from the other team who was covering me for the weekend and briefed her on the admission. She said she would take care of my patients and to enjoy the weekend. It would be difficult to get many tests done on the weekend; before the advent of advanced imaging technologies of today such as CT scans and MRI, little could be expected immediately. The surgical registrar, Akuma, would be doing his rounds the following day, Saturday.

I dashed off to my room, changed out of the hospital clothes, and caught the bus heading towards the subway station, dreaming of my upcoming weekend in the company of my girlfriend. It was close to seven o'clock.

I had a wonderful weekend in London and returned to my quarters at the hospital at around ten in the evening on Sunday.

On Monday morning, I walked breezily into the ward to begin my day. I saw Akuma and a nurse at the far end of the room leaning over a patient. I walked up to him to see that he was attending to the gentleman I had hurriedly admitted late Friday evening. He was hooked to several IV lines and to a monitor displaying his blood pressure, heart rate, and ECG. He had a tube protruding from his nostril and taped to his cheek. He looked frail, but awake and alert. He nodded slightly to me and closed his eyes. The scene spoke volumes to me; my heart sank. I knew I had blundered somehow, but I wasn't quite sure how. Akuma walked with me to the nurses' office and asked if I knew what had happened over the weekend. I said no.

Then he told me the whole story. On Saturday, while doing his ward round, he had noted this patient was barely responsive, and the nurses had reported his blood pressure dropping over the previous few hours. On examining him and getting an urgent X-ray of the abdomen, he had called Mr. Hendry, who came out and confirmed that this man had perforated an ulcer and developed peritonitis (inflammation of the abdominal cavity and lining). They had taken him immediately to the operating theatre and opened his belly, which confirmed their clinical diagnosis. They had poured fluids and blood into him to maintain adequate blood flow, by feeding a catheter into his central veins from the neck, while he teetered between life and death. Fairly extensive surgery had been required to repair the perforation. He was still unstable and fighting for his life.

They had somehow managed to trace his wife and daughter, who had been out of the country. They had flown in and had been by his side since. I felt increasingly filled with guilt and horror at my own incompetence and prepared myself to receive a verbal lashing from Mr. Hendry. He had thus far apparently held a rather high opinion of me. After the morning round that day, we were due in the theatre for another full day of surgery.

I walked in with Akuma into the operating suite to find Mr. Hendry, who had just completed a short surgical procedure, sitting and reading his *Times* newspaper. He looked up at us and said, "Good morning, Azim. Did you have a nice weekend?" I said, "Fine, thank you, sir."

Did I detect an undertone of sarcasm in his voice? I couldn't be sure. I tried to blurt out a few words of an explanation about my botched-up case, how I thought he didn't look very ill, I thought he had a wasting disease with no apparent signs of a surgical emergency, etc. I was sure his steely gaze would burn into my brain, as if to say what have you learnt so far?

I was not prepared for what he did say. He smiled, a rare thing for him. His eyes as they gazed at me over his pince-nez were gentle and kind. He said, "Yes, I know. I think he is going to be fine. You should talk to his family and reassure them." He started humming a tune under his breath, walked into the operating room, more cheerful than most people had seen him in a while. It was as if a heavy load had been taken off my chest. Akuma and I joined him to go through the day's operating list.

The balance of my six months passed quite quickly. I had grown fond of the old rambling hospital scattered on the vast site, its beautiful buildings, mature trees, and long walkways. I had made many friends and had memories of patients, doctors, friendly nurses, antique vehicles, medical rounds; I drove to the nearby town and to the Chase Farm Hospital for clinical meetings. It was time to move on to the next rotation in medicine. Your consultant normally writes a reference letter that supports your application for the next house job. I was somewhat anxious about what Mr. Hendry would write for me. I was asked to pick up the letter from his secretary on my last day at work.

I walked into her cubicle. She was a kindly soul called Mary, whom I had not seen much of. She pulled me aside and handed me an envelope. She said conspiratorially, "That's the best letter of reference I remember him writing. He must have liked you." I felt relief pouring through me; at least I had a good chance of landing one of the three jobs I had applied for. She then handed me a slim blue booklet. It was a reprint of an important paper Mr. Hendry had published in the *British Journal of Surgery* on the technique and results of a "highly selective vagotomy," an operation he had pioneered and used frequently, before the advent of newer medication in current use for the treatment of peptic ulcers. He had signed the inside page.

The next phase of my education as a junior doctor involved securing a post as a house physician for a period of at least six months. For this, I elected to work in a small town outside London, where the community hospitals provided a range of clinical services with a few consultants. I chose to accept a position offered to me in Nuneaton, an old market town in northern Warwickshire in Midlands. It derives its name from a priory for nuns, granted to the nuns by the Lord of the Manor. Its markets and industries originally included leather tanning, silk weaving, and later coal. It is where the famous Victorian writer George Eliot lived. The hospital I joined was named George Eliot Hospital, which along with the Manor Hospital became the base for my housemanship.

The doctors' quarters were located on the second floor of the old Manor Hospital, which was like a manor house. It is where Mrs. Mary Williams, a lovely and maternally dedicated housekeeper, served us, the few junior doctors, our meals, including excellent Yorkshire pudding and roast beef.

The Manor Hospital catered to the area's medical and surgical emergencies, while the larger George Eliot Hospital functioned more as a general hospital. The consultant I was attached to was Dr. Bernard Schmidt, whose special interest was gastroenterology, diseases of the digestive tract.

An urbane, cultured man, he, like Mr. Hendry in London, had a lasting influence on my career. His attention to clinical details, his sound reasoning, and his interest and research in gastrointestinal diseases helped me build a sound foundation in clinical medicine and seek further training in medicine. He was later joined by another consultant physician, Dr. Ken Hollingrake, a brilliant clinician with a special interest in heart diseases. He helped me broaden my interests in cardiology and to look into residual respiratory diseases caused by coal dust, which had been a major occupation of many of our patients.

I am indebted to him for greatly facilitating my mother's urgently needed heart surgery by one of the finest heart surgeons of our time, Mr. Magdhi Yakub at the Harefield Hospital, a centre of excellence in heart surgery.

The letters of reference given to me by Drs. Hollingrake and Schmidt smoothed my path towards landing several positions as senior house officer and registrar in medicine at various hospitals in England and Wales. In Wales, I ended up doing a stint in Abergavenny, a quaint market town surrounded by the Brecon Beacons, at one of the few remaining tuberculosis and chest disease sanatoria in the U.K. Here I was usefully able to apply my knowledge of tuberculosis acquired in Africa and obtained good exposure to chronic diseases and respiratory medicine under Dr. Neil Thomas, a renowned tuberculosis specialist.

That was also the time I took off to get married to Nilu in Wrexham, Wales, and we have been happily married for over forty-five years.

Pluralism in Health Care: Introduction to Aga Khan Health Services

We travelled back to Kenya, where, after our honeymoon, I got acquainted with the expanding work of the recently established Aga Khan Platinum Jubilee Hospital in Nairobi. Post-colonial Kenya was seeking to dismantle some remnants of the colonial-era race- and colour-based health and education services. Aga Khan Hospital was one of the first large private hospitals to open its doors to all regardless of colour or race. On the guidance of His Highness the Aga Khan, diversity was fostered amongst the medical staff and the administration was largely based on merit and inclusion of staff of different backgrounds. In-house training programs were developed in nursing, medicine, nutritional services, hospital management, and paramedical fields. Patient welfare programs were substantially enhanced; modern hospital systems in areas such as medical records management, modern hospital pharmacy practices, and laboratory quality assurance programs were introduced, and new medical and surgical specialties and techniques were developed. Diagnostic capabilities were substantially advanced by the installation of state-of-the-art imaging and laboratory tests.

There was also, noticeably, a remarkable multi-communal voluntary input into many aspects of patient care and services, which added tremendous gratuitous value to the care paradigm and helped to moderate costs of care quite significantly.

My short acquaintance with Aga Khan Health Services of the time left me impressed by the conscious effort being made by a private non-profit organization to introduce best practices and modern methods and standards in health care, as well as questions of access to high-quality health care and equity in a part of the world where the society in rapid transition was grappling with issues of social equality. I must admit I was a little intrigued by the magnitude of their challenge and their efforts in tackling that undertaking. Once again, the question of providing access to high-quality and affordable health care, where even basic health care was lacking or unevenly distributed under the extant national health services, became of paramount importance in my mind.

A New Perspective: Crossing the Pond

It was time for me to move on to continue my higher education in medicine. I soon undertook an extensive tour of universities and teaching centres across Canada, from Halifax on the East Coast to Vancouver on the West Coast, in order to seek opportunities for the next phase of my training. I was gratified to have received acceptance for the residency program in one of the most prestigious teaching hospitals in Canada, and indeed in North America, the Toronto General Hospital in Ontario. It was and remains a major teaching unit of the Faculty of Medicine of the University of Toronto.

The Toronto General Hospital, fondly called TGH, has a remarkable record of clinical and research achievements. Amongst its "firsts" can be counted the development and first clinical use of insulin for diabetes in 1922; clinical use of anticoagulant heparin in 1935; first external pacemaker in open-heart resuscitation in 1950; first successful heart valve transplant in 1955; first coronary care unit in 1965; first single and double lung transplants in 1983 and 1986, respectively; and many others. When I joined in 1975, I was not fully acquainted with its illustrious history, but certainly came to be exposed to the works and teachings of remarkable physicians and surgeons and researchers associated with the hospital.

Recognizing my wide-ranging interests in medicine and health care, I chose family medicine as my primary area of specialization, because of its broad and comprehensive approach in the practice of medicine, to complement my over two years of general medical and surgical exposure in the U.K. The over two years of postgraduate residency in Toronto also involved rotations through the adjoining world-class Hospital for Sick Children and several other hospitals and clinics. I received a wide range of exposure to many clinical medical and surgical disciplines and left feeling confident in my clinical maturity. I remember Dr. Griff Pearson, an eminent thoracic surgeon; Dr. Robert Stone, the residency director; and Dr. Jim McHatty, a gastroenterologist who proved to be a great mentor and friend. From them and many others, I got, by total immersion, a sense of "American" medicine, which differed in some significant ways to the British system I was accustomed to. My residency included placements at several training sites.

I recall spending a month at a small hospital and health centre created to serve isolated First Nations communities. Spurred by the global influenza epidemic of 1918–19, and a tragic railway accident in 1920 and other unmet medical health needs, the Sioux Lookout Zone Hospital was born. In the 1940s, tuberculosis in surrounding northern First Nations communities reached epidemic levels. The federal government of Canada built and operated a sanatorium. The hospital gradually expanded to provide a wide range of inpatient curative and outreach preventive services, respecting the traditional customs of the communities. The time spent at the central hospital and health centre, as well as visits to isolated communities gave me a deeper understanding of cultural beliefs and practices surrounding holistic healing and echoed my days in Africa. I would accompany the extraordinary public health nurses to remote settlements – often mounted in Skidoos, motorized snow vehicles – to visit outlying families or fly in by ski-mounted small planes to remote village clinics, piloted by dauntless pilots. These were invaluable lessons in the health care challenges of isolated or marginalized communities.

There were other placements as well, in smaller towns and cities in Ontario. Training rotations in smaller cities and suburbs broadened my understanding of medicine and health care and local variations.

I remember spending a month in the city of Midlands, where Hollister King, a dedicated leader in family medicine and experienced physician was my preceptor and mentor. Midlands, a popular tourist destination situated on the southern end of Georgian Bay's thirty-thousand islands in central Ontario. Transient tourists and cottage owners required medical care for injuries, accidents, and illnesses. The town had a busy general hospital, where family physicians provided most of the care.

In Oakville, an upscale city on Lake Ontario, Don Butts, a compassionate and dedicated physician and chief of staff of the hospital, and a lover of classical music, wrote a glowing testimonial for me on completion of my placement with him, which opened many career choices for me.

Independent Practice: Freedom and Responsibilities

However, I was soon to learn that the cloistered environment within medical training programs is quite different from the real-life work of independent practitioners. Some attractive offers were coming my way, but at the suggestion of one of my professors, who thought my academic and clinical abilities could prove to be useful in rural or smaller centres, I accepted a position as an associate physician with a group practice in Williams Lake in the central interior region of British Columbia. The town depended primarily on forestry, logging, mining, and ranching.

The group I joined, Atwood & Associates, was led by a well-loved and remarkably worldly and affable elderly physician, Dr. Hugh Atwood. His partners were an agreeable, diverse mix of highly experienced doctors, each with a special interest area, ranging from anesthesia to orthopedics. They looked to me to provide consultative input into modern medical management of complex patients in the clinic and the community hospital, the Cariboo Memorial Hospital. However, I learned a great deal from my colleagues and from the range of people, which included a significant number of Indigenous people, and the diverse clinical presentations. For me, this was the real period of transformation into a more competent general clinician, yet more aware of my gaps in critical knowledge, the awesome responsibility attached to the role of a physician, and the need for lifelong learning.

An opportunity to pursue further knowledge in medicine came my way a year later when I was offered a study award by the College of Family Physicians of Canada to obtain experience in medical oncology (cancer medicine) at the Tom Baker Cancer Centre in Calgary, Alberta. The program enabled me to study primary care aspects of oncology, including early detection, prevention, and continuing care of patients with malignant diseases. Eventually, this led to my establishing a general medical practice in Calgary with hospital privileges at several major hospitals, including the Children's Hospital, and visiting privileges at the Tom Baker Cancer Centre.

My first independent family practice took root in a pleasant suburb of Calgary, a rapidly growing city and major hub of the Canadian oil and gas industry. As the practice grew, I accepted staff appointments in a number of area hospitals, which enabled me to continue my professional development through numerous university and hospital programs. My interests also took me to many countries to attend international conferences on a wide area of interest.

I remember on one occasion attending a medical conference at Temple University in Philadelphia. While in Pennsylvania, I decided to visit the Amish community, centred around Lancaster County, to observe their way of life. The Old Order Amish are a reclusive Christian fellowship of European origin who have maintained their simple way of life – governed by a code termed "Ordnung." They renounce modern technologies and amenities and live in Amish settlements, homesteads, and farms. Their distinctive attire, their horse-drawn buggies, and the charming countryside where they live are matched by their gentle ways and self-sufficiency. While I did not engage in learning their specific health issues, they were reminiscent of ways of life I had observed elsewhere and respected.

It is in Calgary that I established a thriving practice of family medicine, and about eight years later, I had my first formal introduction and later engagement with Aga Khan University and the Aga Khan University Hospital.

CHAPTER 2

ETHICAL UNDERPINNINGS: IMPACTING QUALITY OF LIFE

No man who believes that all is for the best in this suffering world can keep his ethical values unimpaired, since he is always having to find excuses for pain and misery.

Bertrand Russell, Philosopher

The World Health Organization defines health as a "state of complete physical, mental and social well-being, not just the absence of disease or infirmity." By this definition, no nation has achieved this utopian state of health and well-being; indeed, many parts of the world are experiencing a widening imbalance in the state of health of their people, a growing disparity in access to balanced health care.

Each nation has a fundamental interest in and responsibility for maintaining and improving the health of its people. Countries face formidable challenges as they strive to provide high-quality health care that is cost-effective, equitable, relevant, and sustainable. Success in meeting these challenges often involves balancing competing priorities and values in a complementary and mutually reinforcing manner. For instance, the care of individual patients needs to be balanced with more comprehensive public health measures, since both are essential components of health care. Each component can be more effective when working in synergy with the other. Providing the highest quality of health care needs to be balanced with cost-effectiveness and at a cost that society can afford. Few, if any, developing countries have achieved that balance, as competing economic and global forces intrude into the national agendas, relegating essential and equitable health care into the dustbin of national priorities.

As an example, currently, India spends one percent of its GDP on health. Some 4,300 Indians die per day due to the nation's poor quality of health care in non-pandemic times. The ratio of hospital beds to population is six hospital beds per ten thousand in population. The quality of private health care is drastically inconsistent, yet widely promoted to the better-off. Profiteering is rife. Seventy percent of health care costs are paid out of pocket. Civil society's role in helping prioritize equity delivered through evidence-based policy-making is mostly unsupported and undervalued. A similar picture emerges in neighbouring Pakistan and other low- and middle-income countries across the world. This picture of health care and health systems inadequacy is highly prevalent in developing countries but is not confined to the underdeveloped world, as the recent global health crisis caused by the COVID-19 pandemic has starkly demonstrated.

Prevailing State of Affairs: Health Care Delivery Challenges

These inadequacies do not necessarily mean that the world of health care delivery is populated predominantly by heartless entrepreneurs and unprincipled corporations bent on enriching themselves at the expense of captive or marginalized populations – abetted by hapless, ineffectual, or feckless politicians – in a milieu of inefficient regulatory infrastructure. Myriad factors enter into the resultant state of affairs: the piecemeal and poorly-coordinated developments; public, private, and for-profit construction of health services; the challenges of ensuring quality and accountability; and barriers to universal access amongst them. We inhabit an overcrowded planet with shrinking and often mismanaged resources, yet we share a common destiny.

Health is a complex and often messy process with multiple social, economic, cultural, and technological dimensions. The quest for sustained, complete physical, mental, and social well-being for all is continuous and dynamic. Strategies to improve quality, equity, relevance, and cost-effectiveness in health care are unlikely to be entirely successful. Yet, these aspirations still motivate those dedicated to human development and social justice.

The science and practice of medicine changes constantly; medical knowledge increases exponentially, yet knowledge becomes outdated or obsolete within a few years. The history of medicine is replete with practices and procedures, once mainstream, that would now be considered cruel and absurd. To the flux of extant information, many layers of misinformation, distortions, and unscientific extrapolations build like grime on a stately structure, offering nostrums and quick fixes, often for the profiteering and exploitation of the unwary, the gullible, or simply those marginalized from mainstream health services. Not uncommonly, ideas and practices cross national and regional boundaries and leap across continental divides, often uncritically adopted.

Medical education itself has a checkered history; it has been influenced by tradition, culture, religion, and geography, as well as overtly or covertly by notions of race, innate notions of intellectual superiority and inferiority, and privilege. The education of doctors and other health professionals in the modern era has to adapt to society's changing needs and conditions, as well as advances in science and technology and the neuroscience and psychology of higher education. Long-established pedagogic vertical top-down learning methods need to shift to a paradigm of self-directed learning, problem-based learning, and reflective learning. The science and practice of medicine changes constantly; medical knowledge increases exponentially and becomes outdated or obsolete within the ever-shortening span of a few years. The "art" of medicine and health care, the humanistic and ethical foundations, often lags these developments.

In a world progressively driven by free markets, private enterprise, and profits, medical education and health services have not escaped the attention and participation of profit-seeking entrepreneurs. For-profit medical schools, anathema to generations of medical educators, are cropping up in permissive locales, especially in the Caribbean, Central and Eastern Europe, Brazil, India, and other profit-conducive locales. Of the 191 new Indian schools in the past three decades, 147 are private, and most of them are for-profit schools. A similar situation is occurring in Brazil, where private medical schools' growth far exceeds the growth of public schools. These enterprises' ownership is often unclear, anonymous, or through private investors and private equity fund investments.

Medical education in the U.S. reached a milestone with the accreditation in 2007 of the first for-profit medical school since Abraham Flexner's time. The *Flexner Report of 1910*, under the aegis of the Carnegie Foundation, transformed the nature and processes of medical education in America, eliminating proprietary schools and establishing the biomedical model as the gold standard of medical training.

There are questions about the quality of medical education and about the social accountability and ethical foundations of institutions. There are, understandably, questions as to the core purpose of medical education: Is it to produce health care professionals that a population needs, or to deliver a profit, or both? Private health care delivery has progressively taken over medical care provision in large parts of the world, but it tends to focus on clinical services that are built around technology-oriented care and that are profitable. Primary care, preventive care, mental health, and other high-needs areas remain largely neglected or left to underfunded government-run public health services. In many countries, aspects of health care are increasingly outsourced, with much diminished oversight or input.

Disturbing Realities: Tracing Chasms and Bridges

Given the role and mission of higher education institutions, they are a vital part of society's development and make a particular contribution to future sustainable development. Consequently, each higher education institution necessarily sets strategic goals for transformation and reforms, taking into account the development trends in each country in this age of globalization.

The role of competent health care practitioners in modern health care systems cannot be overstated. Policymakers, planners, economists, administrators, and managers lay the groundwork on which health services' structure rests. But it is the health professionals – be they physicians, nurses, or paramedical providers – each with their particular skill sets, who translate and apply their knowledge and skill to people's care. They are the fundamental edifice on which the level of satisfaction and outcome in clinical care is obtained, provided they are given adequate resources in an enabling framework of service.

An unsettling awareness of the imperative for social action in large parts of the developing world was taking root in my mind. In the background of my comfortable surroundings, on occasion, there were fleeting snippets of news about the "Third World" in newspapers and on television – laced with light undertones of reproof and cynicism, more of pity than empathy – that flickered into and lodged into the back of the conscious mind. The perfunctory coverage usually focused on the seemingly unceasing litany of natural disasters, communal or ethnic violence, political upheavals and consequent heavy-handed responses, population displacements, and periodic famines. This reportage was often uncritically lumped into a generic basket of implied mismanagement, incompetence, wastage, and a lack of democratic participation in line with the Western model and expectations.

Coverage of populations struggling to scrape out a living or for a share of their dwindling national natural resources – often in the face of unscrupulous exploitation, concessions, and corruption of the advanced industrialized nations – and the growing divide between the privileged and the marginalized were rarely explored in any depth.

Medical journals like *Lancet* tried valiantly – but ultimately vainly – to report and to shame the industrialized world of abetting and perpetuating the chronic "brain drain" of trained health professional – doctors, nurses, health managers – who tracked to the "greener pastures" of the West, lured by better working conditions and substantially better wages, at a great loss of skills and knowledge to the developing countries.

The story widely propagated by the aid industry and governments of the rich world was that of benevolent goodwill on the part of the developed world extended towards their less fortunate brethren in the underdeveloped Global South. The narrative highlighted the generous sharing of technical and management know-how, usually through well-endowed non-governmental organizations (NGOs) and networks. Little was said of the true nature of financial assistance, which included not just the conditions and selectivity of aid, but also foreign investments that furthered their political and diplomatic agendas, and favourable trade flows to support corporate business interests. It fails to underline unrecorded flight capital, nor the soft power relationships between former colonial powers and former colonies, nor how the "beneficiary" was designed as a beneficial post-colonial construct. Outflows of money from poor countries to rich countries were rarely underscored in debates about development aid, which recent studies have shown far outstrip incoming finances; effectively, wealth transferred from the poor to the rich is at least double that from rich to poor societies.

The history of "development" is checkered with large, crumbling "white elephant" projects: huge, urban public hospitals, which often gobbled up more than half of the country's health budget, yet remained out of reach for the vast majority of local people; dams, highways, stadiums, presidential palaces, often undertaken to prop up the regimes of autocratic but compliant rulers. They, in turn, for significant national budget support programs and other frills, were quite prepared to turn an uncritical eye to the exploitative trading and business ventures of the local elites and their international corporate partners. Arms sales to developing countries flourished, and favourable terms of access to natural resources were wrangled.

For decades, critical areas in need for development – such as health, education, environment, sustainable agriculture, rural development, social and gender equity, progress towards strengthening local management competencies – remained off the mainstream of national development agendas. There were five-year development plans that were regularly published, but social progress remained sketchy and uneven. And it did not deter the proliferation of large networks of donor-funded multilateral, bilateral, and special-interest aid agencies and NGOs of all stripes. The many well-documented failures of the aid industry in international development and its overall ineffectiveness are hotly debated in the academic and public arena.

This was also the time at the height of the Cold War. The scramble for ideological influence over newly emerging and decolonized countries, particularly in Latin America, Africa, and Asia, who were testing the extent of their newfound social, cultural, and economic "freedoms," was at a fever pitch. Western models of the free market, capitalist versus socialist Marxist dogmas, were being explored as the opposing visions of their nation-states' progress. Western powers and alliances were foisting and promoting their wares and goods and services, the Communist–Marxist axis countering with their own menu of development ideology based on socialist, state-controlled collective policies. Underpinning much of this ideological and market scramble lay the global strategic security tensions of the time, the silent threat posed by nuclear weapons proliferation, and the alarming rate of research and development of all varieties of weapons of mass destruction and means of delivery. By and large, the developing countries held vast untapped natural resources, under-educated cheap labour forces, and strategic geography. The choices the nations' sanctuary made in the second half of the twentieth century set their course for development for decades to come, including their socio-economic and cultural future and defence allegiance.

Ethics of Health and Development: Making Health Tangible

Given the plethora of factors that impact health care availability, effectiveness, and efficiency, how can national health systems structure and optimize available resources – both material and human – to make health tangible to its populations?

Much is known about social determinants of health, the quality of information and science that impact the societies' health, and the essential infrastructures that enable the development of healthy and productive societies. In most developing countries – and in many industrialized countries – there remains a chasm between the desired and the prevailing state of affairs in health, as in many other social and economic goals.

The efforts to promote equitable and ethical human development is not new. Efforts to alleviate or improve the human condition is as old as humankind itself. Perhaps the earliest philosophical formulations for this ideal in Western thought can be attributed to Aristotle. In his *Nicomachean Ethics,* he describes the happy life intended for humans by nature as one lived in accordance with virtue. And in his *Politics,* he describes the role that politics and the political community must play in bringing about the virtuous life in its citizenry.

The Universal Declaration of Human Rights (UDHR) was adopted by the United Nations General assembly in 1948, which subsequently led to the formulation of the International Bill of Human Rights – which was completed in 1966 – and enshrined thirty articles of basic human rights. The UDHR begins by recognizing that "the inherent dignity of all members of the human family is the foundation of freedom, justice, and peace in the world" (138th plenary meeting). It declares that human rights are universal, to be enjoyed by all people, no matter who they are or where they live.

In more recent times, efforts such as establishing the National Health Service in the United Kingdom at the end of the Second World War are examples of national attempts to bring in social justice and equity into national development agendas funded by general taxation. Social and welfare departments became central in many more progressive countries in the postwar period. However, a social and economic progress model that values fundamental human rights, such as access to adequate and affordable universal health care, remains elusive in most low-income countries.

Many national and international organizations have developed plans and platforms to foster development, with mixed results. In the year 2000, world leaders came together at the U.N. to adopt the United Nations Millennium Declaration, committing their nations to a new global partnership to eliminate poverty with a series of eight time-bound targets, which came to be known as the Millennium Development Goals (MDGs). Goals 4, 5, and 6 dealt directly with health-related objectives: reducing child mortality, improving maternal health, and combating HIV/AIDS, malaria, and other diseases. These goals were formulated amongst other interrelated goals of reducing poverty, achieving primary education, and ensuring environmental sustainability.

There were several concerns expressed with the MDGs, such as that Goal 8 (global partnership for development) focused more on donor achievements than on development successes. Others did not address within-country inequalities, and insufficient emphasis was placed on the environment and agriculture. The process of MDGs has been accused of lacking legitimacy, underemphasis on human rights, and adverse effects on secondary and post-secondary education because of its sharp focus on providing access to primary education. But many lessons were learned, amongst them the acceptance that a "one-size-fits-all" model will not sufficiently respond to individual health care profiles of developing countries. However, the MDGs did mark an important milestone in global mobilization to achieve a set of critical social priorities worldwide. There is a widespread feeling among policymakers and civil society that some progress against poverty, hunger, and disease is notable.

In 2015, the current framework for sustainable development, termed the Global Sustainable Development Goals (GSDGs), was launched under the aegis of the United Nations, as an effort to continue the progress under the MDGs, which ended in 2015. All U.N. members adopted the GSDGs in 2015 as a universal call to action to end poverty, protect the planet, and ensure that all people enjoy peace and prosperity by 2030. The stated goals fall into seventeen thematic areas.

Sustainable development is the idea that human societies must live and meet their needs without compromising future generations' ability to meet their own needs. The GSDGs emphasized targeting people, planet, prosperity, peace, and partnership.

Experts have identified sixteen significant challenges the world is facing today, among which human capital development takes a special place. These challenges also include peacekeeping, culture and morality, underdevelopment, urbanization, and environmental degradation.

But fundamental questions of the state of the world at the beginning of the twenty-first century, the vast disparity between the "developed" North and the largely "developing" South, remain unanswered.

The questions of the nature, the ethics, and history of global aid and development – and its misplaced priorities – remain largely unbroached in development discourse. Are there foundational, structural, primordial, or intrinsic elements in the story of human development, in the disparate power trajectory of the two hemispheres – particularly in the last one or two centuries – that resulted in stark inequalities in the world as it is today? Did the inconvenient truths of history – such as slavery, colonialism, racism, and the single-minded exploitation of people and resources for the material enrichment of the able and powerful – leave a lingering and indelible imprint on the ultimate imbalance in the world of today? Can the path of widening inequalities and degradation be stopped and reversed if the best of human spirit and intellect is used in the service of the goal of a just world? Are the inequalities between nations and regions, and within nations themselves, surmountable if a spark of the conscious awakening of the realization of a common destiny for humanity and the planet is ignited and fanned by reason? Can we imagine a better future; find or re-ignite a shared ethic or philosophy of comity, cooperation, inclusiveness, or pluralism; or achieve a global consensus on social justice and basic rights?

Some studies have revealed that high anxiety – personal, communal, national, and regional – as a consequence of fear or ignorance of the "other," is pervasive and contagious. But so is hope! As far back as the twelfth century Averroes (Ibn Rushd), an Andalusian polymath, jurist, physician and philosopher wrote *"Ignorance leads to fear, fear leads to hate, and hate leads to violence. This is the equation"*

No simple answers or theories serve to explain the failure to attain a more even and just world. However, progress has been made in some areas of development by metrics of economics and technology. Staggering advancement in science and technology as it applies to medicine and health care has had its impact. Still, its availability and application remain patchy and selective, primarily determined by income levels: a significant majority of people in low-income countries remain deprived of its fruits.

Therefore, modern medicine and health care often appear cold, clinical, and impersonal – politics-, technology-, and market-driven – but bereft of empathy, compassion and the human touch. Thus, the imperative to "humanize medicine," to undergird global health care with ethics, moral values, respect, and fairness, would appear to be pressing, yet remains an idealistic distant dream. Good health, an archetype of a measure of the quality of life, remains elusive, entangled as it is in the matrix of factors that define progress in the modern world.

Beyond the Basics: Scaling Up Medical Care

Many causes of human suffering remain unaddressed or insufficiently confronted in the poorer countries of the world. Poverty, lack of access to basic human needs, and fragile and underfunded health systems account for much of this neglect. Lack of adequate nutrition, shelter, and access to clean water and an environment not conducive to health still account for much of the preventable human suffering, disability, and death. Neglected tropical diseases (NTDs) pose a devastating obstacle to health and remain a serious impediment to poverty reduction and socio-economic development.

NTDs are a group of diseases that cause substantial illnesses for more than a billion people globally. They impair physical and cognitive development, contribute to mother and child illnesses and death, and limit productivity. Many of these diseases are caused by parasites; most of them are treatable by drugs. Conditions such as elephantiasis, river blindness, bilharzia, and Guinea worm disease and hookworm infections fall in this category. Others, such as trachoma, the world's leading cause of blindness, are related to overcrowding, lack of clean water for hand-washing, and environmental hygiene, and can be controlled by a strategy that combines medication, surgery, face-washing, and environmental change.

Scaling up health requires universal coverage against neglected tropical diseases and depends to a large extent on enhanced access to free essential medicines and more robust, well-planned, financially sound, and efficient health systems. Global and multilateral agencies and some non-governmental organizations help prioritize the public health needs of poor and marginalized populations and provide technical and strategic guidance in key areas.

Amongst many other areas of underdeveloped or neglected public health concerns are mental health and psychosocial disabilities. The overwhelming majority of people with mental health problems are living in poverty, have poor physical health, and are subject to human rights violations. They are subjected to stigma and discrimination daily and experience extremely high rates of physical and sexual victimization. Frequently, people with mental disabilities encounter restrictions in the exercise of their political and civil rights. They are restricted in their ability to access essential health and social care and face disproportionate barriers to attending schools and finding employment. Two-thirds of people with HIV/AIDS have depression, while rates of mental disability amongst the homeless can be greater than 50 percent, but their mental health needs are commonly not addressed. Studies have shown an association between poverty indicators and the risk of mental health; the most consistent association is with low levels of education. Factors such as the experience of violence, insecurity and hopelessness, and rapid social change contribute significantly to mental health challenges.

Mental health issues cannot be considered in isolation from other areas of development, such as education, employment, emergency responses, and human rights capacity building. People with mental disabilities are not only missed by development programs but can be actively excluded from these programs. This is in spite of the fact that an explicit goal of development is to reach the most vulnerable.

Yet much remains to be done to lift the quality of life from treatable and preventable diseases. These are not problems where large corporations prefer to invest since they are not lucrative markets for research and development. An enabling environment of public–private enterprises of variable quality in addressing vast inequalities is underway in parts of the world, but calls for more concerted and ethical efforts at setting socio-economic and political priorities are required if the world is to attain a conscionable degree of balance and justice.

The biggest enemy of health in developing countries is poverty.

Kofi Annan, former Secretary-General
of the United Nations

CHAPTER 3

IMPETUS AND INSPIRATION: FORTUITOUS ENCOUNTERS

There is nothing by which a Man approaches nearer to Perfections of the Deity than by restoring the sick, to Enjoyment of the Blessings of Health.

Cicero

I suppose there was no one moment of awakening of the realization that medical education had a far greater potential role to play in enhancing the well-being of people than is often assumed.

My venture into issues of health and development in the developing world in Asia and Africa was perhaps serendipitous and circumstantial, but at its core, it sprang from the wellsprings of the tenets of my faith and my immersion since childhood into a particular ethos of service and sharing.

The usual career pathways of physicians followed a familiar pattern: practising one's lucrative art and science within the familiar and protective surroundings of a hospital, clinic, or office with well laid-out routines, rules, and processes – one patient at a time! Except for some public health physicians and socially conscious policy academics, few ventured to ponder the deeper questions of the greatest good for the greatest numbers – the questions of equity, moral imperatives, human dignity, or, indeed, the relevance of knowledge.

Concerns for far-off places – mostly known for their interminable suffering resulting from a scarcity of competent basic human services, poor sanitation and degrading environments, poverty, famines, and an inequitable distribution of resources – rarely clutter the average Western physician's busy mind. Such concerns fail to distract from the hard-earned and well-deserved rewards that society tends to heap upon a medical practitioner, particularly in the age where purported dramatic scientific progress in the conquest of disease and pain more readily captures the public imagination.

But each individual has a choice regarding his or her inclination to – or not to – involve himself or herself in the broader concerns of society. This applies more particularly to those fortunate enough by circumstance or determined effort to have obtained an excellent professional education, and to have been nurtured by an ethos of sharing one's good fortune, talent, and knowledge that could potentially serve in the relief of humanity's many and diverse ills.

Such an impulse for physicians is a moral and an individual one. It is often compelled by an ingrained sense of values, purpose, egalitarianism, personal morality, and/or altruism in varying degrees, commonly underpinned by an ethic of faith, social justice, and a spiritual calling. This proclivity is, consciously or unconsciously, accrued over time, awakened by conglomerations of the individual nature and means suited to their temperament, condition, and opportunity.

For me, it seemed almost an epiphanic realization one day that "it is more important what you do *with* your life than what you do *in* your life." The faith of Islam, in which I was brought up, enjoins respect for human dignity and relief to humanity through social action and philanthropy, underscored by a universal ethic and a recognition of common humanity.

All the years of training and almost a decade into medical practice in Calgary, Alberta, Canada, had only served to heighten a nagging sense that my education was not being adequately applied to obtain a sufficient sense of professional fulfillment and intellectual stimulation. The prevailing conditions of practice within the universal and publicly funded health care system in which I operated, and where a substantial proportion of presentations had to do with disorders of material plenty, poor lifestyle, stresses of life and relationships, and chronic degenerative diseases – interspersed with frequent presentations of minor or trivial conditions – left me dissatisfied professionally and emotionally and spiritually.

My medical practice was sound and in high demand; the usual stream of patients, hospital visits, and occasional house calls occupied my days and some nights and provided the material provision of a good life – by all measures, a picture of enviable professional success. Yet the sense of underutilization of the full measure of knowledge and skills, diligently acquired over the years, grew into a pervasive sense of ennui and disquietude and restlessness.

In the early eighties, little of the interconnectedness of global humanity had yet to consciously coalesce into a coherent personal philosophy. Still, I reasoned a more catholic perspective of the state of the world through wide-ranging reading, travelling, attending scientific conferences, and participating in groups concerned with issues of security and justice, particularly regarding issues of health and development.

Formative Years: Deepening Global Consciousness

I developed an interest in understanding the potentially horrific consequences of the arms race and nuclear war, initially as a medical and public health issue. I soon realized the hopelessness of any medical response to such a cataclysmic event.

The consequences of the global arms proliferation have far-reaching health, economic, social, and psychological implications, not only for the nations directly involved in massive nuclear arms build-up, but also for developing countries deprived of economic and technical assistance, senselessly channelled into an increasingly burdensome and unstable weapons race. The global arms race can be visualized as a cancer in the global village. Global public health expenditures are well below military expenditures, and this imbalance is much more marked in the developing countries, even though their need for health care is much greater than in the developed world. In 1981, more than $500 billion was spent on arms worldwide, which works out to $1.4 billion per day, or about $1 million per minute. Applying this "meter" to the successful ten-year campaign to rid the world of smallpox is equivalent to the cost of five hours of the global arms race. During this time, malaria, which affected over 300 million people throughout the world, could have been eliminated for the price of half a day of the arms race, or one-third the cost of a nuclear submarine!

The global effects of a major thermonuclear exchange would be the collapse of all organized human activity, leaving a cold, desolate planet. Physicians and other health workers, by virtue of their unique position of trust, can make substantial contributions towards disarmament and world peace.

My growing appreciation of these realities led me to join physician and scientific organizations that propped up to educate the public on this immense threat to the continuation of humanity, indeed to all life on earth. I joined the International

Physicians for the Prevention of Nuclear War (IPPNW) and a related organization, Physicians for Social Responsibility (PSR).

The IPPNW was founded in 1980, an inspiration born of the Cold War by
a small group of Soviet and American doctors, who reasoned that the common
interest and the fate of humanity were more powerful than the ideological divides
between them. This organization was awarded the Nobel Peace Prize in 1985. The
knowledge I acquired while learning the scientific, clinical, and social aspects of
this global threat prompted me to undertake several speaking engagements with
interested physicians, health care workers, students, and the interested public. I
wrote a paper, *"Nuclear War and the Public Health,"* for discussion amongst physicians, professionals, societies, and enlightened public policymakers.

By fortunate concatenations of circumstances, in 1984, I found myself invited
to Chateau de Bellerive, in Collonge near Geneva, the home of Prince Sadruddin
Aga Khan, the founder and president of a think tank, Groupe de Bellerive, and a
non-profit organization, Bellerive Foundation. These organizations were devoted
to a wide engagement in issues under the leadership of Sadruddin Aga Khan, often
working in concert with international institutions, bilateral aid organizations, and
U.N. agencies such as UNICEF and UNESCO, to improve the human condition
on issues ranging from economic justice, environmental protection, wildlife con-
servation, deforestation, and desertification. Other areas of concern for Bellerive
were questions of global and regional security – particularly the prevention of
nuclear war – and other humanitarian and ecological concerns.

Prince Sadruddin had served as United Nations High Commissioner for
Refugees (UNHCR) from 1966 to 1977, during which time he refocused the agency's interest beyond Europe and prepared it for an explosion of complex refugee
issues. His wide-ranging interests and activities had established a lifelong career
in international service. His deep involvement in humanitarian and refugee crises
went beyond Eastern Europe, to territories of Palestine and to Vietnam, Angola,
Algeria, Biafra, Chile, Burundi, and Uganda. He had acquired a deep understanding of humanitarian issues. He also served as the coordinator of humanitarian
and economic assistance programs for Afghanistan, Iraq, and Kuwait – a legacy of
remarkable endeavours in the service of a more humane and just world.

When I received a phone call from his secretary confirming the time and place
of our meeting, I was naturally very excited. The place for our meeting would
be at his lakeside chateau in Collonge-Bellerive. Upon arrival at the stately

seventeenth-century lakeside chateau at the appointed time, I was received by, I assumed, a Nubian butler and shown into a large wood-panelled library, tastefully decorated in an eclectic European and Oriental motif, with grand vases, oriental carpets, and other art pieces arranged around the hall. The tall windows afforded a serene view of Lake Geneva and the further shore. During his lifetime, the prince had assembled one of the finest and most diverse collections of Islamic art in the world, which included Arabic, Persian, Turkish, Indian, and African pieces. As I sat in a luxurious chair, the butler brought in a tray with an array of delectable pastries and an ornate teapot and set it down on the table.

At that moment, Prince Sadruddin walked in, a strikingly elegant looking man in a dark-blue business suit, with a large shining forehead and a serene aura. He smiled kindly, shook my hand warmly, and gestured me back to my chair as he took his seat across from me. Thus began a few hours of the most eye-opening range of discussion in my life. I believe he saw in me a passionate dilettante in the complex and interconnected issues of development and human rights, with budding and unformed interests in the areas of nuclear disarmament, public health, and social equity. His patience and gentle guidance propelled me later in my career to acquire sounder and more in-depth knowledge on these issues.

Before my departure, he presented me with a copy of an *International Colloquium on European Security*, organized by the Groupe de Bellerive, underscoring the perils of the nuclear arms race, and the then-failed attempts to reach arms control agreements between the principal opponents of NATO and Warsaw Pact countries. I departed, my head swimming with questions of moral dimensions of peace, responsive actions to promote environmental preservation, and human development.

I considered joining an advanced degree program at Harvard University in international health, as it was then called. This in no small measure was inspired by my appreciation of the work and ethical framework of a particular organization, the Aga Khan Development Network (AKDN), with which I came to become significantly associated in my career. I involved myself with voluntary participation in some community development events, sponsored by the Aga Khan Foundation, the principal agency of the AKDN, which was particularly involved in some countries in Asia and Africa.

That is when I was invited to meet with Joel Montague, the director of social development programs at the secretariat of His Highness the Aga Khan at

Aiglemont, near Chantilly, north of Paris. My wife and I were received at the station and driven to the gated wooded complex a few kilometres from Chantilly station. The large, beautiful secretariat consisted of several French colonial-style buildings. During my meeting, I met with several senior members of the secretariat staff and division heads from various sections of the secretariat.

Mr. Montague, a tall, urbane American, described in some detail the development goals and agenda of the network, in particular the early stages of construction of Aga Khan University and Hospital in Karachi, Pakistan. This was to be the largest and an "apex" project of the network and had an ambitious agenda to bring in training and high-quality service in medicine, public and community health, health care management, and local human resource development. This was thrilling information, although I was vaguely aware of the plans to establish the university in Pakistan that would cater to the needs of the region as well as other parts of the developing world.

Over lunch in the charming staff cafeteria of the secretariat, which offered a tranquil view of well-tended gardens and gently rolling wooded hills of the estate where a few thoroughbred horses grazed, I mentioned my plans to take further training in international health and development. Mr. Montague smiled understandingly. After lunch, back in his office, he pulled out a file that held a long list of people pursuing advanced public health and international development degrees at many prestigious universities and said the new institution would require people with a wide range of skills, forward-looking people with creative ideas, systems thinkers, people with leadership and management skills, and excellent clinicians and role models. He seemed to imply that the scope, breadth, and depth of the new and ambitious project called for individuals of special qualities and tenacity, vision, and fortitude. Later that day, I left awed, my head swimming with dreams and mixed emotions.

My attempts to reconcile the material with the spiritual and to converge modernity with tradition and humanistic values through meaningful pluralization of action proved to be a difficult act up to that point in time. To me, the model of humanistic, inclusive, and respectful engagement embodied in the principles and ethics of the AKDN and enunciated by its charismatic founder and leader, His Highness Prince Karim Aga Khan, resonated with my own convictions of a fulfilling life.

The Aga Khan simultaneously holds a position of spiritual leadership for a wide diasporic global faith community, spread out over twenty-five countries, with a substantial presence in Canada, the U.K., and the U.S. In his vision, I found full intellectual, psychological, and emotional resonance with my psyche and my search for meaningful action.

In particular, I drew inspiration from His Highness's numerous speeches and public utterances, particularly one in which he states, "Islam is an all-encompassing faith, urging an individual to achieve a balance between material progress and spiritual well-being. But no man, woman, or child can hope to achieve such a balance in sickness, illiteracy, or squalor."

Amongst the vision and many profound insights proposed by His Highness were his articulation of the state of decay of the very foundational institutions once considered beacons of hope and progress in the developing world. These institutions had eroded into a miasma of apathy and political interference, sometimes catering to the needs of narrow interests of particular groups at the expense of the broader community. This decay of standards, chronic underfunding, and human resource drain decreases the capacity of developing societies to deal with the major issues confronting them today and into the future. Vital policy changes were necessary to foster competent and effective institutions in order to release human creativity and energies in myriad forms, to seek local and workable solutions. For me, one call for action arose from the profound conviction that:

> *Knowledge is linked to action,*
> *So, one who knows acts,*
> *As knowledge calls for action*
> *And will depart*
> *If it is not answered.*

> *Imam Ali, First Shia Imam*

Exhilarating Introduction: Heightened Perspectives and Splendid Vistas

I believe I met Shamsh Kassim-Lakha in early 1984 when he walked into my clinic in Calgary accompanying his lovely wife, Khadija. On their visit to Canada, she had developed a fever, and a local friend had suggested that she be brought to my clinic, believing I had some experience in tropical medicine. As it turned out, she had a type of tropical fever, which we were quite satisfactorily able to deal with.

At that time, Shamsh was the chairman of the Owners Representative Board (ORB), the body charged with the planning, construction, commissioning, and initial staffing of Aga Khan University and Medical College and its affiliated 721-bed teaching hospital in Karachi, Pakistan. This apex institution of the coalescing Aga Khan Development Network agencies had been in the planning stages for more than a decade, and SKL, as he was known to his colleagues, was leading a small group of dedicated and competent people as they travelled, consulted, and negotiated widely to bring to fruition this bold and extremely demanding venture. Aga Khan University (AKU) was been granted a charter by the government of Pakistan in 1983 as the first private international university in the country.

In my conversations with him, I found Shamsh Lakha to be highly canny, intelligent, tireless, perspicacious, and entirely committed to this challenging enterprise, as he outlined AKU's proposed goals and potential reach. In later times, I saw him as a visionary leader, a role model, a generous mentor, an accomplished administrator, and a high achiever, who demanded no less from his subordinates. He very kindly invited me to visit Pakistan to see for myself the environment of AKU's potential impress, its construction and progress to date, its recruitment efforts, and its planned innovative architectural and structural features.

This my wife and I undertook later in 1984. We were well received and accommodated in a lovely guesthouse and given a fairly extensive tour of Karachi. At that time, Karachi was a sprawling metropolis, with numerous bazaars and markets laid out irregularly in an ever-expanding network of narrow potholed streets feeding into a growing number of wide highways and tree-lined avenues. In common with many exploding cities in developing countries, it had its share of squatter settlements, slums, and transient outlying population clusters, often locally referred to as *Bustis*. It was nevertheless a fairly modern, attractive city with many colonial-era buildings, grand residencies tucked behind high walls set on the Arabian Sea coast, and large expanses of golden sandy beaches and coves. It is located near the mouth of the Indus River; it is also a bustling port, full of all manners of marine vessels, including dhows, countless fishing vessels, oil tankers, cargo vessels, and local passenger transports. There was a large port community surrounding it, which I later had many occasions for interaction with.

Many excavations pockmarked the eighty-four-acre AKU site and half-completed buildings, laying the foundations for the main University Hospital, college buildings, and staff and student residences under construction. The control centre was a series of single-storey black wooden temporary buildings that housed the project administration offices, the medical and nursing school administrations, the site architects' offices, and various support functions. The lead architect's firm of Tom Payette and Associates of Boston, Massachusetts, also had its presence locally.

Dr. Chevez Smyth, the founding dean of the Faculty of Medicine, was travelling at that time. Shamsh introduced me to Dr. Camer Vellani, the recently appointed associate dean in the Faculty of Medicine. Dr. Vellani, elegant and soft-spoken, a native of Karachi, had recently returned after spending many years in the U.K., and had ably taken charge of the Medical College, which had recently started its first class in medicine in premises rented from the College of Physicians and Surgeons of Pakistan. As I got to know Dr. Vellani over the years, I came to admire and respect him tremendously; I have rarely had the honour to meet a more dedicated, committed, and selfless physician in my time. He was an outstanding clinician and a highly respected teacher. Indeed, I owe much of the support and encouragement in my future work and initiatives to him; he became a guiding light and an inspiration to me and remains so to date.

Our first meeting, however, was relatively brief. He had no illusions about the tasks ahead, and it was evident that AKU was seeking to build a faculty that demonstrated exceptional talent, potential, and creativity. Part of the challenge resided in establishing a model institution that was modern and progressive, but respected cultural imperatives, valued ethical responsibilities, and strived for excellence in a region where standards in education and health care had degraded to a level that had become a drag on society's progress. I grasped the order of the challenge, yet felt an odd thrill course through me at the potential this vision encompassed.

Shamsh Lakha had recommended and arranged for us to visit the Northern Areas of Pakistan, a remote region tucked high in the Karakoram Mountains. The Aga Khan Foundation (AKF) was extending its programs and reach into these far-flung regions. We flew into Islamabad, the modern capital of Pakistan, in the foothills of the Himalayas. The site of the capital, located on the Potwar Plateau close to Rawalpindi, with which it constitutes a metropolitan region, was selected in 1959, and planned construction proceeded over several years. It is an attractive planned city, with tree-lined thoroughfares and gardens, and modern facilities and buildings.

After a short and pleasant stay in Islamabad, we flew to Gilgit, in Gilgit-Baltistan, which was formerly known as the Northern Areas. We were lucky in that the flight took off as planned from Islamabad, as it is often delayed or cancelled. The reason is that the Nanga Parbat peak on the flight path is nearly five thousand feet higher than the maximum altitude of the turbo-prop plane; if there are clouds around the peak, the pilot cannot see the peak, and the flight ends up aborted. This happened to me once on a visit to the region at a later date, when the flight had to turn around quite close to the aerodrome of Gilgit. The flight to Gilgit is considered one of the most dangerous and harrowing in the world, as it squeezes between steep rock cliffs.

The road trip from Rawalpindi to Gilgit of about six hundred kilometres by jeep can take anywhere from twelve to twenty hours, depending on the road and weather conditions, landslides, and the experience of the driver. In some places, the jeep tracks inches away from sheer drops and sudden death.

The flight in a Pakistan International Airlines (PIA) small Fokker aircraft was filled with the most memorable vistas of my life, flying through massive mountain peaks of the Himalayan and Karakoram ranges. Gilgit-Baltistan is home to all five of Pakistan's "eight-thousanders," peaks that are taller than eight thousand metres (over 26,200 feet), and more than fifty peaks above seven thousand metres (over 22,900 feet). The region is home to some of the world's highest mountain ranges. The main ranges are the Karakoram and the Western Himalayas. The Hindu Kush lies to the west and the Pamirs mountains to the north. Among the highest mountains are the K2, also known as Mount Godwin-Austen (height 28,251 feet), and Nanga Parbat, the latter being one of the world's most feared mountains. I had the incredibly good fortune to be allowed into the small aircraft's cockpit, and the friendly crew pointed out from their vantage point the K2 and the Nanga Parbat and other peaks in the distance as the plane weaved its way through treacherously close mountain peaks.

Here, amid the wind- and snow-ravaged gorge and cliff, two ancient continents collide. Their mighty offsprings – the Himalayas, Karakoram, Hindu Kush, and Pamir Mountain ranges – jostle, thrust, and heave in a titanic and relentless struggle. This desolate yet stunning region is the "Roof of the World." The Pamirs and this region of Northern Pakistan share connected communal histories, and in later years, I had the occasion to visit the Pamir societies centred around Badakshan.

In this treacherous and forbidding perpendicular wilderness, there is scant sanctuary for productive human societies. And yet, beneath the glaciers and chasmic gorges flow rivers that nourish tiny hamlets and villages, where a precarious human existence is etched out by sheer determination and adaptability.

We landed at the small airport at Gilgit, made of a series of hut-like structures and old shipping containers, situated between some of the most dramatic mountain scenery. Gilgit is the capital city of Gilgit-Baltistan and is located in a broad valley between the Gilgit River and the Hunza River. Gilgit was once a Buddhist centre; it was also an important stop on the Silk Road. It is today a major tourist destination and serves as a hub for mountaineering expeditions in the Karakoram range. We were met at the airport by an AKF vehicle and driven through the small bustling town to a charming inn at the foot of a tall peak, the Rakaposhi, rising to an elevation of 6,700 metres (nearly 22,000 feet).

In Alberta, we were used to the tall peaks of the Rockies, but being so closely surrounded by massive snow-capped mountain grandeur, glaciers, and fascinating rock sculptures, as well as icy streams amid patches of barren land, engendered an emotion that bordered on spiritual wonder and awe. The harsh physical and climatic conditions of the isolated high valleys – fierce summer heat, bitter winter cold, virtually no rainfall – are matched by its vistas of breathtaking grandeur. The mountainous Northern Areas is totally unlike any terrain I was accustomed to.

The scattered populations eked out a hard-earned living on small plots of rocky, barren land, mainly by growing fruit such as apricot and apple, creating micro-irrigation channels, and keeping some sheep and goats amid the scant vegetation. Poverty was rife; life expectancy, particularly of children, low.

The following day we boarded a crowded minibus to Karimabad, located in the Hunza Valley on the west bank of the Hunza River to the north of Gilgit. Its older name is Baltit. It is situated at an elevation of 2,500 metres (8,200 feet) and is the Hunza District's administrative capital. The town was a caravan halting-place for people travelling through the Hindu Kush mountains to the Vale of Kashmir to the south and is set amid Rakaposhi's snow-clad mountain peaks, glaciers, and deep gorges. The town is made up of stonewall steep slopes on large terraced hills. The scant floral vegetation in the area consists of roses, pansies, lilies, zinnias, and trees such as apple, apricot, walnut, mulberry, willow, and poplar.

Hunza was formerly a princely state, ruled by a Mir, a hereditary princely ruler until the early seventies. The Xinjiang autonomous region of China borders it to the northeast and Pamir is to the northwest. The Karakoram Highway (known by its initials KKH) runs from Rawalpindi through the Khunjerab Pass to Xinjiang, and is one of the highest paved roads in the world, passing close to Karimabad.

We arrived in Karimabad late in the autumn evening and felt the chill of the mountains. Along the way, we were surprised to see small roadside markers and signposts close to streams and irrigated fields that said "AKRSP." The letters AKRSP stand for the Aga Khan Rural Support Program.

In time, I was to learn a good deal about the efforts and projects undertaken by this non-profit company established by the Aga Khan Foundation in 1982. It was established to help improve the quality of life of the villagers of Gilgit-Baltistan and Chitral to the East of Gilgit. It is founded on the belief that the local communities have tremendous potential to plan and manage their own development once they are organized and provided access to necessary skills and capital. Its focus is on social and economic domains. Its key areas of early activities had to do with small infrastructure projects such as bridges, roads, irrigation channels, micro-hydroelectric units, planting millions of trees, and other small projects. Its objectives are community mobilization to foster inclusive and competent local organizations and increase income and employment opportunities, particularly for the poor and vulnerable, including youth and women.

We were shown to a small stone-and-wood-constructed, dilapidated guest house, perched on a cliff. The view from here was stunning in all directions as far as the eye could see. We were met by a youngish man and his flushed-cheeked wife, both wearing traditional Hunza skullcaps. While they could not speak English, they were extremely hospitable and soon made us feel at home. As far as we could tell, we were the only guests at that time. After several hours of a bone-jarring, but fascinating ride from Gilgit in the minibus, we were chilled to the bone and hungry. They set about trying to scramble us a meal. Before long, they laid out for us a supper of freshly cut chicken, naan, rice, and very sweet tea. Soon after enjoying this repast, we headed to bed, fully clothed and shivering. Nilu and I put on our sweaters and jackets and huddled tightly together through the night. We were not well prepared for the biting chill we experienced on our first visit to the area.

The following day, we visited the Baltit Fort, which was then in a dilapidated state (later fully restored by the Aga Khan Trust for Culture), the former residence of the Mir of Hunza. We were also shown a number of other project sites initiated by the AKF, including a girls' school, a primary health centre, and narrow moun-tain tracks connecting people and small farms and orchards. We saw several water channels for irrigation carved out of rocky hills and a few fruits stands by the roadside. We were very graciously received in the one or two households that we entered of the several that we got invited to enter. We saw the last of the summer fruit, mostly apricots and apples, laid out to dry on the houses' rooftops. Staring at us were rosy-cheeked, grey-eyed children; beautiful women in traditional long dresses and bright hand-embroidered caps; men in their baggy trousers and over-coats. Older people with deeply furrowed, but kindly faces greeted us in their native greetings and smiled as we walked the small town.

Over the next day or two, we visited several other adjoining valleys and villages, some located as high as 2,800 metres (9,100 feet) above sea level. The drives, in some parts over suspension bridges, narrow cliff-hugging roads, overlooking deep gorges with silvery strips of rivers visible out of the jeep's window, left us breathless and thankful for the incredible skill of the driver, who quite calmly negotiated his way forward. At one point, we saw a tractor lying on its side deep in a ravine, half-submerged into a river.

We left with a good deal of empathy and respect for these remote regions' hardy people, who continued to retain their good humour, warmth, and hospitality under incredibly difficult conditions.

Upon our return to Karachi, I shared my experience with Shamsh and thanked him for giving me this opportunity to better understand the network's vision and ambition.

~·~

Back home in Calgary, our thoughts kept drifting to the visions we carried in our minds and hearts. It added to the emotional tumult and dissatisfaction I was feeling with the value of my work in my life's comfortable surroundings. Many of my friends wanted to learn from our foray into understanding the exciting devel-opments taking place in Pakistan. I ended up making one or two presentations to groups of interested Ismaili professionals and shared our excitement in the work of the Aga Khan Development Network, particularly the vision, goals, and objectives of Aga Khan University, which had received its charter in 1983. A group of physi-cians and dentists felt they wanted to make a material contribution to the further development of the university, and a fundraising initiative took place. Soon, a substantial corpus of funds was gathered.

In early 1985, an invitation was extended to the group to send a delegate to the opening ceremony of the first phase of the university and hospital campus. His Highness the Aga Khan and the president of Pakistan were to attend. The group unanimously proposed I attend as their representative to this ceremony in Karachi.

Privilege and Opportunity: Broadening Horizons

As a result, Nilu and I found ourselves again in Karachi in 1985. There was almost a festive mood close to the campus site: oleander trees in vivid pinks and reds were in bloom, and a few flags lined the street. It was a magnificent gathering. The main ceremony was held under a bright *shamiana*, a huge tent, the sandy ground covered in carpets that seated hundreds in rows of chairs. The brass band played music. There were a large number of international guests, major donors, diplomats, and public officials in attendance. The formal proceedings went smoothly. Numerous celebration events were held over several days, including local music festivals and cultural shows. The splendid and architecturally unique hospital and university buildings were toured by visitors, entering through a high, dramatic archway. The inner drives within the campus were lined with trees and flower boxes. The newly laid lawns were not yet mature.

I found myself invited to several medical gatherings and conferences over the next few days, where some of the newly joined university heads and leaders were present. I did not realize that some of us were being subtly probed for possible positions with the university.

Dr. David Ulmer had recently joined from the U.S. as the dean of the Faculty of Health Sciences, replacing Dr. Chevez Smyth, who had given years of sterling service to the university as its founding dean. He had recruited a number of expatriate faculty and lured quite a few well-qualified Pakistanis from abroad. There was Dr. Farhat Moazzam, the new professor and head of the Department of Surgery, a brilliant and feisty pediatric surgeon trained in Florida who had returned to her native Pakistan, lured by the prospect of contributing to surgical education through working with a new medical college that promised innovation in training and service. Then there was Dr. Dennis Mull, a professor in the Department of Community Health Sciences (CHS) and director of the Community Health Centre, the main outpatient clinic of the hospital. He was a professor of family and preventive medicine from the University of California, Irvine, and had joined the CHS Department over a year ago. He was a friendly middle-aged American physician with some experience in working in South Asia.

Dr. Mull got to talking to me and asked me probing questions, particularly about my work and interests. He asked if I would be interested in visiting the CHS Department and meet with the preceptors the next day at their departmental meeting. These were young doctors who undertook the task of conducting the field-based training of the medical students for the department; they were also on the path to acquiring higher education in community health sciences, including public health and primary care. He mentioned that many were interested in learning more about the specialty of family medicine, which, while well established in the West, was not yet developed in Pakistan and the South Asia region.

I joined the departmental group the next day, which had gathered in one of the newly opened wards in the main hospital building, as there was no permanent space yet allocated to the CHS Department. In one side room, there were about eight or nine young men and women gathered, who I gathered were the preceptors, and another man and woman engaged in some discussions. Dr. Mull introduced me to the group. Soon I was drawn into their discussion, which related to an issue arising in trying to set up a primary health care (PHC) field site in one of the poorest areas of Karachi. Soon the conversation turned to my work and background, and the place of family medicine in the health care system in Canada, the U.S., and other Western countries. They were keen to learn about opportunities for training in public health and family medicine in Canada. One young man in particular, Dr. Arjumand Feisal, had his heart set on obtaining further specialized training in family medicine in the future. As there were no established programs of training in family medicine in the region, he was looking forward to programs in the U.S. or Canada.

After about an hour and a half pleasantly spent with this enthusiastic group, on my way out I was taken into another side room, which was set up as a temporary office. There Dr. Mull introduced me to Dr. John Bryant, the professor and chair of the Department of Community Health Sciences.

This was my first meeting with the person, who in the days ahead, would have a profound and enduring transforming impact on my life, my destiny, and my trajectory into the arena of global health, health systems development, and medical education. Little did I know at that time of the career of passion and contributions to health in the developing world of this striking, tanned, tall American with finely combed, greying, wavy hair in a short-sleeved shirt, who stood up to greet me. Over the next few years, I got to know him a lot better, and my respect for him as a man of vision, vigour, compassion, and faith continued to grow.

Dr. Bryant, a Navy pilot in the Second World War, had a stellar medical and public health background. Following education and graduation from the University of Arizona and Columbia University, he worked in research at the National Institutes of Health in the U.S. and the Max Planck Institute for Biochemistry in Munich. He later joined the Rockefeller Foundation to study health in developing countries. He published a ground-breaking book, *Health & the Developing World*, a landmark assessment of the problems and vast inequalities in health care delivery in the world's less economically favoured nations. The book's systematic approach, fair assessment, and stark conclusions stunned many of its readers and helped inspire an entire generation of students in public and international health. He later transferred his focus from teaching and research in clinical medicine to teaching health to people at the community level and reaching populations that were not served. He became the dean of the School of Public Health at Columbia University. He represented the U.S. government as the principal delegate to the WHO.

In 1978, he led the U.S. delegation to the International Conference on Primary Health Care in Alma Ata, Kazakhstan, then part of the U.S.S.R. This conference ultimately led to the fundamental doctrine of "Health for All." He served as a consultant to the World Health Organization and many other organizations around the world for many years. He was a recipient of many awards and honours. He retired from AKU in 1993 as professor emeritus, and later, with his wife Nancy, continued to offer voluntary services in Africa in organizing community programs for the care of orphans and vulnerable children in Kenya.

We had a relatively brief conversation on that occasion, during which Dr. Bryant briefly outlined the work of the department, which was still in the process of establishing field training sites for the first-year cohort of medical students. The curriculum of the Medical College was unique, in that 20 percent of each of the full five-year curricula was spent directly in the field sites located in the poor squatter settlements around Karachi, as well as in the rural areas of the province of Sind. These impermanent settlements, known locally as *katchi abadis*, were to be, by direct immersion, the learning grounds of the principles and determinants of the social, economic, preventive, and clinical aspects of health care. This was a bold experiment, an untried method in medical and nursing education in a region with vast inequalities in access to health care.

I left impressed and moved by the enthusiasm, the desire to learn, and the seeming commitment to an innovative community-based medical education paradigm of the young faculty. The next few days were a quick blur of engagements, exciting presentations, and tours. Nilu and I were sad when it was all over too soon, and we had to depart for home, but we left feeling more enriched and enlightened by the perspectives expressed, which encompassed hope, possibilities, and new opportunities and bold new directions envisaged by the incipient new institution.

> *You can count how many seeds are in an apple, but not how many apples are in the seed.*
>
> *Ken Kesey, American novelist*

CHAPTER 4

ANATOMY OF A DEVELOPMENT NETWORK

Founded and guided by His Highness Prince Karim Aga Khan, Aga Khan IV, the Aga Khan Development Network (AKDN) brings together a number of development agencies, institutions, and programs that work primarily in the poorest parts of Asia and Africa. The central feature of the AKDN's approach to development is to design and implement strategies in which different agencies participate in particular settings to help those in need achieve a level of self-reliance and improve the quality of life. Its essential features include following a guiding ethical framework, strengthening civil society, encouraging respect for the environment, fostering gender equality, promoting pluralism, improving the quality of life, finding sustainable solutions, alleviating poverty, and supporting volunteerism.

> *The Aga Khan Development Network (AKDN) is a group of private, international program non-denominational agencies working in over 30 countries to improve living conditions and opportunities for people in some of the poorest parts of the developing world. The Network's organizations have individual mandates which range from fields of health and education to architecture, rural development, and the promotion of private-sector enterprise. Together they collaborate in working towards a common goal – to build institutions and programs that can respond to the challenges of social, economic, and cultural change on an ongoing basis. The Network brings together a number of agencies, institutions, and programs that have been built up over the past 40 years and, in some cases, date back to the early 20th century. AKDN*

agencies conduct their programs without regard to the faith, origin, or gender of the people they serve.

AKDN statement

The network's work in three broad areas – economic development, social development, and cultural development – and in each broad domain has several agencies and programs that serve to actualize its mission. While personal morality is paramount, the function of ethics is to foster self-realization by giving oneself, for the common good, in response to God's majesty. It derives its impetus from the ethics of Islam, which bridges two realms of the faith, the spiritual and the material. This holistic approach rests on ethical underpinnings and includes ethics of a sustainable environment, pluralism, empowerment, cultural restoration, relief of poverty, and intellectual pursuit for the purpose of the search for new and useful knowledge for the enhancement of the quality of life.

The essential components of the ethical framework are the following:
- Ethics of inclusiveness
- Ethics of education and research
- Ethics of compassion and sharing
- Ethics of self-reliance
- Ethics of respect for life and health care
- Ethics of sound mind
- Ethics of sustainable environment
- Ethics of governance

So, what are these ethical principles? In a sense, they are universal principles that inspire and define the work of the AKDN. The Aga Khan has underscored these principles as "cosmopolitan ethics" and "pluralist values" for the advancement towards a just and more balanced world.

We inhabit an overcrowded planet with shrinking resources, yet we share a common destiny. Weakness or pain in one corner has the tendency, rather rapidly, to transmit itself across the globe. Instability is infectious. But so is hope! It is for you – the leaders of today and tomorrow – to carry the torch of that hope and help to share the gift of pluralism.

The Aga Khan, Gatineau, Quebec May 2004

The ten agencies that constitute the Aga Khan Development Network work to improve people's welfare and prospects in the developing world in Asia and Africa. Some programs, such as specific research, education, and cultural programs, span both developed and developing worlds. While each agency pursues its particular mandate, all of them work together within the network's overarching framework so that their different pursuits interact and reinforce one another.

A significant portion of the funding for development activities comes from part-nerships with national governments, multilateral institutions, and private sector partners. His Highness the Aga Khan provides regular funding for administration, new programs and country initiatives, and some core activities. The Ismaili com-munity contributes invaluable volunteer time, professional services, and substan-tial financial resources. Other funding sources include income from user fees and endowment funds. The Aga Khan Foundation holds several regular fundraising activities in Canada, the United States, the United Kingdom, and Portugal. The project companies of the Aga Fund for Economic Development – the only agency of the AKDN that works on a commercial basis – operate as businesses, but all surpluses are reinvested for further development initiatives.

Transcending Borders: Multipronged Development

One of the principal agencies of the AKDN is the Aga Khan Foundation (AKF), which was established in 1967 and registered in Geneva, Switzerland. It brings together human, financial, and technical resources to address the challenges faced by the poorest and most marginalized communities globally. Its six major thematic areas and objectives include gender equality and inclusion mainstreamed through-out all programs: agriculture and food security, economic inclusion, education, early childhood development, health and nutrition, and civil society. The AKF has helped to pioneer the "multi-input area development" (MIAD) approach, which leverages multiple AKDN agencies' capabilities to deliver its social, economic, and cultural interventions in targeted geographies to accelerate development over time.

Other agencies deal primarily with health care, education, microfinance, cul-tural preservation and restoration, and economic progress. Of note is Aga Khan Education Services (AKES), formalized as such and registered in Geneva in 1986. It operates more than two hundred schools and educational programs in Africa, Asia, and the Middle East. However, its infrastructures were laid in the long tradition of promoting education in the Middle East, South Asia, and East Africa. The first schools were established in the early part of the twentieth century in South Asia and in Zanzibar in East Africa by Sir Sultan Mohamed Shah, Aga Khan III.

Similarly, Aga Khan Health Services (AKHS) has a long history of serving essential communal needs in health, particularly in areas of maternal and child health. In the modern period, its seeds were planted during the time of Aga Khan III when a maternity home was established in Karachi, Pakistan, in 1912. It operates one of the largest non-profit health care systems in the developing world. It consists of more than two hundred health centres, diagnostic centres, and hospitals, including two university hospitals, secondary and tertiary hospitals, and a referral network. Many of its units are benchmarked to the highest international standards, including ISO and/or JCI accreditation. It, along with Aga Khan University (AKU) and the AKF, delivers quality health care to over five million people annually and works closely in planning, training, and resource development. AKHS works closely with AKES and the Aga Khan Agency for Habitat (AKAH) to integrate health issues in special projects.

Social and economic development are not enough to ensure holistic development, and therefore the cultural branch of the AKDN complements the other two. The basis is how through culture you can help for a positive change in society. In the broad realm of culture, the AKDN agency, Aga Khan Trust for Culture (AKTC), oversees several units and programs, specifically to do with the physical, social, and economic revitalization of communities in the developing world. It includes the Aga Khan Award for Architecture, the Aga Khan Historic Cities Program, the Aga Khan Music Initiative, the Aga Khan Museum in Toronto, and several other initiatives, some of which are online. Some beneficiaries of the initiatives particularly benefit from job creation and restoration training in programs that target the built environment, parks, recreation, and the reclamation of historic sites and the heritage of traditional arts and music.

To complete the suite of agencies for integrated development are the Aga Khan Agency for Microfinance (AKAM), the Aga Khan Agency for Habitat (AKAH), and the Aga Khan Academies (AKA).

The AKAM brings under one umbrella microfinance efforts conducted over more than sixty years. It provides loans to over three hundred thousand clients for housing, health, and education through self-standing microfinance institutions. The AKAH attempts to address threats posed by natural disasters and climate change. Its efforts are also directed towards environmental stewardship, water and sanitation, and safe housing. The AKA is dedicated to an integrated network of eighteen schools called the Aga Khan Academies to expand access to education of international standards of excellence. Several academies are opened and functioning or are planned to open in locations in Africa, South and Central Asia, and the Middle East, to promote understanding amongst cultures and sectors of society and to emphasize leadership development, ethics, pluralism, and social responsibility.

The only for-profit institution that is part of the AKDN, the Aga Khan Fund for Economic Development (AKFED), carries out economic development by promoting entrepreneurship and building economically sound enterprises in the developing world. It often works in parts of the world that lack sufficient foreign direct investment. The AKFED operates a network of more than ninety separate project companies employing over sixty-five thousand people. It is active in eighteen countries in parts of Africa, South Asia, and Central Asia. The profits generated by the AKFED are reinvested in other economic and social development initiatives.

The AKDN is a multisectoral development network and an NGO, born of a long history of communal social and economic empowerment. The AKDN's functions, intrinsic values, and vision that drive it are not merely of a transnational NGO nature. They are defined by the vision of the Aga Khan, the Ismaili Imam, as a vehicle for the realization of the social and humanitarian ethics of Islam in an entirely non-denominational, merit-based, pluralistic, and effective manner. It has not adopted any nationalist ideology or political ideology, but rather is driven by a humanistic ethos.

Health Beyond Medicine: Profiling Aga Khan University

Higher education is provided by two international universities: Aga Khan University and the University of Central Asia.

The University of Central Asia (UCA) was founded in 2000 under an international treaty and charter in three countries in Central Asia, with His Highness the Aga Khan as the founder and chancellor. UCA primarily serves the people of mountainous regions in the countries of Central Asia, who because of their unique needs, culture, and isolation need specific approaches to issues of development.

Since 1980, Aga Khan University (AKU) has been making a difference in the developing world by enabling young men and women of all backgrounds to realize their potential and by creating innovative solutions to pressing problems. Its programs and campuses are now spread across six countries, and the university is both a model of academic excellence and an agent of social change. Its underlying premise is to educate leaders, embody excellence, discover what works, serve the community, empower women, foster pluralism, and foster connections between private and public sectors, the developing and developed world, urban and rural, ideas and faith. It has a myriad of partners and supporters, including many universities and United Nations agencies, such as the World Health Organization and the World Bank.

Like all network institutions, the university is non-denominational, and admission to its academic programs is based strictly on merit. Currently, with eleven teaching sites spread over eight countries, AKU serves as an agent of change. Its expanding suite of faculties and programs includes two medical colleges, the School of Nursing, teaching hospitals, the Institute for Education Development, the Institute for the Study of Muslim Civilizations, the Institute of Human Development, the Graduate School of Media and Communications, and a Faculty of Arts and Science.

AKU derives its inspiration from the great tradition of Islamic learning at the height of Islamic civilization, from Spain to India, from North Africa to Afghanistan. Starting in the ninth and tenth centuries, higher learning academies were born in Baghdad and North Africa – Qarawiyyin in Fez in Morocco, Zaytouna in Tunis, Al-Azhar in Cairo – the last established by the Fatimid forefathers of the present Aga Khan. Al-Azar, Oxford, Heidelberg, and Harvard are in AKU's bloodlines. It is therefore fitting that Harvard University played a lead role in its conceptualization, along with McGill and McMaster Universities of Canada, but it is strongly influenced by its times and its location. It is these intellectual, spiritual, and contextual forces that define the central ethic of the university.

It took almost twelve years of planning, thinking, and wide consultation before construction of its flagship campus buildings started on an eighty-four-acre site in Karachi. It has made significant contributions architecturally and aesthetically and to its cultural environments and has earned international plaudits for its functionality.

This not-for-profit organization's approach seemed to be in accord with my quest to balance my values with purpose and professional satisfaction. My future engagement with a few agencies that constitute this development organization was, thus, a consequence of the fortunate conflation of an imperative of a personal search for meaning and purpose with an institutional philosophy and ethos that provided the conditions and provisions for its attainment.

It is necessary to say something about the founding principles, vision, and goals of Aga Khan University and its Faculty of Health Sciences (AKU-FHS), with which I was most involved.

In a region undergoing major social and political adjustments, AKU – an important component of the Aga Khan Development Network (AKDN) – is an agent of change. As both a national and international institution, AKU faces many challenges. Through its high academic standards in programs relevant to the needs of the developing societies, it works as a dialogue partner with governments on issues of health and education policy and on its delivery of critical social services at the local and regional levels.

Its first faculty, the Faculty of Health Sciences (FHS), comprises the School of Nursing (AKUSON), opened in 1980, and the Medical College, started in 1983. The idea of establishing a higher learning institution extends back several decades. Initially conceived to establish a hospital and medical college, its conception later transformed into a full-fledged university with plans to have a campus and reach many parts of Asia and Africa. Early planning, which began in the early years of the sixties, began with Harvard University's participation in the U.S.; McMaster University in Canada, particularly for its nursing education program; and McGill University in Canada for its community health sciences and services. The University of Malaysia and some other regional institutions were also involved in the university's early conceptualization and planning.

The role of McGill University in the planning of the medical college was to translate the broad purpose of embracing primary care and community health as the top priority of the new AKU Faculty of Health Sciences in an advisory and consulting capacity. Local field teams and visiting experts undertook extensive studies of data available on health status, health outcomes, health resources, human resources for health, morbidity and mortality, demographics, and socio-economic determinants of health in Pakistan.

It became quite clear that many essential data sets were inadequate or lacking and that correcting for much of that lack of information should become a priority function for a community-oriented health sciences institution. A proposal emerged that proposed "community modules" as the cornerstone of the Aga Khan Medical College's pedagogic strategy, in which the "community" becomes the principal site for education and training, in contrast to the hospital-based "teaching around the patient" approach as practised in most conventional medical schools.

If AKU succeeds in producing the desired kind of physicians, and the curriculum achieves a status of excellence as an innovative resource for meeting the health care needs of the developing world, it would serve as a model much needed for transformation in health sciences education. Its deliberations to create a health sciences education facility that placed quality, relevance, and context as its core values were steadfast. But the traditional model of hospital-based, technology-dependent medical education, so deeply ingrained in most universities both in the developed world and, by its blind adoption, in the developing world, was still the dominant model, despite the growing realization of its severe limitations in meeting the health needs of the large majority of populations in many parts of the world.

The Alma Ata Conference of 1978 had declared primary health care (PHC) as the key to achieving "Health for All" by the year 2000. In its long history, the Aga Khan Health Services facilities and programs were substantially immersed in providing primary health care services, including immunizing hundreds of children in the remotest parts of the globe, such as the Northern Areas of Pakistan. Maternal and child health programs, health education, and school health programs had been operating in a number of Asian and African countries for decades.

The Aga Khan Foundation (AKF), in partnership with the World Health Organization (WHO), jointly organized a conference in Karachi in November 1981 that examined "The Role of Hospital in Primary Health Care." This international conference aimed to deliberate on the tensions between the material and human resource allocations between these two necessary holistic health care components and to propose possible solutions. The meeting was co-sponsored by the Canadian International Development Agency (CIDA). Dr. Hafdan Mahler, the director-general of the WHO, summed up the essential qualities of mutually supportive collaboration between hospitals and primary care. Its conclusions offered mechanisms whereby a more balanced approach to education, research, and service could be fostered in transforming health care.

Other international conferences were held through the eighties by the AKF, AKHS, and AKU in collaboration with partners such as the WHO, UNICEF, the International Child Health Foundation, and the National School of Public

Health of Portugal. These conferences contributed to the intellectual foundations for advancing medical education, primary care, community care, and human development.

The founder of AKU, Prince Karim Aga Khan, conceived the progressive development of an integrated modern health care system, built on the network's past experiences, its historical values, and its human capital. He was under no delusion regarding the magnitude of the work involved at all levels and the role that AKU could play, the cooperative and collaborative efforts necessary by multiple stakeholders and putative beneficiaries in order to succeed. He conceived the new medical college and its teaching and service facilities as a possible prototype for widespread dissemination if shown to be effective.

Thus, AKU's solid intellectual and conceptual base for educational components and research, including humanities and social sciences, which equips the students for the practice of curative and preventive medicine, was essentially consolidated. The Medical College's Department of Community Health Sciences (CHS) works with communities in both urban and rural settings. It seeks to assist communities in developing their own leadership and resources so as to create self-sustaining health systems. The curriculum was thus problem-based learning, fostering problem-solving skills, progress from information to more complex concepts and skills, and a capacity to evaluate, criticize, and recommend changes, while integrating curative with preventive and developing leadership skills.

To achieve its objectives, the department established several PHC field sites in the *katchi abadis* (squatter settlements), each looking after approximately ten thousand people. These sites are developed in various settings – urban, rural, and mountainous areas – where poverty, underemployment, poor housing, overcrowding, a lack of adequate environmental sanitation, and low literacy levels are common factors for high morbidity and mortality. This teaching and service program's backbone is young doctors and nurses, locally recruited, who also serve in junior faculty positions as instructors and senior instructors.

The CHS program's preceptors served as community health doctors, tutors for small groups of medical students, field directors, and researchers while furthering their own education and leadership skills. The AKUSON had a parallel structure for nursing leadership development, though integrated with the medical care and education program.

AKHS and AKF have initiatives underway that, ideally, should dovetail with

AKU's long-term vision for the health sector and human resource development in Asia and Africa, guided by a shared health strategy and goal for the development of societies. In essence, AKU needs diverse "training complexes," both within the Aga Khan network and in the public health facilities that provide a range of learning opportunities, experiences, patients, programs, resources, and interactions crucial for high-quality education. Of no lesser significance is the imperative for the AKDN to engage in public sector development and capacity building – through the interface of public–private partnerships and collaborations – primarily through knowledge generation and translation, technical support, and resource mobilization that is mutually beneficial.

Let the beauty of what you love be what you do.

Jalal ad-Din Rumi, thirteenth-century Persian poet and Sufi mystic

CHAPTER 5

THE ROLE OF THE ACADEMIC HEALTH
SCIENCES CENTRE: DOCTOR AND SOCIETY

You were born with wings,
Why then prefer to crawl?

Jalal ad-Din Rumi, Persian poet and Sufi mystic

It was Saturday afternoon when my wife picked up the phone call from Dennis Mull. This was now about six weeks after our return from our last visit to Karachi. I had settled back into the busy routine of my practice, somewhat wistfully. After exchanging a few pleasantries with my wife, he asked to speak to me.

Dennis greeted me warmly and said that I seemed to have impressed quite a few people during my visit, and in particular, the preceptors of the CHS Department. He asked if I would be interested in considering accepting the assistant professor position in the Department of Community Health Sciences and associate director of the Community Health Centre (CHC), which AKU was looking to fill. I later learnt that another candidate had been strongly considered for this position, apparently another expatriate physician. It was noted by some senior people that I was an "idealist and passionate" in their interview notes.

He did say that compared to the comparatively high earnings of a physician in Canada, the compensation package on offer, while generous by local standards, would seem relatively meagre, but would prove to be quite adequate given the low cost of living in Pakistan. He gave candid examples of the relative cost difference, in the order of several-fold, of Karachi's haircut price compared to a large city in California. The same applied to the cost of housing, food, and local travel and entertainment. Most of this we had already gleaned during our sojourn in Karachi, albeit subconsciously.

While excited and gratified by this offer, we were apprehensive of its consequences on our life and future. We had much to show for materially in Canada, by the usual metrics of success. We had two young daughters, ages five and eight, and the impact on their young lives was a consideration, as was the cost of private education in Pakistan, which Dennis had not directly alluded to but hinted at. He left his phone number with us and suggested we think about it and call him.

Surprisingly, it took us very little time to reach our decision! We all agreed that change and a new challenge, while possibly momentous and life-changing, was due in our lives. We soon set the wheels in motion for the big move. Within two months, having hastily sold our home and my beloved Jaguar, and transferred my patients to a new doctor, we were ready to move.

Crossing Continents: Excitement and New Beginnings

The Swiss Air flight to Geneva gracefully landed us in that beautiful city, known for its multilateral agencies and many international organizations and, in particular, the United Nations and the World Health Organization. It is also where the Aga Khan Development Network's several agencies, such as the Aga Khan Foundation, Aga Khan Health Services, and Aga Khan Education Services, were headquartered. We planned to spend a few days sightseeing and visiting some of these entities. On my visit to the Aga Khan Health Services office, I had a delightful meeting with Dr. John Gillespie, the senior program officer. He shared with me the vision and objectives for health development in the countries where they operated. Dr. John Tomaro of the AKF was also very helpful in providing an overview of their efforts to foster growth in the third world and of the health programs supported by the AKF.

After a few pleasant days spent in Geneva, we flew to Istanbul. This bustling ancient and historic city at the crossroads of Asia and Europe introduced the children to a glimpse of life in a pluralistic Asian culture. The streets, bazaars, museums, and mosques all impacted their curious minds and shaped some of their interests and education in the future. The girls were gobsmacked by the vibrancy of daily life, the local cuisines, and the Turkish Airlines billboards proclaiming the joys of flying on the *Turk Hava Yolare*, the name for Turkish Airlines in the local language. The lilting singsong rendition of this name amused them to no ends, and they persuaded me to change our onward flight to Karachi from Swiss Air to Turkish Airlines. They soon learnt that the meticulous and sanitized Swiss Air environment was not matched by the airline of their choice and to be alert to the risk of the latent deception of sweet iterations of words.

Karachi was hot and humid when we arrived. We were met at the airport by AKU staff and soon whisked off to the AKU guesthouse, which was to be our home for almost two months until we were finally settled in our first home. Our "suite" in the charming old guesthouse consisted of two rooms, a common dining and sitting room furnished with well-worn stuffed old English-style sofas, a few chairs, a television set on a high stand, an old radio, and a bookshelf holding a few old books on travel, local history, and novels in English, Urdu, and French. A door led to a small, walled back garden, where a few flowering plants of jacaranda, frangipani, and hibiscus and fruit trees grew. The guesthouse served to accommodate visitors from various parts of the world who from time to time arrived to work as consultants, those on a multitude of short-term assignments, and newly joining staff and faculty such as ourselves. In our time at the guesthouse, two or three visitors arrived and stayed for short periods. The guesthouse staff included a cook, a "bearer" (helper/cleaner), and two Pathan *chowkidars* (security guards). They were consistently courteous, helpful, and discreet. We managed to communicate with them in broken Urdu and English. It took a bit of getting used to an entirely different cuisine.

The girls soon found a way to amuse themselves, creatively making dolls and toys with empty Coke bottles and other odd bits and pieces around the guesthouse. We all eagerly waited for our container's arrival and our luggage, which contained the girls' books and some of their favourite toys and mementos.

A friendly and well-informed representative of the university's Hospitality and Housing Department showed us around Karachi – the schools, markets, and supermarkets. One supermarket, in particular, Agha Supermarket in Clifton, seemed to cater to the expatriate community of Karachi and was recommended to us. The Hospitality and Housing Department lined up several homes for us to check out. My wife was taken to some shops selling furniture and essential household goods.

I had taken some pains to acquaint myself somewhat with Pakistan, a country in the South Asia region. My earlier visits and general interest in the history, geography, and cultures of South and Central Asia – that swath of the Indian sub-continent that included India, Pakistan, Afghanistan, Bangladesh (formerly East Pakistan), Nepal, and Sri Lanka – had given me a broad perspective on this ancient land and its strategic location, as well as the development and political challenges, many shared by its neighbouring countries in the region.

With a population of over 220 million, it borders India, Afghanistan, Iran, and China. Its long coastline along the Arabian Sea and the Gulf of Oman offers it close historical and current contact with the Middle East. The territory that now constitutes Pakistan was the site of several ancient cultures and intertwined histori-cally with the broader Indian subcontinent.

Ancient history involves the Neolithic site of Mehrgarh and the Bronze Age Indus Valley civilization, notably Mohenjo-daro and Harappa, which along with Mesopotamia and Egypt and Minoan Crete, is considered one of the oldest civilizations in the world. It was home to kingdoms ruled by different faiths and cultures, including Alexander III of Macedonia and the Mughals. Its turbulent modern history included its birth in 1947 with independence from the British Empire and partition from India. It shares many challenges in common with its neighbours in the region. Over time, a deeper appreciation of the region's socio-cultural and historical contexts proved crucial in my involvement in the develop-ment objectives of the AKDN.

Grand Design: Form and Function Reshaping the Complex Care Paradigm

I almost immediately plunged myself into taking charge of the Community Health Centre (CHC). The label Aga Khan University Medical Centre (AKUMC) is used to describe the 721-bed teaching hospital (AKUH), of which the CHC is an integral part, and Aga Khan University (AKU) comprising the Medical College, the School of Nursing (AKUSON), and male and female housing. The CHC was the first unit of the AKUMC to open its services to the public.

In congruence with the medical centre's grand architectural style and marble façades, the CHC is beautifully designed and situated in one corner of the medical complex's continuous interior spaces surrounding the observer. The striking geometric design of the whole medical centre, whose diverse physical and functional requirements were incorporated into an organic whole, offers the different functions represented through the identification of appropriate entrance portals, fountains, changes of level, and vistas. The architectural experience consists of movement through portals, transitional spaces, and courtyards. The CHC is entered through an open entrance from a large quadrangle – which is partially covered by trellises of bougainvillea, jacaranda, and other flowers – opening into a large courtyard. One side of the courtyard housed the main clinic space, comprising about ten consulting rooms, a small operating room, and a treatment room. Adjoining it are offices for the medical director and the nursing manager and an office occupied by the welfare officer, where there was always a line of needy or disadvantaged patients and their families seeking assistance with the cost of care through the hospital's Patient Welfare Program. One side of the courtyard held the patient registration counter, a small outpatient satellite pharmacy, and a teaching seminar and meeting room. The patients and their families sat on pink marble benches that lined the courtyard. In the middle of the courtyard was a small fountain, which was not turned on most of the time to conserve water. The square was an ideal space for patient waiting and contemplation.

The CHC was originally called the "filter clinic" by the planners. The thinking was that this low-cost outpatient service would "filter" hundreds of people passing through it – patients with "simple" fevers, coughs, respiratory illnesses, rashes, diarrhoeal diseases in children, etc. – and refer the more serious cases to the Consulting Clinic (CC) or for inpatient care, where a whole range of medical and surgical specialists would be based and where more in-depth consultations and diagnostics tests would occur. Of course, this meant the costs would be considerably higher for the patient, while still subsidized to an extent.

The CHC was staffed by about six or seven junior doctors, referred to as RMOs (resident medical officers). These were a diverse group of young doctors of varying training and experience levels who had obtained their basic medical education in one of Pakistan's medical schools. It was my job to supervise their clinical practice, mentor and guide, and enhance their knowledge and skills. In this, I was ably assisted by Rukhshana Zuberi, a bright and committed Pakistani physician. Her experience of medicine's normative practice in Pakistan and the relative deficiencies in applying modern scientific principles in medical education proved to be very valuable in our efforts to improve the quality of care in the CHC. She had been appointed assistant director of the CHC before my joining. As a senior instructor in the CHS Department, her passion for improving the medical staff's knowledge base and practice was invaluable.

There were also nurses and nursing assistants, clerical staff, and support staff. The nursing manager, Ishrat Jaffer, an early graduate of the AKUSON program, was a dynamic and iron-willed leader, protective of her team, yet a firm disciplinarian. Her oversight of nursing care and training, historically a weakness in the country's care paradigm, and her managerial skills added a great deal to our efforts to enhance care and training in the ambulatory setting.

I was given very little information on the complex internal and external dynamics that impacted the centre's functioning, concept, vision, and objectives. All this I was to learn by quick and total immersion into the management and supervision of the unit. In effect, as time would tell, this served me well. Since I was not a party to the long and arduous deliberations on the vision, goals, planning, conceptualization, management, and operations of the centre, I found myself relatively unencumbered by heavy-handed officialdom or straight-jacketed by preconceived notions. I was able to improvise and innovate to nimbly solve problems, particularly as they related to questions of quality of care, the flow and waiting times, the costs, and patient outcomes and satisfaction.

The CHC served as the main ambulatory primary care clinic for patients of all ages with all manner of undifferentiated problems seeking care at the hospital. It had been operating for at least two years by the time I joined the organization. My early assessment of the mission and the profile of the CHC led me to reach some important conclusions that served to guide the future development of this critical unit.

To state it succinctly, the population groups that presented to the CHC consisted mostly of low- to middle-income patients, who showed not for short minor acute illnesses, as was initially thought, but for more severe or unresolved advanced clinical presentations or chronic problems, which they had neglected or for which they had previously sought care elsewhere. It also served as the entry point to the hospital's advanced clinical services for the sick, indigent, and marginalized patients referred from the CHS Department's prototype teaching field units located in the *katchi abadis* – impermanent or squatter settlements – in some of the most impoverished areas of Karachi and Sindh.

There were other users of the CHC also, middle class and better-off economically. They found the pleasant ambience, the relatively low costs of quality service, and access to a range of sophisticated diagnostic tests and to some of the best specialists in the city to be a highly satisfactory medical service option for themselves and their families.

And the CHC was expected to do a good deal more. As a unit under the Department of Community Health Sciences, the Medical College's largest department, it also served as a clinical teaching unit and a putative research unit for the departmental students, preceptors, and scholars. It served as a vital outpatient teaching site for medical officers and medical and nursing students of AKU.

The financial model of AKU/AKUH also presumed a certain level of generation of income to enable its broader mission of serving low-income populations with quality care and access. Hence, there were efforts and programs to enlist "corporate clients" who could provide a minimal, steady income level. This service entailed providing basic clinical care for employees and their families, pre-employment physical examinations, preventive care and immunizations, and other interventions for a list of rostered companies. The corporate health service users included Suzuki Motors, the Japanese consulate, Cyanamid Pakistan, and many other large industrial and business companies. The CHC also provided medical care to the students and staff of AKU and AKUH in some rudimentary way.

I quickly realized that the smorgasbord of services delivered in the unit posed enormous operational challenges and created unrealistic public and institutional expectations of the CHC, which was still in its relative infancy. These included the broad and diverse range of services and outcomes expected, the high expectations of the unit's quality and efficiency of service, the unrealistic income generation projected, and a portal to a broad spectrum of the population, many of meagre economic and financial means. Compounding the image and function issue was the underlying institutional desire to project an image of modernity, innovation, good care quality, sophistication, ethical and philanthropic underpinnings, and the institution's generous predisposition. Much of this purportedly highly ambitious agenda had resulted from the imperative to satisfy multiple stakeholders and planners and address perceived needs and deficiencies in health care without adequate regard to the availability of necessary trained human resources and the political and cultural environment in which it operated.

I surmised that the manifold goals and objectives – some potentially incongruent – emerged from the lofty mission, goals, and vision of the non-profit philanthropic institution; the input of multiple external experts; and the urgency of making an immediate impact. The many tensions inherent in these ambitious and diverse demands had begun to manifest themselves. Clearly, this was a front unit of the AKUMC of which much was expected, and on which rode dreams and high expectations.

Many pressing operational and quality issues seemed to revolve around complex and bureaucratic processes surrounding patient care delivery; many were imported and unfamiliar in Pakistan's existing medical service paradigm. These included new and untested medical records systems, financial tracking and support mechanisms, and relatively inexperienced nursing and support staff. Added to these were issues such as the institution's crucial teaching mission, burgeoning demand, and the unintended fragmentation of service components – physically and operationally – such as laboratory, imaging, and pharmacy, much of this unfamiliar both to service users and providers. While in keeping with the organization's processes of quality control and audit, these elements led to significant delays and bottlenecks; for many users, it resulted in some disorienting pathways to receiving care.

I tested the following questions: Is it a model that holds that the CHC is a "machine," a machine that can be optimized by breaking it into its constituent parts, optimizing each and putting them back together to make an optimally running whole? Further, can the machine be improved by pursuing increasing levels of efficiency in each constituent part? Since the definition of "efficiency" in medical care is somewhat abstract, I considered the myriad human dimensions at play as critical determinants of quality and efficiency; a mechanical analogy would be insufficient to address the challenges.

To mitigate some of the process issues and impediments to quality care and patient satisfaction, we conducted several "time-motion" studies and patient-needs surveys. We looked at both the clinical quality concerns and presentations, as well as non-clinical roadblocks.

The feedback was very telling. The lessons learned enabled us to redesign and streamline patient flow patterns, prioritize patients based on their clinical urgency and complexity, and assign more experienced nursing and management staff to expedite care and flow. I trusted this initial collaborative exercise to Dr. Waris Kidwai, one of my more experienced RMOs; the nursing manager; a research assistant; dedicated volunteers; and hospital management representatives. It also served as an essential educational, research, and planning exercise for the organization, one of the many efforts to improve patient care in the years ahead.

Dr. Amin Haiderali, a brilliant young man, freshly qualified from the first batch of graduates of the AKU Medical College, later undertook several further studies under my supervision as part of his internship, which added considerably to our understanding of demographics, costs, and consultations. These studies yielded important information on diagnostic services' utilizations, medication prescriptions, and the levels and types of clinical problems we were dealing with daily. The studies confirmed that over sixty percent of patients presenting had already seen between two and four other health care providers before presenting themselves to the CHC, when their problems remained unresolved. This unexpected complexity, severity, and diversity of clinical issues added to the many operational challenges confronting the CHC. We also learnt that often the only source we could use to reconstruct the patient's medical history was little pieces of crumpled papers that patients preserved and carried with them, consisting of old prescriptions, occasional scribbled hospital notes, or a lab or X-ray report, which they instinctively recognized as valuable information. They called these bits of paper *purchis*. There was no organized system of medical records in the country; the AKUH was the first to attempt to introduce this method routinely, which in days ahead proved invaluable in clinical care, service planning, and research.

The following vignette may illustrate the interplay of diverse factors surrounding many patient visits to the CHC. One afternoon, Dr. Renee D'Souza, a young and caring RMO working at the CHC, asked me to see a family seated in her consulting room. I entered and greeted a family cluster of four in the room. Renee introduced me to the family and gave me an outline of the problems she was facing. A man in his late thirties, his lined face looking older than his stated age, was accompanied by his wife, a tired-looking shy lady, a boy of about eight, and a frail elderly lady, probably in her late sixties. I learnt this man, Mr. Ramzan, was a fruit seller in Sindh's interior, and the family had made a costly and challenging journey to Karachi the day before, as both his son and his mother had been sick for several months. Visits to several local practitioners and *Hakims* (faith healers) had proved to be fruitless in resolving their problems. He had spent a considerable amount of his meagre earnings buying various medications and "tonics" recommended to him.

Mr. Ramzan told me that his son developed a fever every night, had frequent diarrhea, and had lost weight. He missed school frequently due to his illness. He also expressed worries about his mother, who was becoming increasingly frail, hardly ate anything, had bone and joint pains, and seemed to have little energy. He mentioned he had three other children at home and often lost time from his work.

Detailed history and examination and a few well-targeted tests led us to conclude that the boy suffered from a chronic intestinal infection, which led to some liver inflammation. His elderly mother's problem was medically quite complicated and would require several additional diagnostic tests and specialist consultations. The probable diagnosis was a malignant disease, likely affecting the bones, liver, and possibly other body parts. We gently shared our impressions with Mr. Ramzan, who was shocked at the implications of these conclusions. He was also worried about how he would cope financially with his two loved ones' anticipated care costs.

He later confided that, given his limited financial ability, he had surmised that he might have to choose between trying to seek treatment for his beloved son or his mother, whom he adored. His wife, who worked as a cleaner in a small rural township, also visibly affected, was trying bravely to support her husband. We directed our efforts to assuage the family's emotional and economic burdens while bringing all our clinical resources in treating both patients. They both needed inpatient care, which we arranged, ultimately with very significant financial assistance from the Patient Welfare Program.

While not all cases were of this level of social and economical and medical intertwining, they were by no means uncommon in the cross-section of patients we were dealing with. It was a damning testimony to the relative neglect in the provision of medical care and decades of underinvestment in health, poor health care infrastructure, and the lack of competent service availability and affordability nationally and, indeed, regionally.

With increasing experience, and informed by several surveys and studies, we assimilated the complex interplay of the significant process impediments. The mismatch between the level of clinical efficiency and the clinical demand was evident, and these were often at odds with the societal traditions, culture, and expectations. The users' socio-economic realities appeared incongruous with the lofty stated goals and mandate of the CHC and its relationships to the university, the university hospital, the community, and society.

I immediately set about rectifying several aspects of the medical care process. The clinical reasoning skills and competence of all doctors and other care providers need to be significantly uplifted. It included increased supervision of clinical care and mentoring the RMOs and junior medical staff. Simultaneously, I attempted to create an environment conducive to improved work satisfaction and learning. With the nursing manager, clerks, pharmacists, and hospital management, I tried to streamline patient flow and introduced a triage mechanism that prioritized care according to urgency.

Over time, several self-study groups, committees, and task forces were set up by the organization to define further this integral unit's central mandate and future directions. I wrote several documents and analytical reports and made presentations to the Medical Centre's senior planners, administrators, and governing bodies proposing mission-critical adjustments to serve users and providers' diverse constituencies. I was tasked to chair a critical multidisciplinary CHC committee that attempted to rebalance, harmonize, and redirect future development, as well as to foster continuous quality improvement, training, and research culture. The focused and concerted effort soon began to show results. Ongoing surveys over the coming months showed increasing patient satisfaction, cost containment, and promptness in service.

I was appointed director of the CHC after Dennis Mull's departure less than a year after I joined the organization. Dennis Mull had planted the initial seeds of the concept of "family medicine" within the curriculum. I was passionately committed to this concept, as it was my own chosen specialty, and I had supported this vision in my early interactions with the institution. During my previous visit to Pakistan, I had promoted this notion of comprehensive primary care to the Pakistan Medical Association, to the embryonic College of General Practice of Pakistan, and at the WONCA (World Association of Family Doctors) conference in Hong Kong. There was mounting evidence worldwide of the benefit of advanced structured training in clinical and preventive medicine and its impact on improving population health by combining health promotion and disease prevention and scientifically sound clinical medicine, if adopted widely.

Enhancing Clinical Competence: Fostering Critical Thinking

I was concerned about the level of clinical training and the proficiency of the CHC medical staff, including the RMOs and preceptors. As was usual in Pakistan and other countries in the region, medical education, as in other professional education fields, tended to be outmoded and consisted of more rote learning – that is, the passive absorption of vast amounts of information, without significant critical thought and problem orientation. This colonial legacy of traditional higher education modes had not undergone any considerable revitalization informed by advances in educational and cognitive sciences, problem-based learning, and critical thinking.

One of my earliest initiatives was establishing regular, formal continuing professional development for all junior doctors working through the CHC and CHS field sites. We launched regular sessions of essential learning three times a week. All junior doctors were required to participate in and upgrade their clinical skills and maintain their staff credentialling and promotion. Among the programs I scheduled were seminars such as "Patient Management & Therapeutics", "Appropriate use of Diagnostic Tests," a journal club, and other sessions such as weekly case discussion rounds. The objective of embedding these intense educational exercises was to foster intelligent diagnostic formulation; the cost-effective use of tests, drugs, and procedures; and founding care decisions based on critical evaluation of scientific evidence.

In partnership with the Pharmacy Department, we developed a hospital formulary to guide proven and cost-effective drug therapy. Similarly, with the clinical laboratory, we developed guidelines for the appropriate use of laboratory and imaging studies, including urgent notification of critical abnormalities on standard laboratory tests.

The students and staff of the Medical Centre were users of the CHC for their own medical care. To upgrade the quality of comprehensive care provided to them, we formally established Student Health and Employee Health Services, each guided by advisory committees. I chaired these committees for several years and appointed dedicated physicians to each to manage the respective services. I believe this resulted in a marked improvement in the quality and scope of care and satisfaction. It enabled us to introduce periodic health examinations, regular screening for specific users – such as food handlers, laboratory staff, cleaners, and nurses – and immunizations for common conditions such as tetanus, hepatitis, typhoid, and tuberculosis.

Interestingly, the restructured process enabled us to detect many "silent" conditions, such as high blood pressure, diabetes, hepatitis, and kidney disease. Early treatment of these disorders results in reducing long-term complications of the disease. User health education became an integral part of the service and served as a valuable educational exercise for medical and nursing students.

Wherever the art of Medicine is loved, there is also a love of Humanity

Hippocrates

CHAPTER 6

TRAINING DOCTORS FOR TOMORROW: ADDRESSING QUALITY AND RELEVANCE

First, it must be a pleasure to study the human body, the most miraculous masterpiece of nature, and to learn about the smallest vessel and the smallest fibre. But second and most important, the medical profession gives the opportunity to alleviate the troubles of the body, to ease the pain, to console a person who is in distress, and to lighten the hour of death of many a sufferer.

Rudolf Virchow, German physician, "the father of modern pathology"

Our initial efforts had been directed towards restructuring and aligning our internal processes to optimize outcomes of patient contacts with the CHC. But we could not escape the conclusion that a broader enabling environment for effective care was critical in order to have a wider impact on the health of communities and populations more generally. This would entail boldly extending the reach of our institution beyond our walls and disseminating our methods, experiences, lessons, and standards much more extensively.

Bridging the Quality Chasm: Promoting Continuing Professional Growth

An interesting observation of our internal assessments led us also to evaluate patients' referral patterns to our services at the CHC from community-based physicians, both from the private and public health sectors. One study had shown that on a visit to a practitioner, an average of five or more medications were prescribed to the patients. Of these, there were more than half that were essentially "tonics" or vitamins; "therapeutic" drugs made up the rest of the prescription. More often than not, the patients spent their limited financial resources buying the cheaper "tonics," rather than the essential treatment medications. Hence, there was often little response to treatment. Also, patients were often prescribed injections and intravenous therapies, it being assumed, by and large, by the practitioners and the consumers that treatments were more effective when delivered with a needle. The resulting delay in proper diagnosis and treatment led to many seeking cures of their unresolved illnesses at our doors.

I enlisted Murad Verjee, the manager of marketing for the hospital, and his staff to survey the education interest and requirements of medical practitioners in various communities in the urban and rural areas of Pakistan. Khairunessa Ahmed, then Murad's dedicated assistant, toiled tirelessly to print and organize the survey instruments expeditiously.

We surveyed a large and diverse segment of health practitioners in different settings. We visited a number of doctors' offices and clinics and were always cordially received. The needs and interest surveys were surprisingly frank and hopeful; there was clearly hunger amongst the practitioners to upgrade their knowledge. They freely admitted deficiencies in their practice and training. Many admitted to their inability to help patients with complex or advanced problems, yet still attempted to alleviate the patient's disability and suffering to the best of their ability and available resources. Referral networks to private and public hospitals were patchy and irregular.

Most had limited or no access to reputable sources of continuing medical education; available literature was usually slanted towards pharmaceutical substances' uncritical promotion. Available courses tended to be sponsored mostly by foreign and a few local pharmaceutical companies, promoting their expensive drugs. There was no national drug formulary in use; diagnostic laboratories were not standardized or regulated. There was no mandated regulatory requirement to maintain competence and registration as a licensed medical practitioner.

However, it was heartening to note that a large proportion of the practitioners recognized their need to upgrade their mostly outdated knowledge base and clinical skills. Our survey indicated that the areas of knowledge most sought were advances in diagnosis and treatment for common diseases: rational, evidence-based drug therapy; appropriate referrals for specialist assessment and treatment; and emerging clinical technologies, among others.

Armed with this encouraging information, I drafted an upgrading course outline for community doctors and widely consulted the university faculty for their input and participation. There was an equally gratifying response from the AKU faculty to this venture; unfailingly, all those approached agreed to participate in any program to impart and share knowledge with their external colleagues.

This deliberation on the community-based medicine practice's state led to the tentative launching of our first formal continuing medical education endeavour for outside medical practitioners in the later part of 1986. We titled this program "Update in Clinical Medicine." It was held twice a week for three weeks and covered important topics such as childhood illnesses, infectious and diarrhoeal diseases, undiagnosed fevers, respiratory infections, hypertension, tuberculosis, and diabetes. We attempted to make these courses as interactive and case-based as possible and had encouraged the attending course participants to bring forth cases from their practice for discussion.

While the faculty presented and guided the discussions, we were pleased to note the attendees' increasing direct participation in seeking solutions to clinical problems common in their practices. It was traditionally typical for a top-down hierarchical education mode to impart knowledge; I encouraged our faculty to make our format more participatory, problem-solving, and case-based learning – a form of learning rare in the region. This exercise led to lively discussions amongst the participants and the faculty; some participants later expressed an unwonted feeling of "liberation" from the tyranny of "experts who claimed" superior knowledge.

Our initial hope was to attract about fifty to seventy participants to our first venture into this new direction in improving clinical practice more broadly beyond our institution's walls. But we were overwhelmed by the response. The number of applications to our course exceeded three hundred, despite the unreliable means of distributing our course application forms. Most applications came from the province of Sindh, where we were located, but we had several applications from other parts of the country.

Given the limitations of our capacity and our endeavour's tentative nature to mount a large-scale education enterprise, beyond the central goal of training doctors within our own established and emerging training programs, this was a daunting undertaking. Yet most among our faculty, administration, and planners freely supported our larger mission of impacting the broader population's health by means of bold and innovative steps. Therefore, we admitted around 180 participants in our first program, promising to accommodate others into future programs. At the end of the course, we handed out a beautifully designed "Certificate of Attendance," signed by the dean, Dr. David Ulmer, and me as the course coordinator. This certificate gave considerable pride to the recipients and a new sense of self-confidence, dignity, and value. We conducted a post-course survey, seeking feedback on such programs' value and desirability and received our effort's enthusiastic endorsement.

Soon after our project's successful conduct, the board of trustees of Aga Khan University met with the full faculty at a luncheon in the charming lobby of the Private Wing of the AKUH. I was deeply gratified and touched when His Highness the Aga Khan, the chancellor and charismatic founder of Aga Khan University, graciously expressed to me his pleasure and support for this new effort to broaden the institution's quest to educate health professionals in the country. He was pleased with AKU's first continuing medical education (CME) program response and acceptance by the medical community and encouraged its continuation and expansion to serve as a resource and a change agent. When introduced to him by the university president, I was amazed by how much he knew about me, recalling my work over time and my work with the organization. The only time I recalled a previous encounter – a very fleeting encounter – with him was several years prior in the cafeteria of the Aga Khan Secretariat in Paris upon a visit with his senior staff members.

He asked me to prepare for him a document that outlined the opportunities, goals, and strategies of continuing professional development, not only for Pakistan but also for the region at large, and more broadly for other developing countries. His vision was that Aga Khan institutions should ultimately serve as a resource for and provide access to community physicians, local health care institutions, and all population segments, giving priority to programs that address unmet needs. As a result of this resounding endorsement, I prepared the requested document over the next few weeks and forwarded it to him through the dean's office, bypassing the usual vetting procedures normally in place. I titled the document *Continuing Medical Education: A Statement of Mission, Opportunity and Strategies of the Aga Khan University.*

To conduct this venture most effectively, I proposed and received ready institutional support to establish an Office of Continuing Medical Education (OCME). For over four years, I served as the founding director of the Office of CME. We conducted at least twenty more CME programs over the next three years, targeted towards fostering better management of women's health problems, nutrition, mental health, eye and ear diseases, skin disorders, heart and lung disorders, and preventive care, amongst others. We emphasized imparting knowledge and skills that we felt could contribute most significantly to beneficent effects on the population's health.

$$\sim \! 9_{\! 6} \! \sim$$

An elegant, well-dressed gentleman walked into the CHC compound one morning and asked to see Dr. Jiwani. He was shown to my office by a unit clerk, while I was attending a patient with an RMO in a nearby examination room. When I came into my office, he introduced himself as Pat Cronin, but said little else about himself, except a passing reference to his current position. He was somewhat terse but pleasant when we met. I got to know him and his illustrious history much better later. The senior medical advisor to His Highness the Aga Khan's Secretariat; son of A.J. Cronin, the famous British novelist; and a former dean at the School of Medicine at McGill University in Canada, he was very involved in health services development for the Aga Khan Network.

His father, Dr. Archibald J. Cronin, of Scottish descent, was a successful physician and general practitioner who worked as a medical inspector of mines in the 1920s and '30s, where he pursued the link between coal-mining dust and chronic lung disease. His most famous novel, *The Citadel,* raised controversies about medical ethics, the self-serving state of the predominantly private medical care in the U.K. in the pre-war period, and moral conflicts between the individual and society. His writings exposed the inequity and incompetence of medical practice at the time. He advocated a national public health care service, and he is considered a major contributor to the eventual establishment of the National Health Service in the United Kingdom at the end of the Second World War.

Patrick Cronin had a distinguished history in medicine himself, as a physician and professor, as well as in fostering the education of medical students and doctors from many developing countries in the Middle East, Asia, and Africa through exchange programs. In his capacity as a medical advisor at the Aga Khan Secretariat, he furthered the development of the AKUH and Aga Khan Health

Services more generally, with a particular interest in continuing the professional development of practising physicians; hence, our paths were bound to cross given our common commitment to that end.

He said that he was aware of changes that had taken place in the design and functions of the CHC. He ventured that it appeared that the service model had significantly shifted since I took charge of running the unit. He asked if I was aware of how much planning and consultation had gone into planning the CHC and how many experts were consulted.

I said yes, I had some idea of the complex nature of planning that had taken place. However, I countered, I was the one who was at the front line of care at the CHC and in contact with the day-to-day realities of the CHC and its myriad issues and challenges. It was crucial to adjust and adapt in significant ways, including the numbers and nature of clinical care provided at the CHC. I was aware there was a shift in the model from the one originally planned.

He smiled. He said he approved and had heard favourable comments from various sources about the progress taking place in the CHC. We chatted for a while, both now perceptibly relaxed. He was very interested in the education efforts we were making to uplift the house staff and community physicians' clinical competence. We got to know each other rather well in the days ahead. He invited me to participate in and to consider widening the scope of continuing professional development of AKHS network physicians, which I did with some gusto over the coming years. A few months later, he invited me to participate in a CME course he organized in Mombasa for Kenyan medical staff of Aga Khan Health Services and hospitals. It was the first of many programs I got involved with.

Supporting Community Health: Extending Clinical Partnerships

A major concern revolved around improving health providers' knowledge and skills located among the seven CHS field sites. These field sites in *katchi abadis* (informal settlements) were involved in training AKU's medical and nursing students and in providing some primary care of the defined populations. People in these impoverished communities usually sought medical care from diverse providers – traditional healers, faith healers, herbalists, homeopaths, "pharmacists" (medicine shop owners) and others, and a few licensed general medical practitioners. The concern expressed by the CHS Department was the highly variable quality of care the patients received from these sources, and the imperative to improve their knowledge, understand their limitations, and refer to more qualified care when indicated.

Since our nascent efforts were directed only towards enhancing medical doctors' professional competence, we had vigorously directed our efforts towards that group. The objective was that more skillful clinical problem management would ultimately improve users' health outcomes and foster healthier populations. It was beyond our means to undertake an enterprise encompassing transforming or uplifting care provided by non-physician "healers." But we did not wish to disparage the services of these non-conventional healers, since they formed the cultural and psychological bedrock of health care for a large segment of society who trusted and relied upon them for their basic care.

However, it must be noted that there is considerable scientific skepticism of traditional healing practices and the potential for harm. There may be some presumptive benefits to traditional practitioners' care, such as Unani, naturopathy, herbal medicine, and faith healing. In Pakistan, as in India, a large majority of people seek initial treatments from these sources. Various private foundations and "research" institutions exist in Pakistan in support of Unani (meaning "Greek") medicine, which traces its roots to the Persio-Arabian pseudoscientific system of medicine in addition to its Hellenistic roots. One such research institute, the Hamdard Institute of Medical Sciences & Research, had a powerful impact on Pakistan's traditional healing practices and held a respected status in the country.

As our experience in providing community-based physicians' professional development grew, we could more effectively target the learning objectives.

Fostering Synergies: Linking Network Health Services

A special interest to me was the ongoing professional educational development of medical and ancillary staff attached to the units of Aga Khan Health Services of Pakistan (AKHSP).

The AKHSP, in its long history of almost a century of providing health care, had established numerous programs, projects, and units in urban, rural, and remote mountainous regions of Pakistan. Their activities primarily revolved around providing a broad spectrum of primary care, including immunizations, environmental sanitation, health education, nutrition, growth and health monitoring of infants and children, maternal care, and basic curative medical care. Over the course of time, the organization had found it necessary to enter into providing a higher level of clinical care. It, hence, had established several maternity homes and diagnostic and treatment centres.

Their first maternity centre, the Janbai Maternity Home, established in Kharadar, Karachi, was established almost a hundred years ago by Sir Sultan Mohamed Shah, Aga Khan III, grandfather of the current Aga Khan, and served later as a model centre. The diagnostic centres were the primary locus of clinical curative care. They were staffed by a range of general practitioners and specialists, as well as auxiliary staff such as nutritionists, physiotherapists, and health educators. I had visited several of the AKHSP units over time and was struck by their vision and efforts to provide high-quality, cost-effective care to large segments of populations. The leadership and support staff, primarily made up of volunteers, were dedicated and inspired.

I had always seen the need to support and foster synergy between the health systems of the AKUMC and the AKHSP, our sister agency in health care. The relationship between the two agencies of the AKDN was, on occasion, somewhat fractious. As the newer entity, AKU housed the advanced technical and intellectual capital; the AKHSP had a long experience of public health needs and the harsh realities and challenges associated with improving large populations' health.

When I was approached by Aziz Currimbhoy, the chairman of the AKHSP, to provide upgrading educational programs for the health professionals of the AKHSP, I felt the need to consider their unique needs, their history and experience, and their distributed service locations. Aziz was a passionate, perspicacious, and savvy leader who had been involved for decades in the Aga Khan agencies' global work, including AKU's planning and other projects. He also sat on the board of the university. Sophisticated, erudite, and with almost a military bearing, he was nevertheless modest and generous and highly committed to furthering the reach and development of the AKHSP. Despite his seniority in the institutional hierarchy, he would often wait patiently for his turn amongst other patients when he sought medical consultation with me at the CHC. In my time at the AKUMC, I only treated him at the CHC, not at the Consulting Clinic or the Executive Clinic, at his insistence.

In several of our new CME programs, we gave preference to the AKHSP practitioners and their particular educational needs. Linking referral, diagnostic, and specialist support undergirded the CME efforts. As our growing support of the AKHSP grew, I found myself more drawn into a broader academic engagement with the global AKHS facilities, particularly in East Africa, India, Central Asia, and the Middle East in the years ahead.

In 1987, a group from the Aga Khan Health Board from India visited Karachi to seek consultation and input into formulating a viable health plan to provide cost-effective, comprehensive care to a large middle-class population residing around the Prince Aly Khan Hospital in Bombay.

The Prince Aly Khan Hospital, an AKHS India facility, has a long and illustrious history. The team leader, Dr. Sultan Pradhan, a prominent oncologist and cancer surgeon, outlined their vision and objectives and the challenges faced. They were particularly interested in drawing on the lessons from AKU, the AKHSP, and the CHC and CHS in linking ambulatory care to secondary and tertiary levels of care and on quality control and resource questions. It was one of many fruitful consultations between AKU and the more comprehensive AKHS network that I was privileged to participate in and to foster.

Expanding Roles: Onerous Responsibilities

The CHC was beginning to shape up nicely. We could demonstrate measurable improvements in quality of care and patient satisfaction. Our in-house education programs were demonstrating greatly improved clinical management of patients. Besides, I had organized for some specialist senior residents in training to hold weekly consulting sessions at the CHC to support the care provided by the RMOs, somewhat to the disapproval of hospital management, who would have preferred patients to be referred to the Consulting Clinic. We had residents from surgery, internal medicine, pediatrics, gynecology, psychiatry, orthopedics, and ophthalmology holding low-cost consultations in the CHC. In addition, several senior consultants offered to see patients in the CHC periodically. Flow patterns had improved; costs continued to be reasonably contained. A level of more complex medical care could be provided to patients who needed them at the CHC. For the medical residents in training, the CHC afforded significantly enhanced learning opportunities. The clinical departments were supportive of this educational and service linkage.

Some of the RMOs who worked in the CHC during my supervision and tutelage distinguished themselves in their own right and by their efforts. I took great pride when, in years to come, Dr. Waris Kidwai was appointed professor and chair of AKU's Department of Family Medicine; Dr. Nilofer Ali, a shy, young CHC medical officer, later became a full professor of family medicine; and Dr. Masood Kadri, another RMO, obtained master's- and doctorate-level education in the U.S. and rose to the rank of professor in the CHS Department. Many other RMOs and preceptors proceeded to obtain advanced education in family medicine, public health, and health services research from prestigious universities like Harvard and Johns Hopkins in the U.S., Karolinska in Sweden, the London School of Hygiene and Tropical Medicine, and other institutions. They went on to hold senior positions at AKU, other Pakistan universities, and also in many other countries and institutions.

But ambulatory services in the Consulting Clinic and the Emergency Department, lacking sound clinical and administrative leadership, were experiencing problems. I was approached by the senior hospital administration to take overall charge of all ambulatory services of the AKUH. Bill Borton, the director-general of the AKUH, took me to dinner to persuade me to assume a more significant hospital administration role. He was backed in this by Shamsh Kassim-Lakha, the president of the AKUMC, with whom I had a long association.

The dean, David Ulmer, had cautionary counsel for me, fearing further drift into administration would increasingly distance me from the clinical and academic arena, which he stated was my proven forte. But it was Jack Bryant, whom I held as a role model, and for whom I had the greatest admiration and affection, whose guidance meant a great deal to me. Jack, in his remarkable career, had held highly significant clinical, research, and administrative positions globally. He was universally respected for his many contributions to global health and justice, institutional development, and health sciences education. Jack, the Community Health Sciences Department chair, my home department, invited me to dinner. As was his custom, he was forthright. He stated my contributions to upgrade the competence of the preceptors and RMOs and to improve teaching and research in the CHS field sites were highly appreciated by the department and by AKU broadly. My move further into hospital administration could mean less effort and time available for academic and departmental work. He further ventured to say that he could practically assure me a pathway to high positions in global health with prestigious international organizations such as the WHO or other U.N. bodies if I wished in the future. Shamsh had informed David and Jack of their desire to draw me into greater administrative and strategic planning roles on the hospital side.

I was torn between accepting an expanding administrative and planning role that Bill Borton assured me was an invaluable asset to have in my "back pocket" for career progression and my love of clinical medicine, teaching, and academia. I agonized over this offer to increase my hospital administration participation, while fully conscious of the possibility this could impact the degree of my academic involvement in the university's many exciting developments. This apparent tension between AKU and the AKUH may seem somewhat confusing and arbitrary.

A brief note on the entities may help clarify the apparent duality. Each of the two institutions was an independent registered entity, governed by separate boards: the Owner's Representative Board (ORB) for the AKUH, and the Board of Trustees (BOT) for AKU. The Faculty of Health Sciences of AKU related to the AKUH by an affiliation agreement. From 1988 onwards, the two entities functioned synergistically as the Aga Khan University Medical Center (AKUMC). Shamsh Kassim-Lakha, who was the chairman of ORB, was appointed president of the Executive Committee of the AKUMC. Shamsh brought years of leadership experience and was well placed to balance the tensions between service and academics and the long-term sustainability of its ambitious programs.

After almost two years at the helm of the CHC, I accepted the position of Administrator of Ambulatory Care. I reasoned that accepting this position was not in conflict with my passion for human resource development through education to impact population health. It seemed to me to be fully in accord with effectively linking hospitals to communities and their needs. I saw the pressing need for synergy and harmony in community care and hospital care into a continuous spectrum of care levels according to need.

The ambulatory care services encountered about eight hundred patients a day. Counting accompanying relatives and friends, over two thousand people passed through the concerned departments. Therefore, it was a locus of short, but often intense, human interaction between sick and anxious patients, relatives, and hospital staff, including registration clerks, unit clerks, nurses, doctors, students, laboratory staff, technicians, pharmacists, and welfare and finance officers. In addition, numerous hospital systems had to work in a coordinated and supportive manner. Therefore, the ambulatory care service was a complex of human and systems behaviour, any of which may have broken down at any point, resulting in unsatisfactory outcomes for the patient and, indeed, for the institution.

In this new role, I initially focused my energies on improving patient care in the Consulting Clinic and Emergency Department. The experience acquired in the CHC proved invaluable.

For enhancing the efficiency and effectiveness of emergency services, we introduced a multipronged approach: tutorials in emergency medicine for doctors and nurses, weekly clinical conferences and case reviews, focused education programs, and patient-needs surveys. We recruited trained emergency medicine specialists, developed scientific care and referral pathways, and upgraded ambulance staff and first responders' training.

In the Consulting Clinic, new services were introduced, and undergraduate and postgraduate training were streamlined. We introduced an Executive Health Service to complement our existing Corporate Health Service program, as there was considerable demand for health screening, early detection of disease, and health maintenance. Although this service proved to be a significant revenue generator for the medical centre, I was determined to pursue only scientifically sound and evidence-based screening of healthy people as a model of service befitting an academic medical centre. The objective was to detect, treat, and educate. It involved diagnosing diseases in early stages, particularly in those at high risk and whose outcomes could be modified by lifestyle changes or early treatment; conditions such as high blood pressure, colon cancer, and diabetes fell into this category. Our goal was to research the scientific basis of health screening while providing a much-needed service in a region undergoing rapid health transition to degenerative and lifestyle diseases of affluence. We recruited seasoned and well-motivated "honorary consultants" in delivering this service, conducted under carefully developed scientific guidelines. I provided clinical and administrative leadership and oversight to the program, which included the participation of dietitians, exercise trainers, counsellors, and nurses. These service users were mostly business executives, consular staff, professionals, expatriates, and political elite.

There is a tendency in the South Asia region to use "executive health" as a wide-ranging catch-all consultation and screening process that often lacks scientific validity but is a highly lucrative private service. This service has proliferated widely in Pakistan, India, and other developing countries.

The AKUMC credentialled several prominent and well-established specialists who were given the designation as honorary consultants. They complemented the full-time faculty in teaching and service roles and contributed to the medical centre's revenue streams. However, tensions between the full-time university staff and the honorary consultants soon emerged, partly resulting from different expectations and culture of practice and degrees of freedom, and mode of compensation. I proposed and created an Office of Physician Relations (OPR) to address these issues. Murad Verjee was appointed to manage the OPR, the Marketing Department, and the Office of Continuing Medical Education (OCME).

The question of the AKUMC's relation with outside physicians was a complex one. While we wished to encourage local physicians to avail of our advanced diagnostic and therapeutic services and enable admission of patients under their care as necessary, the AKUMC's physician care model was strictly governed by appropriate credentialling, quality standards, oversight mechanisms, and frequent reviews as befitting an academic institution.

My new role, thus, called for a much more expansive suite of responsibilities. It included the overall supervision and accountability of the OCME, the OPR, marketing, all the ambulatory services (the E.R., CC, CHC, Dental Department), and the Pharmacy Department. The Pharmacy Department was very ably managed by Lateif Sheik, an American-trained pharmacist. Lateif had undertaken several initiatives, such as decentralizing pharmacy service, introducing a safe chemotherapy drug formulations program, and periodically updating the hospital formulary. We introduced a Pharmacy and Therapeutics Committee that oversaw medication acquisition based on its evidence of effectiveness and cost-effectiveness. We introduced a pharmacy internship program to enable new graduates to receive supervised experience early in their careers and provide career pathways, a novelty for Pakistan.

Two competent assistant hospital administrators, Aslam Jindani and Steve Rasmussen, both well trained in health management at U.S. schools, valiantly continued, with their staff, to attempt to address the numerous issues that invariably attend a new university hospital complex's accelerated passage into maturity. Pakistan's normative chaotic health care environment presented many problems and challenged our formative years' operations and plans. There was no shortage of detractors, some plausible calls for process improvements, and many unreasonable expectations in care outcomes. Not unexpectedly, some issues were instigated by private hospitals, who sensed competition from a new, technically advanced university hospital.

Private medical care, uneven in its quality and content, was – and is – a lucrative and growing health care industry in Pakistan and most rapidly developing countries. It targets the elite, expatriates, and the well-heeled business, professional, and upper-middle classes. A thin upper crust of society, these users disparaged the poorly funded public health sector; they tended to be accustomed to gratification on their terms. Yet it was a user sector that contributed to the financial sustainability and long-term viability of the AKUMC and its vision of broader public good, a change agent, and a model for excellence in health care and education.

I continued some clinical practice by holding a few regular clinics in the CHC, the CC, and occasionally in the Executive Clinic. I was determined to continue teaching and mentoring to the extent possible, but it was a tricky balancing act between administration, clinical practice, teaching, and strategic planning. There were other demands on my time. I wrote numerous reports and concept papers, made board presentations, met with many visiting dignitaries, and participated in quite a few standing and ad-hoc committees and task forces. There were frequent academic and diplomatic visiting delegations, with whom I conferred and shared our development trajectory. I recall visits from the Universities of Khartoum, Malaysia, Bangladesh, and many others, as well as visitors from Canada, the U.K., the U.S., the U.A.E., and Egypt.

A critical task force, named "The Self Study Group," carried out an analytic task to redefine a set of goals for the medical centre a few years into its existence. The group underlined the mandate and essential focus, priorities, and strategies to achieve its long-term impact and goals. It strengthened the AKUMC's resolve and efforts to include all segments of the population, establish and maintain excellence in education and service, and extend counsel to national health systems in areas of the institution's distinctive competence.

Family and Community: A Suitable Environment

My family, in the meanwhile, was well settled into their new routine. The Hospitality and Housing Department had found us a lovely, spacious Spanish-style bungalow in the upscale "Defense 5" area of the city. I was provided a Toyota Corolla and a driver. However, I preferred to drive myself around through Karachi's chaotic traffic conditions. Still, it allowed my wife and the children a degree of mobility in having a semblance of everyday life. We hired, on advice from the housing people, a Pathan *chowkidar* (security guard), Hakim Khan, who would quite readily have laid his life for the family's protection, and a "bearer" who served as cook, cleaner, and gardener. In the desert-like conditions of Karachi, water shortage was a daily fact of life, which we had to learn to adapt to and practise general economy in all aspects of our life. Nilu, out of necessity, became an expert at coaxing bowser (water tanker) purveyors to deliver water twice a week to our residence; at other times, she hassled the Cantonment Water Board into providing a tanker of water at particularly demanding times.

The girls enrolled in the British Overseas School, where the headmistress, Mrs. Elizabeth Mirza, an Englishwoman, enforced a tightly disciplined British school curriculum, which included field trips to interact with local communities. On some weekends, they showed outdoor films and held dance and music festivals on their ample grounds. Interestingly, my daughters, Nadya and Aliya, learnt very typical Scottish Highland dancing and some local dances at this school.

Nilu spent a lot of her time at the hospital gift store in a voluntary capacity, along with Khadija Lakha, Sayeeda Vellani, and other senior executives' or faculty wives. The proceeds from the gift store were rolled into the Patient Welfare Program of the medical centre.

There were a number of expatriate senior management staff working at the hospital, mostly from Canada. Zaheer Janmohamed, director of human resources, had done ground-breaking work in establishing human resources policies, recruitment procedures, and a vision for human resources development. Mussadiq Umedali, head of finance; Nizar Sheriff, head of facilities construction; and Farooq Nurmohamed, the facilities resident architect all made significant contributions to the very early stages of AKU's and AKUH's planning and development. Al-Nasir Visram, a lawyer by training, was involved in the crucial resource-development initiatives. The late Zaher Lalani, a dedicated pioneer and factotum, joined in AKU's embryonic stages and filled multiple roles in his time. They formed part of our social group, along with many local Pakistani and other communities.

The founding of AKU attracted many well-qualified Pakistani nationals from several countries where they had obtained their higher training, and some had established their homes. They identified passionately with the mission and vision of the AKUMC in bringing high-quality, compassionate, and equitable medical care and community development to Pakistan, with its long-term goal of disseminating a scientifically sound and relevant model of education and service widely in

Pakistan, the region, and the developing world. Dr. Farhat Moazzam, a prominent pediatric surgeon, returned from Florida to become the first female to assume the chair of the Department of Surgery in Pakistan; Dr. Rizvi returned from the U.K. as head of obstetrics and gynecology; and Amin Suria as head of pharmacology and many others returned who wished to contribute to the development of their country. In the early years, the faculty mix included many visiting faculties from the U.K., Canada, and the U.S., who contributed their experience and wisdom in many basic sciences and clinical departments. The Departments of Laboratory Medicine, Radiology, Medicine, Surgery, Gynecology, Physiology, and Anatomy benefited greatly from their unstinted contributions during the formative years of the institution. I fondly recall Robbie Robinson, a retired professor of obstetrics and gynecology from Dalhousie University in eastern Canada, who, with his lovely wife Lillian, devoted several years of devoted service to AKU in periods of a critical shortage of highly qualified specialist clinicians and faculty.

Responding to Demands: Venturing into Environmental and Occupational Health

Our outreach to community physicians, business corporations, physicians, and managers involved in occupational and employee health programs, including those in the manufacturing, hospitality, and fishing industries, had attracted the attention of the pharmaceutical and health care industries in Pakistan. Our primary objective was to extend education upgrading to those involved in the crucial working-class's care in various industries and service sectors and to market our clinical services to the industry.

Occupational health was a relatively underdeveloped health care field, with few trained specialists in environmental, occupational, and industrial health available. We received many requests to provide advisory and consulting services in this vital but underdeveloped health field to various industries and businesses. Murad brought several requests to my office, but we lacked the requisite time and the full range of expert resources to accede to these requests. There were a few requests that we accommodated. The airline industry had a few "flight kitchens" established to provide catering and meal services to local and international airlines. KLM Airlines ran one large kitchen in Karachi. We accepted their request to inspect its kitchen, review its hygiene standards, and make pertinent recommendations. The AKUH had sophisticated food-handling and dietary standards in place, overseen by well-qualified dietitians. We visited the KLM facility, which proved to be of quite a high standard, and recommended additional quality-control measures. Our corporate health program through the CHC provided skilled health screening and preventive care, which an increasing number of corporations signed on to over time.

One corporate health consultation I vividly recall was undertaken at the request of an American petroleum company operating in the Sindh province of Pakistan. This company, Union Texas Petroleum (UTP), was involved in oil and gas exploration and drilling and had established four field sites for the preventive, environmental, and occupational health and first-level clinical care of its employees. Accompanied by two executives of the company, I flew in a small company-owned Piper Comanche over the desert expanses of the interior Sindh to Kashkeli in the Badin District of Sindh. Kashkeli was the district's main health centre, which they wished to expand into a more comprehensive health centre. I spent a full day reviewing their four facilities, which were of quite decent standards, but stocked some inappropriate medications while lacking other useful drugs. They also lacked properly trained front-line health staff, except for two nurses at their main centre. I provided a detailed report and recommendations to Ms. Claudia Woods, R.N., M.S., the company occupational, environmental, and corporate health administrator, which was very gratefully acknowledged by the company. We trained some of their staff in a malaria control training program at the AKU campus.

While this form of consultation provided some income in the form of consulting fees for the medical centre, we did not wish to venture too far into service domains that may have detracted us from our core goals. Nevertheless, we recognized the potential for critical social and economic benefits of improving worker health in large communities by fostering safe environmental conditions in the workplace. Thus, we considered the dispersion of applied knowledge mutually beneficial – by enhancing capability in one critical aspect of comprehensive health systems development, and hence, in consonance with our mission, and by supporting a strand of AKUMC's financial sustainability.

The health products and pharmaceutical industry approached us on many occasions to detail their products, with pleas to add their products in our formulary. As a new and modern academic medical centre, our commitment to remain steadfast to an evidence-based and cost-effective hospital formulary raised anxiety amongst members of this industry. This was a new, hard standard they were not accustomed to in Pakistan and in the region at large. We curtailed their promotion of new drugs on the hospital premises and set firm guidelines for their ability to promote drugs and products. We did agree to limited participation in international conferences, if held by reputable organizations. On one occasion, I attended a European Conference on Diabetes and Endocrinology in Innsbruck, Austria, accompanied by a few other members of the medical faculty, on the introduction of new treatments in diabetes. On my journey, I attended a WHO conference in Geneva on the further developments in the international classification of diseases (ICD).

International Dimensions: Confronting Emerging Challenges

I received an invitation to attend a training program and conference on geriatrics organized by the International Institute of Aging (United Nations - Malta), jointly held by the U.N. Social Development and Humanitarian Affairs and the WHO. There was a budding organization in Pakistan, the Pakistan Senior Citizens Association, that was concerned with problems of aging and the elderly in Pakistan and the South Asia region. They were keen that the AKUMC consider the special needs of the aged in a society with rapid growth and demographic transition. The association requested that the AKUMC consider including courses in the care and special needs of the elderly, geriatric medicine, and healthy aging in our education and service models. This was not a consideration that had been high in the planning priorities of AKU programs or the AKUH, where the emphasis was placed largely on the care of women, children, infectious diseases, and emerging chronic non-communicable diseases. However, our early experience and population studies showed a rising prevalence of diseases usually associated with aging, including cancer, heart disease, arthritis, diabetes, and nervous system disorders such as stroke. Social and economic neglect of the elderly was also on the rise. I agreed to represent Pakistan at the U.N. conference and to foster the academic medical centre's involvement in establishing innovative care and education programs relevant to aging societies.

The conference, warmly hosted by Malta, mainly targeted developing countries, underlined the future trajectory of demographic drift in populations globally, which is now all too evident in the twenty-first century. There were representatives from Egypt, India, Bangladesh, Fiji, Malaysia, Belgium, the U.K., South Africa, Brazil, and other countries.

As the jet banked over the blue expanse of the Mediterranean towards Valletta, dotted by numerous small crafts and larger vessels, I was struck, once again, by the sheer contrasts of colours and shapes, indented with harbours and bays, rock beaches, and beautiful sheltered coves. Some years ago, my wife Nilu and I had visited the island and marvelled at its culture and history. Malta is the navel of the Mediterranean, floating in the sea between Sicily and Libya. An ancient temple-building civilization, with later Phoenician, Roman, Arab, Norman, and Aragonese occupations, it is a collage of cultures and history. The archipelago is made up of three islands, of which the largest is Malta, on which the tiny capital Valletta is located, which was to be our base for the next couple of weeks. Valletta, a UNESCO World Heritage Site with its grand harbour, baroque landmarks such as St. John's Co-Cathedral, and museums, is a lesson in society and architecture's pluralism. The Maltese people, among the most resilient peoples in the world, are proud and patriotic in the face of an ever-changing array of rulers and strong outside influences.

The conference was held in a classical, old palatial building. It was facilitated by the lead coordinator, John Fabri, a proud Maltese health care professional. He represented the U.N. agency as well as the Maltese government. He and his team's capable conduct of the course added spice to the conference, which included visits to local health care facilities, university departments, and research facilities. They peppered the conference with field visits to historical sites, ruins, temples, and great cathedrals, and visits to the island of Gozo, the cities of Mdina and Sliema, and other sites, all of which proved edifying.

The interactive course and open-ended conference highlighted clinical challenges, the social and economic impact of changing population demographics, and evolving national health policy questions. The conference organizers and participants elected me the *special rapporteur* for this conference. The proceedings later resulted in scientific publications and the wide dissemination of awareness in this burgeoning but neglected medical care and social challenge in countries undergoing a rapid demographic transition. The AKU's CME programs added special courses on the questions around elderly care. In my later years, I served in various policy-making and advisory capacities in organizations in several countries concerned with aging, degenerative disorders, and the elderly's neglect.

I appended a visit to Cairo on my return journey to Karachi from Malta at the Egyptian colleagues' invitation. I was somewhat acquainted with the health care system in Egypt but used this opportunity to visit universities and medical centres in another Islamic country, struggling with similar challenges as we were in Pakistan.

A Defining Moment: Ceremony and Renewed Vitality

A momentous event in the history of AKU took place in early 1989. The first batch of medical students emerged as qualified doctors at a historic convocation ceremony held on Karachi's vast AKU campus. The fifty graduates from the Faculty of Health Sciences School of Medicine had completed their five-year undergraduate medical degree course leading to the award of an MBBS degree. The festival-like, open-air ceremony was held with considerable fanfare under colourful shamianas. The graduation ceremony was attended by many foreign and local dignitaries, diplomats, academics, and donors. Amongst the invited dignitaries were the president of Pakistan; the governor of Sindh; the chief minister of Sindh; Dr. Halfdan Mahler, director general emeritus of the World Health Organization; and other distinguished scholars and visitors from local and foreign universities. The brass band played tuneful melodies, one of which was especially hauntingly memorable, artfully merging grand musical traditions of the East and the West. It came to be known as the "Convocation March" and became the signature tune for all future AKU convocation ceremonies.

His Highness the Aga Khan, as the founder, sponsor, and chancellor, accompanied by the president of Pakistan, led the convocation procession, followed by an international board of trustees of the university and invited dignitaries. I vividly recall the enduring thrill of the dignified walk with the rest of the medical faculty in the parade, the faculty robed in uniquely designed green *Jamiaposh* to the raised platform as the musicians played the "Convocation March."

In his convocation address, His Highness thanked the government of Pakistan for its decision to authorize for the first time a private, fully independent international institution of higher education, international faculty, and the unprecedented generosity of donors. He stated that the intellectual, spiritual, and contextual fields of force were beginning to define the university's central ethic. In his words, he reminded us of the university's human mission, its imperative to respond to the needs of the "common man." He said that the exposure of the students to field work in the *katchi abadis* not only instructed them in the techniques of primary care for the poor but also exposed them to deeper truths – our common humanity and worth, humility before great suffering, and recognition of dignity and worth among simple people. It is an ethical education that must underpin the life of a physician. Uncompromising excellence is also an ethical principle. He underlined the imperative of intellectual freedom and expansive enquiry, as well as the university's mission of imparting the most modern medical curriculum with all it means to address the moral and ethical questions of life in our times. To the faculty and leadership, he said to think creatively, to innovate, and to improve.

Three days of intense deliberations followed the convocation. The health conference's themes focused on child and women's health, infectious disease, equity in health care, management and health systems research, health policy questions, social justice in health care, supporting and fostering research, management of emerging chronic diseases, and other topics. The wide participation in these conferences was heartening to note, as public health experts from the public, U.N. agencies, civil societies, universities, and private organizations shared their knowledge and experience, and built supportive networks.

The signal convocation events and proceedings surrounding it injected a new spirit of confidence, renewed vitality, and inspired ambition to aim higher and reach further, and spurred innovation at all levels of the university and its expanding system of facilities and programs. The new graduates were soon absorbed into the ranks of the hospital medical staff as junior doctors, interns and residents, to begin a new phase of their education; newly qualified nurses were readily recruited into the many areas of service clamouring for this crucial asset in health care.

CHAPTER 7

IMPACTING HEALTH CARE:
LEADERSHIP AND PARTNERSHIP

Upon the departure of Bill Borton, Joe D'Mora, a senior health executive from Canada, joined the AKUH as the next director-general and CEO. Joe had an expansive view of the hospital's role in the national health system, a closer working relationship with the AKHSP, and a strategy for enlarging the scope of off-campus service delivery. Our shared concern for disadvantaged populations and for extending the reach of the AKUH beyond the walls to bring skilled services closer to those in need led us to work closely with the CHS Department and the AKHSP. Clinical departments such as pediatrics, obstetrics, medicine, and the clinical laboratory were keen to reach out to extend their expertise to community-based care that was evolving.

The AKUMC was in a rapid growth phase in education and service developments, but occasionally lacked coordination and a delicate balance. The institution's full-time and honorary faculty strength was expanding rapidly. Specialized expertise grew steadily in the medical centre's capability to handle complex care in clinical areas like neurology, neurosurgery, heart and lung surgery, plastic surgery, and pediatric surgery. The suite of postgraduate residency programs expanded to over twenty-two specialty areas.

With new opportunities and the increasing public demand for specialized care and education came some turbulence, which became almost palpable. New challenges surfaced, especially in quality control, cost containment, patient satisfaction, space demands, and facilities expansion plans. As AKU and AKUH consolidated their growth and development initiatives, its evolutionary process gathered momentum. The policymakers, planners, and senior leadership worked tirelessly to address new and emerging issues.

In this milieu, Joe D'Mora asked me to consider expanding my role and responsibilities further. David Ulmer's office as dean and acting rector of the Faculty of Health Sciences also served as the medical director for the AKUH. In these wide-ranging and demanding roles, David needed assistance in the assurance of clinical care quality and the pace of developments in the hospital. Joe asked me to propose suggested roles and responsibilities to help ease some of the stresses within the complex interdependent systems.

The medical centre was poised at a stage where there were significant opportunities and challenges on the horizon, but also threats to progress. The founder had always seen the institution as a reflective and adaptive organization. There was, thus, a need to realign objectives with directions, set clear priorities, and monitor progress towards defined goals. The opportunities stemmed from growing faculty strength and clinical capability, the recent self study groups' studies and conclusions, and the institution's commitment to reappraise, re-evaluate, and redirect resources to meet changing conditions. The opportunities and challenges called for well-planned and committed institutional responses. There was a need to re-examine the institution's medical care model, provide cost-effective care to the needy and deprived populations, and innovate clinical and preventative strategies applicable and acceptable to the institution's served populations. The university medical centre's place in national, regional, and international health care would be determined by its ability to finely balance program developments with needs, demands, relevance, and the exhibition of excellence in its conduct and ethos.

I reflected deeply on the emerging challenges confronting the organization. I concluded that my experience and efforts thus far to interdigitate the education and service missions into a seamless whole could prove helpful in the broader leadership role.

I accepted the appointment as associate medical director of the AKUMC with some trepidation. In consultation with the senior academic and administrative leadership, my expanded role now formalized all my former responsibilities as administrator of ambulatory care and added many special functions. These included monitoring institutional clinical care delivery and facilitating, initiating, and reviewing special programs, including day surgery and special outpatient programs such as ambulatory rehydration therapy in children.

The role also fostered collegial medical staff organization and development to optimize productivity and staff satisfaction and assist in faculty recruitment and credentialling. The liaison role with the AKHS was formalized, broadly in the domains of education and clinical quality upgrading and new initiatives in community health. The position mandated other consultative and advisory roles as needed. It also included working with the clinical department heads to help resolve patient care issues.

The sum of my training, interests, passions, and some limited experience led me to envision a multifaceted role that fostered an enabling environment for progress. My heightened position required me to interact evenly with full-time and honorary faculty, junior medical staff and residents, medical records, nursing services, pharmacy, diagnostic services, patient welfare, finance, and a host of other support services, patients, and their families and advocates. I also engaged at multiple interaction levels with public health authorities and planners, private hospitals, universities, non-governmental organizations, and national and international bodies.

Unstable Environments: Chaos and Challenging Interactions

There were times when there were periodic political disturbances in Karachi and in the province of Sindh. These events usually involved the student and youth wings of opposing political parties, often leading to violent clashes. Large parts of the city came to a standstill; public transport became irregular or cancelled, stranding countless workers, including hospital staff, at home or other sites. The streets became filled with police and paramilitary vehicles. It adversely affected the finely tuned operations of the institution. Many patients could not present for their treatments; staff could not safely travel to the hospital site, so special transportation arrangements needed to be improvised, including arranging for police escorts. A particularly rough period occurred around mid-1988. An outburst of politically motivated tumult reached its zenith, with rival armed groups provoking riots and looting. Yet Karachi continued to function in some fundamental manner, in a state of "ordered disorder."

Karachi, Pakistan's turbulent metropolis, is one of the world's largest cities, with a population of over twenty million. Since the country's creation in the 1947 partition tumult, thousands of predominantly Urdu-speaking "refugees" have arrived.

They became known as Mohajirs. Tensions with the local Sindhi populations rose over time for scarce land and housing and votes and influence. The ethnic and political fault lines dominated the "official" and "unofficial" economy and politics and power structures of the city. Communities of Pushtuns, Balochis, and Sindhis carved out their turf and political space. The country's security situation considerably deteriorated during the Afghan intervention by the U.S. and its allies and Pakistan's participation in that prolonged war to displace the Taliban. Guns and drugs, principally heroin, found their way into Pakistan, giving rise to drug "mafias" and gun runners. Huge numbers of refugees poured into Pakistan, straining the social fabric even further. Compounding the military rule of the time, increasing provincial discord and tribal rivalries severely affected the lives and livelihood of the "common man," struggling to eke out a basic livelihood.

We received people with knife wounds and gunshot wounds in our Emergency Department, some with severe or life-threatening injuries.

One afternoon, I received a call from a frantic emergency room doctor. They had just received a seriously wounded student leader, accompanied by a crowd of belligerent youth, several carrying various weapons. Upon my arrival, I saw two senior staff surgeons examining the patient. They quickly briefed me on the young man's critical condition, who had a wound in his abdomen and a penetrating bullet wound in the head. He was quickly taken to the operating room, where the surgeons worked to save his life. The neurosurgeon, Rashid Juma, a highly experienced surgeon, later described his findings to me. The bullet had penetrated the skull and damaged some vital areas of the brain. He carried out the delicate surgical repair to the extent possible, but the damage could be life-threatening. The patient was moved and carefully managed in the intensive care unit of the hospital.

His friends crowded around the ICU lounge and vowed veiled threats if their leader died. While Shamsh and Joe conferred with the party's senior political leadership and security services, I attempted to reason with the angry youths gathered in the hospital premises. I explained the critical nature of the injuries their leader had suffered and possible outcomes. We asked them to put away their weapons while present in the hospital premises and allow only one or two representative members of their group to visit their critically wounded colleague. We were pretty firm in our demand that the group follow hospital regulations to create the best conditions for the recovery of the wounded. It took a couple of days of suspenseful patience before they fully complied with our requirements, fortunately without any violent confrontations or disturbances on the campus.

Disturbances of this nature affected the smooth operations, projected revenue generation, and recruitment of well-qualified staff for the medical centre. However, the medical centre began to be recognized and respected as a non-partisan, meritocratic, equal opportunity, and progressive institution. The unwavering efforts in building bridges with governmental and non-governmental organizations, civil society, and social and economic organs were yielding dividends. Shamsh Lakha, Jack Bryant, and Camer Vellani, and many others, guided by the chancellor's vision and were at the forefront of advancing its mission, even in the midst of troubled times.

Camer Vellani, the chair of the Department of Medicine and associate dean (and later the rector of AKU), was well-grounded in the harsh realities of life of the teeming millions trapped in poverty and the poor infrastructure for health and education in the country. Slight of build, soft-spoken, and mild-mannered, he belied his tremendous inner strength and toughness. He had a calm temperament, unflappable composure, and clear moral convictions; nevertheless, he was a realist. A well-loved teacher and an outstanding clinician, he was often seen deep in the hospital wards, the emergency room, or his office late at night. His loving, devoted, and remarkably patient wife Sayeeda often despaired of him showing up at family and social engagements on time, if at all.

I often sought out his sage counsel in my many overzealous efforts to introduce new ideas or initiatives. He was always unfailingly courteous and judiciously supportive, grounded but ambitious to attain the institution's goals.

Blueprint for Health for All: The Role of Primary Care

A growing consensus was forming amongst the institution's planners and leaders for the crucial need to extend the AKUMC's institutional infrastructure to address the community's unmet health needs. Camer Vallani, an early champion of linking primary medical care to hospital care, well understood the institution's resource limitations in fashioning an enabling environment to widely impact the vast population's health. However, with Jack, myself, and others, he firmly advocated extending the AKUMC as a model to be replicated widely in the country and establishing outreach facilities, linking community health facilities to the centre in a referral system. We explored the idea of developing a "spoke and wheel" approach, whereby we would develop satellite clinics, frontline hospitals, and outreach programs functionally linked to the central medical centre campus. The CHS Department and the AKHSP were in dire need of this supportive and referral system, as were many other neglected segments of society.

As part of its plan to introduce innovative, structured postgraduate medical education, AKU had started residency training programs in internal medicine, surgery, pediatrics, and other critical needs areas. I championed the concept of family medicine as a core discipline best suited for delivering primary medical care in developing countries. A competent generalist physician could bring holistic medical care for the individual, the family, and the community in the social, economic, and cultural context of recipients. Its inclusion into the undergraduate medical degree program curriculum introduced the students to the core principles underpinning comprehensive care, which took the biological, psychological, environmental, and social determinants of health in their encounters with patients, families, and communities. AKU introduced the students to this integral problem assessment model of patients early in the CHC and the CHS's seven field sites, and then gradually embedded it into the AKHSP clinical sites' work. AKU students were, hence, comfortable with the comprehensive primary care in the community settings.

Some of my fondest memories recall occasional visits to the CHS field sites as a tutor for small groups of medical students and accompanying nursing students and social workers. They visited these centres as part of their primary care and community health courses, often located in the most disadvantaged areas (the *katchi abadis*) of the city or rural communities. We would all bundle up into two or three small Suzuki wagons, which often traversed miles into the sprawling, overcrowded suburbs on unpaved pot-holed roads and narrow lanes strewn with piles of garbage and overflowing drains, ending at AKU's health centre. Among its other functions, these centres served to provide primary clinical care to women and children.

The centres and the surrounding communities provided ideal learning conditions for integrated clinical and preventive medicine. Teaching clinical medicine in these squalid conditions I found particularly rewarding and fulfilling. Still, it was the generous and cheerful nature of the communities, their silent grace in the face of evident privations that I recall best. And I remember sometimes sitting on mats on the floor of tiny ramshackle homes, sipping hot sweet tea from chipped glass tumblers pressed into my hands by kind-hearted housewives. Simultaneously, the nurses and social workers engaged in vociferous discussions with community women on hygiene, nutrition, immunizations, and appropriate medical care, including pregnancy and safe maternity care. My opinion was occasionally sought after.

Family medicine's premise underscored the quest for physical, mental, and social well-being to meet individuals' and populations' most essential health needs. But it required considerable adaptation of the health systems to provide competent care defined by criteria of effectiveness, affordable cost, and social acceptability.

My home organization – Aga Khan University and its partners, Aga Khan Health Services and the Aga Khan Foundation – were clear in their objectives of enabling these underlying principles in its programs and development wherever its reach extended. However, the external realities of health care and health systems in developing countries were often in stark contrast to these ideals. Therefore, the challenge for us was to demonstrate the proposed approach's effectiveness and strive to influence national policy deliberations for equitable, sustainable, and affordable care processes.

Among the many documents I wrote, I put forward a detailed outline of a Postgraduate program in Family Medicine, in line with other accepted postgraduate medical education offerings at AKU. I drafted a model curriculum in consultation with others interested in the project. The World Health Organization (WHO), in partnership with the World Organization of Family Doctors (WONCA), had put out a useful guidebook entitled *Improving Health Systems: The Contributions of Family Medicine*, based on extensive worldwide studies and experience in this field. There was undoubtedly an emerging interest in the idea of family medicine as a discipline and specialty in Pakistan and India, Bangladesh, Sri Lanka, Nepal, and the Middle East. There were nascent Societies of General Practice and Family Medicine in Pakistan, especially in Lahore and Karachi. I received invitations to their meetings.

Arjumand Feizal, a senior preceptor in the CHS Department, had a keen interest in family medicine as a career. He was a confident and passionate young man who had acquired considerable first-hand experience of health problems and challenges facing the population served by one of the first *katchi abadis* field sites, Orangi. Orangi had undergone periodic upheavals of a political and ethnic nature, undergirded by poverty and displacement. Arjumand and I attended the Lahore Society of Family Practice conference, where they honoured me to be the keynote speaker. I was heartened by their accepting the notion of changes necessary in the national undergraduate medical education, and positioning family medicine early in medical students' training. The society was highly supportive of the idea of a formal advanced education program in family medicine and commended AKU for its lead in considering its introduction at the university.

There was a high degree of acceptance of applying principles of comprehensive family medicine by other influential organizations. It was increasingly clear that the fragmentation of medical care into specialties and low-quality primary curative care was ineffective in handling undifferentiated problems regardless of the patient's age and gender. The Pakistan Medical Association held a favourable position on family medicine's values and principles as relevant in the urgency of skilled and comprehensive care of populations in Pakistan. The College of Physicians and Surgeons of Pakistan (CPSP), responsible for the accreditation of postgraduate medical education in the country, supported the idea of awarding postgraduate qualifications in family medicine. Ruksana Zuberi and Fauzia Qureshi of the CHS Department, both serving at that time on the board of the CPSP, keenly promoted the idea of a curriculum model that could enhance medical care across the spectrum of medical needs of society. They and many others shared my vision of training a generalist physician to a higher level and who would provide comprehensive and continuing curative and preventive care of people of all ages, and cost-effectively refer to advanced specialist care where indicated.

The CPSP soon after created a postgraduate Diploma in Family Medicine (DFM). I acceded to their request to serve as an examiner in their first examination. In later years, the college moved to a higher qualification level, offering a Fellow of the College of Physician and Surgeons of Pakistan (FCPS), requiring a longer formal training period.

In the months and years ahead, I would spend most of my career extensively in developing and promoting family medicine in developing societies of India, Egypt, Kenya, Tanzania, Uganda, Tajikistan, and several other countries.

> *Seek the wisdom that will untie your knot. Seek the path that demands your whole being.*
>
> *Jalal ad-Din Rumi, Persian Poet and Sufi Mystic*

CHAPTER 8

ETHICS AND LEADERSHIP

Frontlines of Trauma and Displacement: Pain and Empathy

One day, a young American physician was directed to my office. She introduced herself as Dr. Sharon McDonnell. She had been directed to see me by the university president and the dean. She was the WHO Afghanistan training coordinator and was based in Peshawar. She was on a consulting assignment by the WHO to help plan the retraining and return of displaced Afghan doctors living in Pakistan. The Afghan war had displaced huge numbers of people to Pakistan and Iran. An estimated more than three million people had taken refuge in Pakistan. Amongst the displaced to Pakistan were health workers, including nurses and doctors, who lived in camps scattered in the northern parts of the country, mainly in the Northwest Frontier Province (NWFP), but also in Baluchistan and Punjab. The "Allied" war effort, which included Pakistan and a coalition of other nations, had established frontline hospitals and other facilities along the Pakistan–Afghanistan border close to the Khyber Pass but mainly centred around Peshawar.

She was informed that Prince Sadruddin Aga Khan, who headed "Operation Salaam," (a humanitarian and economic assistance program of the U.N.), had suggested that Aga Khan University could be a source of expertise to assist in the retraining and redeployment of displaced Afghan doctors back into service in a postwar Afghanistan. I had received a copy of the letter addressed to the president of the AKUMC, Shamsh Kassim-Lakha, and John Bryant, chair of the Department of Community Health Sciences, written by Dr. Mumtaz Hussein, WHO senior health coordinator. The letter underlined the critical shortage of trained Afghan health professionals, a vital requirement for Afghanistan's health services' reconstruction and rehabilitation. Dr. Hussein's letter had outlined the critical need for Afghan health professionals to acquire the necessary skills and competence in handling the health crises of Afghans on both sides of the border, including the wounded fighters and civilians of all ages. It made a request for AKU's and AKHS's assistance in providing wide-ranging medical and surgical refresher courses and training, as well as upgrading the managerial skills of Afghan health professionals.

Afghanistan, prior to the Soviet invasion in 1978, was one of the least developed countries in the world. The infant and maternal mortality rates were the highest in the world. The average life expectancy was forty-two years. The Soviet invasion and its resistance had dire consequences on all spheres of life: the economy, social services, and infrastructure. The major causes of sickness and death were infectious diseases, diarrhea, acute respiratory illnesses, childhood tetanus, tuberculosis, malaria, and malnutrition. Inadequate access to safe drinking water, poor sanitation, and lack of access to basic health care further compounded the problem.

The resistance to the invasion and the communist government in Afghanistan was mounted by the Mujahideen (freedom fighters), disparate groups of fighters with varying parties and loyalties. A loose alliance of Afghan parties formed in Pakistan to coordinate and implement military strategy and humanitarian aid. This alliance came to be known as the Afghan Interim Government (AIG), based in Peshawar. There were also numerous U.N. agencies on the ground, as well as many NGOs in Islamabad, Peshawar, and other Pakistan locations. The representative NGOs from the U.S., Denmark, Kuwait, Saudi Arabia, and many other nations tended to be mostly involved in providing education, primary health care, food aid, and rehabilitation of wounded Mujahideen and civilians.

The war in Afghanistan was undoubtedly posing major political, social, economic, and security strains on Pakistan. It was further hampering local and national social and infrastructure developments, yet the government of Pakistan had committed to aid the refugees.

I was intrigued by this immense and daunting challenge the request posed. In its early formative years, AKU was still a young university with limitations on its resources and not geared to undertake sensitive and large-scale education development enterprises. My preliminary discussions with Sharon McDonnell ranged widely on the challenges that Operation Salam and WHO faced, and their expectations of the AKUMC and the AKHS in providing professional development of the health staff, reoriented to provide an infrastructure for the health of Afghan populations. At her request on behalf of the WHO, I agreed to visit Peshawar and adjoining areas to assess the situation on the ground.

Peshawar is an ancient city, with teeming streets and colourful bazaars, notable landmarks and parks. It is a Pushtun majority city, and its long history since the fifth and sixth centuries BC has seen numerous conquests, kingdoms, and dynasties. As a powerful centre during Moghul times, it was a centre of trade and culture during the Delhi to Kabul route of the period and as the northwestern extension of the Great Trunk Road through the Khyber Pass. It has been an important trade route throughout history and the Silk Road between Central Asia and the Indian subcontinent.

I was given a quick tour of the city and shown the major refugee centres, schools, and dispensaries. Over a few days, I visited several medical facilities, tent "hospitals," and public and private hospitals. Some centres resembled M.A.S.H. units popularized in the eponymous television show. I met with several volunteer or sponsored American, Danish, Swedish, and Saudi surgeons at various centres. There were also a handful of Afghan doctors serving at these centres. The largest public hospital in the city was overcrowded, and corridors were lined with stretchers bearing sick and wounded. The few private hospitals in the town were of better quality but lacked adequate operating and diagnostic facilities.

One centre stood out. Named the Afghan Trauma Centre, it was a fifty- to sixty-bed facility operated by the Health Committee of the Afghan National Liberation Front. It had male and female wards; provided orthopedic, plastic, and general surgery; and had an outpatient department. It also provided services such as wound dressing and customized orthotics. It housed basic laboratory and X-ray facilities and provided free food and medicines to inpatients. It had ventured into an organized program of upgrading education for doctors and nurses. There was a visiting American-trained Afghan surgeon who took a lead role in administrative and teaching activities. I met with Dr. Rabani, the deputy director of the centre, who showed me around and shared his views on their needs and issues. Amongst the multiple medical and surgical problems, severe limb injuries resulting from landmines were a significant problem in the combatants and civilians, including children.

Two well-armed Afghan volunteers took me to meet some Afghan Interim Government officials tucked inside an unprepossessing building in a lane. The interior of the offices on the upper floor, decorated in traditional art, wall hangings, and carpets, conveyed a sense of home away from home for the displaced Afghans. There, two heavily bearded turbaned men with piercing eyes greeted me and served some local sweet tea. The younger had a dark beard and dark flashing eyes. I was told he was the minister of health of the AIG. The older gentleman wore a large turban and had a flaming orange-red beard and light grey eyes. He was introduced as a deputy prime minister. They, of course, knew of Aga Khan University and, after an exchange of a few pleasantries, asked me why the organization had not taken a more active role in aiding Afghan refugees and combatants. They assumed we had virtually bottomless resources to assist in many ways. I patiently explained our mission, our programs of our resources' limitations, and our institution's still very early formative stages.

The mission's nominal head, a large, rather portly man wearing an Afghan waistcoat, suggested I visit a "medical school" they had established in another town. He asked me to provide advice on its improvement and further development. The following day, I was driven to a "university campus," attached to a small rural hospital several miles away. My companions showed around their basic sciences labs, library, lecture halls, and hospital wards, which provided the setting for clinical teaching. I also met several students in the labs and library. I was struck at the stark paucity of materials, furniture, supplies, equipment, or any semblance of a well-planned medical school. The library held a few, old, worn-out, out-of-date textbooks; the labs barely had any modern scientific apparatus. The hospital wards appeared to lack an organized ward system and discernable infection control. The pharmacy stocked a few first-line antibiotics and pain medications and not much else. The school head informed me that about seventy students were enrolled in the school, but the school had not received accreditation from the Pakistan Medical and Dental Council. They told me that there was a further smattering of Afghan students in other medical colleges in Pakistan. I later visited two more university medical colleges that had enrolled Afghan students for unrelated issues.

I returned to Peshawar, briefed Sharon on my findings and observations, and promised to provide a report following consultation with AKU authorities regarding the possible role we might play in providing the assistance asked of us. I was conflicted by what I had seen: the degree of privations, belied by the stoic forbearance I had seen in the children, young women, and deeply lined faces of older men and women in various places I visited. They clung to a spark of lingering hope of succour as they lined the corridors of hospitals and clinics or lay in crowded wards, often two or more in a bed. They had a steely determination to reconstitute their shattered lives and their country by any means possible.

I realized I had only acquired a fragmentary view of a complex and tangled multidimensional morass that was Afghanistan and its people during my short visit and cursory acquaintance with its representations. Still, I surmised that a lack of a clear overarching vision and able leadership, political and ideological divisions, and a barely competent civil society impeded their progress towards a quantum of self-sufficiency. The quagmire born of corruption, internecine tribal loyalties, and the shifting sands of internal and external political forces further impaired their ability to progress to a more stable society and forge the national identity they desperately aspired to. I conjured a gestalt of a hardy, resilient, and fiercely independent people locked in an existential struggle against overwhelming odds.

Upon returning to Karachi, I informally shared my findings and views with some faculty and administrative leaders. I endeavoured to patch together a menu of possible educational offerings, a viable plan that might meet approval by concerned parties, considering the effort and commitment required. I proceeded to write a detailed report laying out my observations, possible avenues of engagement, and constraints on our extant resources. There was a general sense at the AKUMC that many of the problems outlined were intractable and solution-resistant in the short-term. However, there was a high degree of empathy for the refugees' plight, particularly for women and children. Here, the heart of health problems lies in the scarcity of essential primary care in all its aspects, including immunization, safe pregnancy care, access to adequate nutrition and habitation and sanitation, access to competent curative care and essential drugs, and effective secondary level hospital care. Much of these social and economic issues lay outside our purview as a private institution. Nevertheless, our own experience and enterprises to date had earned us an image as an institution of excellence when it came to training and program development that could potentially impact large populations.

I proposed a plan in which we offered free instruction for small batches of suitably qualified doctors to our Preceptor Orientations program. The program delivers intensive community health and clinical care courses for new and junior doctors engaged in our field health centres. The program also underscored health management and leadership at the primary and secondary health care levels, an essential skill for frontline doctors. We offered opportunities for some selected

Afghan doctors to attend our frequent CME programs, attend ward rounds, and attend laboratory and X-ray interpretation and clinical decision-making seminars at no cost. AKU faculty visiting Peshawar volunteered to offer tutorials and lectures on their occasional visits to the region. However, we were not in a position to offer admission into our formal medical school training programs at the undergraduate or postgraduate levels, as this was a much more involved process.

Regrettably, our putative partnership did not gel into a long-term sustainable project for several reasons. However, it enabled us to provide some technical and consulting input into the multi-agency initiatives they were undertaking.

Balancing Priorities: Connecting Levels of Care

My days were getting crowded. And they were going fast. There were meetings, frequent visitors, reports to write, patients to see, students and residents to teach, clinics and wards to be overseen, patient and public concerns to be addressed. The AKUMC's Joint Staff Committee met monthly, a meeting of faculty department heads, senior administrators, and invited participants to harmonize, coordinate, and update progress, concerns, and plans. These meetings were sometimes tense, as they often involved questions of resources and priorities. The faculty and the senior management teams had their positions on questions of recruitment, program development, space utilization, and quality concerns. Numerous ad-hoc and standing committees and task forces operated in their spheres of responsibility. I found myself drawn into a number of these deliberations.

It was a thrilling time to be in a position that called for and encouraged wide-ranging clinical, strategic, and tactical planning perspectives. It called for embedding context, nimble adaptation, and a fine balance between competing priorities in all deliberations. Nevertheless, the time devoted to clinical and academic activities suffered despite my attempts to continue engagement in these areas that I loved. I found I was probably spending less than 40 percent of my time in these functions. I recalled with a slight pang of loss Jack Bryant and David Ulmer's sagacity when they had warned me of the romantic allure of position and leadership and the inevitable drift into new territories of medical administration. I attempted to attend weekly clinical conferences and presentations to the extent possible. I dropped into the CHC and the CC every week to hold at least one clinical session of teaching around patients' presentations and encouraged the students and residents to bring challenging cases for discussion. I spent a good deal of time reviewing patient records for quality assurance imperatives. There were frequent meetings with clinical leaders relating to care-concerns and challenges, evolving medical technologies, departmental strategic plans, staff recruitment, networking, and departmental faculty's continuing professional development.

I was fortunate to have support and encouragement at all levels of the institution in all my endeavours. Periodically, I had extra assistance to handle the workload. One that I recall fondly was when one day a smart young man walked into my office. He introduced himself as Mahmud Mitha, a Canadian visiting from the U.S. He had an MBA degree from Cornell University. He was currently pursuing a Master of Public Health (MPH) degree at Columbia University in public health administration. He had been directed to my office for assistance in completing his master's dissertation.

Mahmud proved to be a highly articulate and organized young man who had put together a study proposal on medical administration challenges in developing countries. He presented an outline of his study and asked for my guidance. Over the next few days, we worked through his research project. I assigned him some data sets to assist with his research.

Our primary interest converged when I described our challenges in developing a viable system to link primary care with secondary and tertiary care. AKU worked assiduously with public and private sector facilities to explore relationships and linkages between the community and its frontline hospitals. We were keen to explore the scope of the hospital's services to benefit community health and how that is assured.

AKU and AKF had partnered with the WHO through the eighties in examining the role of hospitals in primary care. More recently, the CHS Department and the AKHSP had also been deeply engaged in further exploring functional partnerships in this critical area of health system development. I had also been drawn into this crucial question since my time at the CHC. Our work on this and other projects led Mahmud and I to work together on health systems development in years to come elsewhere.

Jack Bryant and Camer Vellani were deeply involved in shaping viable partnerships that satisfied our values and standards. The multifaceted challenge included delicate issues of education and training, attitudes, managerial and technical supports, and appropriate resource development and allocation. We visited several existing hospitals and health facilities that could enlarge our education and service network, with a particular view of fostering a secondary-level referral hospital concept, a vital missing piece of health care system development. AKU needed to provide a more extensive and more diverse pool of patients closer to their communities to complement training received within the AKUMC campus.

One particular visit I recall was an exploratory visit to the semi-autonomous Karachi Port Trust Hospital, owned and operated by a parastatal, the Karachi Port Trust. This hospital primarily catered to the needs of port workers and their families and those communities surrounding the port area. Linkage of this nature would be ideal, as it was in accordance with AKU's core values, mission, and goals. If successful, it could leverage AKU's reach while also positioning the AKUH as a tertiary-level referral centre. This exploratory outreach continued for several years.

Forging Closer Bonds: Advancing Special Relationships

Our engagement with the AKHSP facilities was progressing more fruitfully. The medical students and residents and nursing students in training gradually diffused into well-operated AKHSP diagnostic centres and clinics, bringing an academic institution's knowledge base into a more comprehensive network.

The AKHSP was in the process of establishing a referral hospital in the remote Northern Areas of Pakistan. The Singhal Medical Centre, a secondary-level hospital born of the best practices drawn from AKU and the AKHSP, globally served as an effective and mutually beneficial partnership model. On a visit to the centre, I was impressed by the care it offered, especially in maternity care, children's care, and general first-level hospital services and educational opportunities.

Steve Rasmussen, who previously served as an assistant administrator at the AKUH, had moved on, with his lovely wife Zeba, a Harvard-trained physician, to accept the general manager position of Aga Khan Health Services for Northern Pakistan. In late 1989, on his and Aziz Currimbhoy's request, I undertook a consulting visit to the AKHSP's health care network in the Northern Areas, as well as visits to the widely scattered facilities in Gilgit and Hunza and the Punial valleys, including health centres, dispensaries, community health programs, and environmental intervention initiatives. I also visited the government dispensaries and a district hospital, and met officials involved in the public health care system. I reviewed clinical data and the main determinants of illness and disability.

The disease trends and prevalence were predictable and disturbing. The AKHSP's considerable experience in primary, maternal, and child health care had served well in improving morbidity and mortality in the region; still, the population's preventive and curative health needs were broader. Hence, the question of future directions of the development of AKHSP's programs was under deliberation – between focusing on the institution's traditional strengths or evolving the system into a more comprehensive health care service ranging from primary to secondary care, with linkage to AKUMC's tertiary care facility.

My wide-ranging report offered some consultative opinion, but of course, significant resource challenges and considerations, training, geography, terrain, transportation, communication, and regional government plans for broadening and deepening its services were outside our purview. In the years to come, steady but glacial-paced progress continued to be made in the region's health care development. The AKDN's multi-pronged intersectoral approach, in which agencies for habitat, education, and economic arms worked collaboratively, continued to make major strides in development.

An instance of deeper involvement occurred when Aziz Currimbhoy invited me formally to serve as a consultant and academic resource on a task force planning a new hospital and ambulatory care facility in the city of Hyderabad in Sindh province. AKU's role in developing an operational plan, capacity-building, and technical support was crucial for the new health centre and hospital. The proposed Aga Khan Hyderabad Maternity and Child Health Centre (HMCHC) had an ambitious vision and reach. Hyderabad, the teeming second-largest city in Sindh, lying along the Indus River, is a transit between rural and urban Sindh. It is rich in culture, tradition, and history. It was Sindh's capital for many centuries, and its sights include Kolhora and Talpur rulers, royal fortresses, and the colourful Shahi Bazaar.

The Hyderabad Maternity and Child Health Centre sought to support an array of primary care and maternal and child health programs of the AKHSP in Sindh's interior, providing higher clinical-level care, including complex obstetrical and pediatric care. The stunning custom-planned and -built complex, built with local materials and labour, added architectural enhancement to the city. Its geometrical gardens and courtyards, outdoor patients' tree-shaded waiting areas, and the play of light and breeze recalled the much larger Aga Khan University Medical Centre complex in Karachi. The seventy-bed hospital included a newborn intensive care unit, operating rooms, and wards primarily catering to women and children's medical needs. An emergency ward that addressed obstetrical and other critical emergencies provided a much-needed service to Sindh's urban and surrounding rural communities.

As planned, in the months and years ahead, it evolved as a model frontline hospital, a site of excellence in clinical education for medical students, post-graduate residents, and nurses of AKU, and addressed crucial research questions ranging from clinical, epidemiological, health policy, and health systems, to the application of appropriate technologies in health care. The visiting AKU faculty increasingly involved themselves and the learners in crucial areas of family planning, maternity care at all levels, outreach visits, nutritional rehabilitation, child development, community health education, and school health. Early childhood development efforts were added in conjunction with Aga Khan Education Services and the Aga Khan Foundation at later stages.

At the opening ceremony of the HMCHC, His Highness the Aga Khan remarked on the potential benefits such a collaborative effort offered in serving in the leverage of effective partnerships to benefit societies. The joint efforts of many, both from AKU and the AKHSP, helped converge and further both organizations' ultimate goal into developing effective models of care for large populations of rural and urban people. A replicable model of linking primary, secondary, and tertiary care was beginning to be shaped, influencing health policies and resource allocation.

Enhancing Personal Development: Opportunities and Support

My wide-ranging roles and responsibilities also meant that I often felt in need of training and support, particularly in some aspects of administration and management. I continued to maintain a certain level of clinical and academic competence through my various engagements. However, challenges in complex policy questions, strategic planning, conflict resolution, networking and leadership, quality assurance, and resource and time management were areas I felt I needed additional formal upgrading. The institution was always supportive of continuing professional upgrading of its senior academic and leading executives. I was given the necessary support and encouragement to personalize and pursue my education.

The Physician Management Institute (PMI) offered one instance that I recall as an archetypal training course for physician leaders under the Canadian Medical

Association's aegis. I enrolled and attended this modular program held in Whistler, British Columbia, in August 1989. With the family visiting Canada on vacation, I immersed myself in acquiring the requisite skills. The course was interactive and case-based. Interestingly, the participants were all senior medical leaders in Canadian and American health care organizations. They were amazed at the range and complexity of a medical leader's issues in a resource-poor developing country while noting the commonalities of challenges encountered in advanced societies such as Canada and the U.S. The course and collegial support I received revitalized in me the conviction, courage, and confidence to undertake increasing responsibilities and a clearer vision of the direction and the value of our endeavours. In the years to come, I attended many other development programs and conferences targeting physician leaders.

Ethical Challenges: Embedding Guiding Principles

A haunting and transformational challenge came our way one evening as I was leaving my office after a harrowing day at work. I was summoned to the Emergency Department of the hospital. Upon entering the unit, I saw a young child being examined by a pediatric consultant and two residents. The consultant quickly appraised me on the problem. They were assessing a nine-month-old female infant brought by her parents, who were sitting anxiously in the waiting room. The child was labouring to breathe; the breathing was irregular and shallow. The pediatricians reached a tentative diagnosis of polio, involving the part of the brain that affects the breathing muscles and, hence, controls breathing. Her limbs were flaccid and lacked the usual tone of healthy muscles. Her reflexes were absent.

In medical parlance, this is referred to as bulbar poliomyelitis. The part of the brain called the brainstem also controls swallowing, speech, and other functions. The physicians were concerned that this child might not survive without breathing assistance, but for the immediate term, she certainly needed hospital admission and close monitoring. We quietly discussed the problem, which revolved around safely admitting her, monitoring her, and assisting her as she struggled to breathe. The AKUH at that time did not have a pediatric intensive care unit (ICU), although we had a recently established ICU for newborn infants, a neonatal ICU (NICU). This unit would not be suitable for her. There were very few children's ICU units in Karachi, and they were usually crowded and unavailable. We gently broke the news to the parents, a Pathan gentleman with a henna-dyed full red beard and his wife, and a younger man with them who was the child's uncle. He had insisted on bringing in the baby when he recognized the severity of her condition. He said the baby's name was Noor.

In lay terms, we explained that the child's breathing was impaired because of paralysis of her breathing muscles of the chest, and we could not predict how this would evolve over the next few days. We urgently held further consultations with the senior pediatric and neurology faculty and decided to admit the child to the pediatric ward with enhanced nursing and isolation measures. We had reached a consensus that, if indicated, we would move the baby to our regular ICU unit. The family agreed to allow Noor to be admitted under our care; the uncle expressed profuse gratitude, confident in our care and technology.

When I arrived the following day, I found that the child had indeed been moved to the ICU overnight. I found her awake; her large, wide, beautiful grey eyes were quite serene, and she was breathing through the oxygen mask covering her fair-complexioned round cheeks. There were intravenous lines and tubes attached to her tiny body. Nurses were hovering around her, periodically sucking secretions from her mouth. The ICU physician updated me on the child's status. He said it was challenging to maintain adequate oxygen in her blood when on the ward, and a late-night decision was taken to transfer her to the ICU. In the ICU, blood oxygen levels were satisfactory. The neurologist was going to be visiting her later today. I gently touched the child; her gaze remained steady on me. I briefly checked her limbs for muscle tone; they were still quite flaccid.

I walked out of the ICU into the outer waiting area, where a few people were sitting, relatives and families of patients in the ICU. I saw baby Noor's parents and her uncle, whom I had met the night before. I took them aside and updated them on the child's condition. I could see they were pretty tired and had been sitting outside the pediatric ward, and later outside the ICU, for the night.

Over the coming days, I saw the mother sitting patiently and uncomplainingly in the waiting room on most of my visits. She was allowed into the ICU for short stays. The father, after a few days, would only be seen occasionally. The child's clinical condition, however, was not showing signs of improvement. Any attempt at reducing breathing support would result in a drop in blood oxygen level. A small group of clinicians frequently met to determine clinical progress and the likely prognosis of this young child. I met periodically with the head of pediatrics, the nursing director, and other involved clinicians. It became increasingly clear that the breathing problem from polio was likely permanent, and she was most unlikely to breathe unassisted. We discussed the clinical need to perform a tracheostomy, a surgical opening into the windpipe, to attach the ventilator machine to help her breathe.

The medical and nursing staff became increasingly emotionally attached to the beautiful, innocent child, who otherwise appeared well and alive to the world around her. The tenderness and the loving care she was receiving were palpable.

The senior management was, understandably, concerned about the set of issues this raised for the institution, including the continuing occupancy of a critical ICU bed, the mounting cost of care, and the family's inability to contribute to the ongoing care of the child. There was mounting pressure on me to garner an acceptable consensus and a care proposal in the context of the complex social, economic, and ethical imperatives. The Patient Welfare Department met several times with the family on the institution's welfare support system and the level it was prepared to provide, which to date was exceedingly generous.

The father let it be known that he did not see a future for his daughter, and in what must have been an agonizing decision, let us determine her fate. The family would not be able to cope financially or culturally with a girl who could not have prospects acceptable in a conservative, traditional society. The mother, consistently and with quiet dignity, continued to visit and tend to her child, demanding little and caring little for her own needs and pain. Little did we realize this case was to cogently portend questions of the utmost gravity of human dignity, justice, priorities, resources, and fundamental ethics in health care.

At AKU's board of trustees' request, the senior administration had previously striven to work on a preliminary document on an ethics framework as it applied in the AKUMC's context and time and place. However, this case's imperative required an urgent framework to guide the institutional response to challenging situations foreseeable in the future. I found myself located in the centre of this weighty charge. I consulted frantically, seeking input to guide, balance, and alleviate the problem humanely and fairly.

Health care providers' ethical responsibilities in treatment and delivery have raised vital and challenging health care institutions' dilemmas. The growth and sophistication of medical technology, concerns about practical limits on financial resources for health care, transitions in disease patterns, changing attitudes in societies, and unequal distribution of health and technical resources have added complex dimensions to ethical dilemmas. The AKUMC, as a private philanthropic institution working in a conservative Muslim milieu, would be forced to choose between alternatives, make value judgments, and face increasingly complex moral dilemmas in resource distribution, quality of life issues, and the use of technologically advanced clinical systems in prolongation of life.

But the fundamental ethical questions faced by the AKUMC, as an apex institution of the Aga Khan health care system, go beyond those that ordinarily apply to responsive and advanced hospital settings. Among the crucial questions is the challenge of ethically allocating scarce resources – in front of conflicting urgencies, each with a tenable case and a plea – to the greatest ultimate good of the public it serves. This is perhaps the dilemma with the most profound significance relative to the institution's impact on society's advancement towards better health and justice. To take an enlightened approach, we need comprehensive consultations with stakeholders, policymakers, and the public.

My research and some familiarity with biomedical ethics in industrialized societies led me to undertake visits to some established centres with experience and progress into this complex question. I wrote to Professor Margaret Sommerville at the McGill University of Canada, whose work I was acquainted with to an extent. She immediately replied and invited me to visit her centre.

I arrived in Montreal via London, where I had stopped to visit a respiratory unit at St Thomas's Hospital, where research was being conducted on a new model of iron lung, an external breathing assistance device. A suitable version was not available yet for very young children.

In Montreal, I met with Professor Sommerville, an Australian by birth. She was an elegant and gracious lady who headed the McGill Centre for Medicine, Ethics and Law. A lawyer by training, she and her team had done considerable work on the intersection of ethics, health care, and the law. She listened empathetically to the problem I put in front of her and asked many penetrating questions. She freely shared her views on the developments in bioethics, evolving societal trends, and some documents her team had developed when faced with ethical dilemmas. She was very interested in the challenges of establishing bioethical frameworks applicable in the developing society context and informed me of some work done in Egypt along these lines. I was very grateful for her advice and guidance.

Upon returning to Karachi, I set about drafting an outline of a plan to establish an Ethics Committee for the AKUMC and detailed the scope, structure, and process to address challenges like the one we faced with baby Noor. The document more widely sought to embed acceptable standards of professional conduct, consultations, and support. I shared the draft widely with the senior administration and faculty leaders and sought input from religious leaders and civil society.

A much refined and nuanced document made its way to the policymaking board of the institution. The document, titled "Medical Ethics and the Aga Khan University Medical Centre: A Case and a Proposed Model," served as a concept paper in this critical deliberation. The proposal outlined the establishment of a multidisciplinary Ethics Committee; its composition, roles, and structure; and guidance for the medical, nursing staff, and others involved in patient care. With the senior leadership's concurrence and input, I developed and circulated an AKUMC version of a universal "Guide to the Ethical Behaviour of Physicians." The initiatives towards a formalized bioethical framework I consider a signal achievement for the institution, which over time and after different experiences and deliberations resulted in further progress and maturation.

As for baby Noor, she lived on ventilatory support in a ward, well-beloved and adored and schooled by all who saw her. By all accounts, she lived until the age of 12, gradually maturing, the staff lavishing their love on her until her last day, well after I had moved on to other endeavours in my life.

───～୨୧～───

My wide-ranging involvement in the community health, clinical, educational, administrative, faculty development, and service enhancement domains were agreeably synchronized into the rhythm and goals of the medical centre. Over the past several years, I had also had the privilege of illuminating the challenges and growth trajectory of the AKUMC with a number of interested groups and professionals abroad.

Inspired by the Aga Khan's words and the growing international recognition and reputation of the AKU, there was increasing interest from overseas students wishing to do parts of their elective studies at the AKUMC. As well, qualified health professionals, particularly from Ismaili health communities, expressed the desire to seek short-term engagements with the university. Many others sought to offer voluntary services in various ways, in fields as diverse as nutrition and dietetics, pharmacy, medical records, financial systems management, physiotherapy, and laboratory medicine. My office received frequent enquiries seeking suitable opportunities, which I attempted to respond to sympathetically, directing many queries to appropriate departments as necessary. However, at the relatively early stage and in the external conditions in which we operated, AKU was not in a position to accommodate most of these well-meaning requests. In the years to come, professionals and volunteers made significant contributions of their time and knowledge generously under a more formalized system.

———◦c———

After almost five years deeply engaged in the seminal stages of AKU's steep trajectory of growth, I felt it was time for me to consider returning to Canada. I put my request for a timed departure to Shamsh and David Ulmer. While reluctant to accept my intention of moving on, they graciously accepted my timeline for formal departure. However, they wished to create a permanent position to replace my soon-to-be-vacated position, retitling the position to be medical director and associate dean. They requested my participation in the search committee to be set up to identify a suitable candidate for the role. Over the next few months, while tying up loose ends and ensuring continuity and synergy I had laboured assiduously for, I interviewed several highly qualified internal, local, and returning Pakistani nationals for the position. We finally agreed on a returning highly experienced physician executive to fill this role.

Shamsh had said that "the university will call on you again in the future," a statement which in the fullness of time also became a reality when I assumed charge of new developments in East Africa. Those words assuaged some of the pain of separation from the beloved institution that felt like my family, and I boarded the Air France flight to Paris.

Everyone has been made for some particular work and that desire for that work has been put in every heart.

Jalal Ul Din, Sufi Mystic and Poet

(Photo Credit - AKU)

(Photo Credit - AKU)

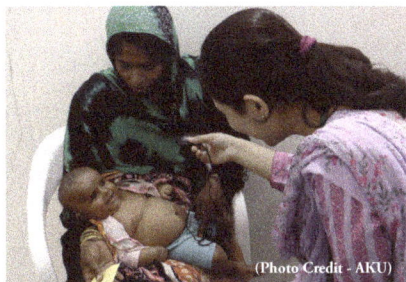

(Photo Credit - AKU)

CLOCKWISE FROM TOP: *AKUH Karachi, Lakeview – Private Wing; AKHS Health Visitors – Pakistan; AKU – FIMC – Kabul, Afghanistan; AKU Students in Rural Community Development – Pakistan; AKU Medical Students Visiting Katchi Abadi – Karachi*

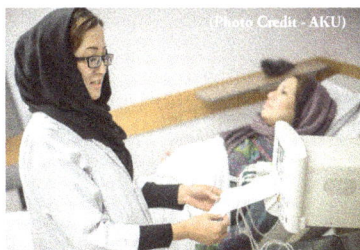

(Photo Credit - AKU)

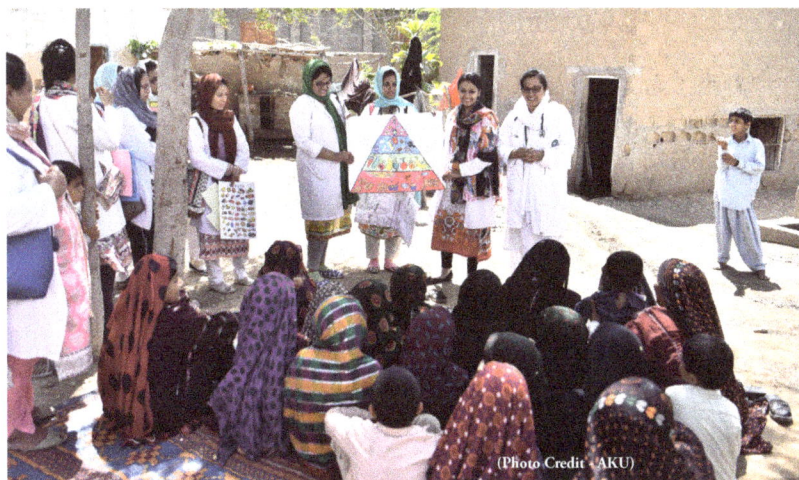

(Photo Credit - AKU)

129

FROM TOP: *Karakoram Mountains – Highways to Northern Gilgit – Pakistan; Karakorams – Baltistan, Pakistan; Karakoram Ranges – Pakistan*

FROM TOP: *The Pamir Mountains – Tajikistan; AKHS Dodoma Health Center, Tanzania; Community Development Work – AKU Arusha Site*

(Photo Credit - AKU)

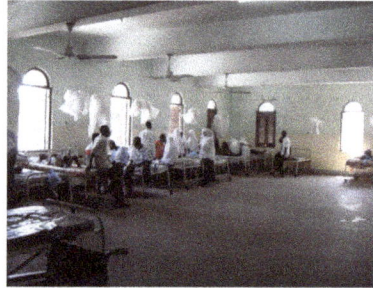

CLOCKWISE FROM TOP: *Rural Development AKF – East Africa; General Ward in Public Hospital – Tanzania; Rural Health Activities – Tanzania; School Health – East Africa*

(Photo Credit - AKU)

(Photo Credit - AKU)

CLOCKWISE FROM TOP LEFT: *Wildlife in Serengeti National Park – Tanzania; New Aga Khan University Hospital – Nairobi; New Aga Khan Hospital, Dar-es-Salaam; Old Aga Khan Dispensary – Zanzibar; View of City of Dar-es-Salaam, Tanzania; AKU-PGME Centre – Tanzania*

CLOCKWISE FROM TOP LEFT: *Dr. Azim Jiwani – PGME Office (Dar-es-Salaam); Author with PGME Students – East Africa; Aerial View – Aga Khan University & Hospital – Karachi, Pakistan; Author with PGME Students and Staff – East Africa; Traditional Life – Rural Africa*

CHAPTER 9

INTERVENING PERIOD:
BROADENING PERSONAL COMPETENCIES

The autumn of 1990 felt like the autumn of my life. The Vancouver weather had turned grey and damp a bit early that year. A few weeks before, we had returned to Canada after spending almost five eventful years in the nearly perpetually sunny and sultry Karachi. Nilu and the girls missed the sun and the heat. Nilu's rheumatism was beginning to act up.

The journey back from Pakistan had been pleasant; we had spent a few wonderful days in Paris on our way back home in a charming little hostelry on the left bank. We recalled the anticipation and excitement we felt five years before on our way to Karachi from Vancouver when we had also spent several days enjoying springtime in Paris. The time had passed on too fleetingly, and nostalgia periodically flooded our minds as we all, in our own way, tried to reconcile ourselves to a new reality.

The girls missed their many friends. They imagined their friends were busy enjoying the last weeks of Karachi's hot and humid summer vacation. They'd be picnicking, swimming, or playing soccer and hockey on the Karachi International American School's (KAS) ample well-kept grounds – if they were not away visiting exotic places in the region. They had recently started their new schools in Vancouver and, as yet, had not made many friends. They were quite sure they'd never make friends like the ones left behind – an enticing mix of cultures and backgrounds – little realizing the privileged status they all enjoyed in the otherwise less-privileged general population of Pakistan. Their initial impression was that the pupils at the Vancouver public school they now attended were less international, less stimulating, and somewhat insular in their interests and outlooks. Walking the shopping malls seemed to be the local thing!

The KAS, a private American school, tended to cater to a diverse expatriate community and children of well-off Pakistani nationals. Nadya and Aliya had attended the school for about two years, which imparted excellent education, but also sensitively instilled cultural and social values, being situated in a traditionally conservative society. Nevertheless, the close-knit school community was usually a beehive of activities – sports days, cultural days, music, drama, and educational outings – hardly representing the society where it was located.

The decision to return to Canada had been a difficult one. For several months, Nilu and I had reflected deeply on our future direction, within and outside AKU. Much had been accomplished, to which, I was told, I had made some worthwhile contribution in the early years of the fledgling institution's life. Yet much more needed to be done. But there were pressing issues to address back in Canada, some of which involved consequences of some imprudent financial and investment decisions I had made in the period surrounding the time when we had hurriedly departed from Canada.

My original plan to engage in global development challenges for two or three years had extended to a stay of five busy, exciting, and fulfilling years, but the imperative to resume life and career back home had also weighed in on our final decision. My colleagues, friends, and the senior leadership of the AKUMC had understood and accepted my reasoning for wishing to return home and pick up the pieces of personal and professional life that I had abandoned five years prior.

We had no home to return to, no established practice, and no fixed career plans. I had some vague idea of pursuing a career that combined my acquired experience in international health, education, and institutional capacity building with the practice of general medicine, preferably affiliated with an academic institution. We were fortunate to have some temporary accommodations and the use of a vehicle for the first one or two months while we waited for the arrival of our container and personal belongings from Karachi. In the meantime, I had gone through the demanding process of professional recredentialling in British Columbia, enrolled the children in local schools, and searched for suitable accommodations and professional opportunities.

I soon found work as a part-time locum doctor with an established family physician in Vancouver. The result was a slow and not very rewarding job. Browsing through the "Physicians Wanted" advertisements in medical journals led me to start a practice of making house calls to homebound patients in the greater Vancouver area. With Nilu acting as my navigator, we would drive many miles through the day, visiting many sick and elderly patients in their homes or long-term care facilities in our borrowed vehicle. There was no GPS to guide our trips; we pored over maps and tried to familiarize ourselves with Vancouver's roads and alleys. Before too long, we had found a small old bungalow to rent and a slightly used vehicle to call our own.

Seductive Opportunity: Poor Professional Fit

Perhaps one of the most unexpected, somewhat tantalising, and ultimately unsettling and educative developments occurred serendipitously around this time. One day, I ran into an old patient of mine, Patrick Pang, a well-connected Singaporean civil engineer. He had been my regular patient in Calgary and frequently travelled to Asia. He said he was delighted to see me; he had been looking for me. He knew I had been abroad, working with a university, but did not know I had returned to Canada. He insisted we meet over coffee as he had important news for me. Over coffee, he told me he had returned from Brunei. He had been consulting for several years on some large engineering projects, including a private hospital built for the royal family and senior government officials. His patron and employer, Prince Jefri Bolkiah, the Sultan of Brunei's younger brother, was seeking to recruit a head of the private hospital and asked Patrick to recommend a suitable candidate for the position. Patrick had thought of me. He said it was a well-paying and privileged position that included looking after the royal family and included considerable international travel. Patrick indicated I would be an ideal candidate for the post! I laughed at the proposition, but he was quite serious. He took my contact details and said he would contact me.

I was surprised when he phoned a few days later to say he had talked to the prince, who was keen to meet me. The prince, who was the finance minister of the tiny oil-rich country on the island of Borneo, had invited me and arranged to pay for mine and my wife's visit to Bander Seri Begawan, the capital of Brunei. While titillated by this unusual opening, and not yet established in any regular full-time occupation in Canada, Nilu and I agreed to check out the offer. Part of the reason for accepting the invitation was an intellectual curiosity of a region I was less acquainted with and to see the state of development in a state primarily funded by the oil and gas economy in Southeast Asia. We had visited several Middle Eastern Gulf states in our time. We were generally disappointed by the wasteful splurging of national wealth on trinkets and baubles of little use to the dispossessed and the marginalized in the region of high need.

A few days later, we flew to Singapore, the closest major city to Bandar, and caught a Royal Brunei Airways flight to Bandar.

With its coastline along the South China Sea, Brunei is surrounded by the Malaysian state of Sarawak and is an absolute monarchy under the ruling sultan. It has a population of about four hundred thousand. It gained independence from the United Kingdom in 1984 and has the second-highest human development index among Southeast Asian nations, after Singapore. Although classified as a developing country, according to the International Monetary Fund, it is ranked fifth in the world by gross domestic product per capita.

Bandar Seri Begawan is derived from Sanskrit, meaning "the aura of gods," and has over one hundred thousand inhabitants. Human settlements started back in the sixth and seventh centuries with a Malayan trading centre and fishing port near the Brunei River banks' current site. During the Bruneian Empire period from the fifteenth to the seventeenth centuries, the Sultanate ruled many parts of Borneo, including the Philippines' southern region and its capital Manila.

As the jet banked, we could see the historical stilt settlement on the Brunei River in the heart of the capital. The city's suburbs incorporate nearby Kampong Ayer (water village), in which houses are built on stilts. It stretches about eight kilometres along the Brunei River. Founded a thousand years ago, the village is considered the largest stilt settlement in the world, with approximately thirty thousand residents and two thousand houses. The term "Venice of the East" for the settlement was coined by Ferdinand Magellan's crew in 1521 while on his last voyage.

One or two government officials at the small airport met us and whisked us off to our hotel. It was hot and humid, but the small, elegant hotel was air-conditioned and central. The following day, Patrick met us and showed us around the small city. I was particularly interested in spending some time in Kampong Ayer to study that population's social, cultural, and health dynamics. He showed us the area somewhat perfunctorily, but he was excited to show us the hospital, the royal palaces, the polo grounds, and the prince's collection of luxury cars. He said, regretfully, that the prince had to travel out of the country for some urgent business, and therefore we would not get to meet him on this trip.

What he did show us was the height of personal hedonism, dissipation, narcissism, profligacy, and intemperance most unimaginable! Patrick took us to what I thought initially was a huge car depot. It held countless rows of luxury cars, from Bentleys, Rolls-Royces, gigantic Mercedes, BMWs, Lamborghinis, to specially commissioned Aston Martins and every conceivable make of luxury car. Patrick said that was just part of the prince's car collection. He said if I took the job, I could expect at the very least to be gifted the largest model of a BMW! What else he showed us was equally disorienting and disturbing. These included palaces with gold domes, luxury homes of the rich and the royal family, the prince's private aircrafts (including a modified Boeing 747 and executive jets), and a fraction of the art collection that included Manet, Renoir, and Degas originals.

While not yet fully constructed or operational, the hospital was a showpiece of modern hospital design and technology. Some of the hospital suites were extravagantly decorated; some had gold-plated faucets, plush furnishings, and ornate telephones.

I learnt that the prince was chairman of the Brunei Investment Agency (BIA), whose holdings included New York's Palace Hotel, Hotel Bel-Air in Los Angeles, and Plaza Athénée in Paris. He indicated, somewhat ruefully, that I could expect to stay in these luxurious hotels in my travels, accompanying the royal family in their private jets on their many sprees abroad as the personal physician to the royalty! He indicated that our children would be sent to a prestigious private school in Singapore, with whom the country had a close relationship. He said he would arrange for me to meet with the prince's top aide in the next one or two days.

Back at the hotel, Nilu and I could not wrap our heads around this level of unseemly ostentation and self-indulgence in a world where almost half the people were deprived of even basic amenities, housing, and health care. It was blindingly clear to us that this was not what I expected by constructive engagement in global health issues! Two days later, without waiting to meet with the prince's officials, we departed for Singapore.

Resettlement: Adjusting to New Realities and Opportunities

I was beginning to appreciate, once more, the challenges to equitable health care even in a developed country like Canada, where there were many significantly marginalized and neglected populations, recalling my experience in developing societies where the problems of poverty and marginalization were stark. Much of what I saw on these visits was a consequence of loneliness, social isolation, malnutrition, and chronic and multiple degenerative diseases, such as chronic lung disease, heart failure, arthritis, stroke, mental illness, and chronic pain.

My reacquaintance with the spectrum of illnesses and aging populations in Canada serendipitously led me towards engagement with several facilities catering to the elderly, persons with dementia, and persons with chronic mental conditions and disabilities. The old Shaughnessy Hospital, then affiliated with the Faculty of Medicine of the University of British Columbia (UBC), was one such facility. This sprawling, old teaching hospital catered mainly to veterans, many of whom had a range of physical, mental, and social disabilities. It was not uncommon to see patients disabled by chronic lung damage acquired in the wars or those with chronic brain injuries or spinal and limb injuries. I got to know several dedicated medical and rehabilitation staff and occasionally did locum work for them. Another facility with a similar patient profile was the George Derby Centre, which catered to veterans' needs, the disabled, and those requiring long-term care. Periodic visits to these and similar facilities began to fill my days while I worked to reconstitute a more regular life as a family physician with an academic interest.

⁓ ꝺ·ꝼ ⁓

Over the following months, some contacts at the UBC Department of Epidemiology and Health Care invited me to share my experience in global health care and education endeavours acquired in my time with Aga Khan University. We shared, compared, and contrasted concerns of challenges confronting health care and medical education in industrialized countries and in resource-constrained counties of the developing world. I was soon offered a position as clinical assistant professor in the department, which allowed me access to the university's many resources.

On one occasion, the university was hosting a public forum that addressed the issues raised by the recent World Bank's *World Development Report,* which focused on health. Called "Investing in Health," it examined the interplay between human health, health policy, and economic development. I was asked to be a panellist to discuss the findings of that annual report. This report examined the controversial questions surrounding health care and health policy. Not being a trained health economist, my contribution was relatively modest, but I underlined the value of good health as an ethical goal in itself. Good health increases individuals', families', and communities' economic productivity, an area of activity that the AKDN was substantially invested in through its diverse activities.

Community Development: Domestic and International Engagements

An event I remember well, mainly because of its atypical setting and goals, occurred when I received an unexpected invitation to attend a conference on community-based development sponsored by the government of Canada and an NGO that promoted community-led development in Canada's isolated communities. I was not yet fully gainfully employed and longed for worthwhile and stimulating engagement. I accepted the invitation as it piqued my curiosity with its rather unusual agenda.

The program was held on Winnipeg's outskirts and brought together those interested in sharing experiences and ideas to foster development in neglected areas of community health in Indigenous communities, including a holistic approach to healing. It brought together a group of about thirty people with diverse backgrounds, including nurses, a few physicians, occupational therapists, health planners, one or two music therapists, traditional healers, and representatives of local indigenous communities. Interestingly, this low-budget program was held in a disused convent – I believe a nunnery – where the male and female participants were provided accommodations in separate dormitories. The conference events were held in a wood-framed hall; the participants were fed in a traditional long dining hall and kitchen expected in a residential school. I confess I felt a little awkward and out of place initially, but the program and camaraderie were engaging and cheerful.

A theme that underpinned deliberations was empowering communities to influence policies; to decentralize management; to ensure access to essential primary health care, ensuring that the poorest have access to care; and to foster respect for traditional community and health practices. Interestingly, one guiding idea was the little-known "Bamako Initiative."

Later a "Declaration," the Bamako Initiative was initially sponsored by UNICEF Director James Grant in partnership with the WHO in 1987. The declaration had to do with strengthening primary health care in sub-Saharan Africa, mainly West Africa, and was adopted by the regional ministers of health. It stated that many countries were burdened by a lack of resources and practical implementation strategies. I was well acquainted with these themes within my training and many years of work, inspired by Aga Khan Development Network's ethos, including exposure to justice and equity issues and empowerment. I suppose my input into the questions of equity, justice, and ethics in human development with dignity and respectful participation struck a chord with the organizers since I was invited to lead several workshops and help develop some documents outlining the group's recommendations.

The conference's highlight was for the participants to attend a "sweat lodge" ceremony at a close-by First Nations reserve.

A sweat lodge is a low-profile hut, typically dome-shaped or oblong and made of natural materials. Traditionally, the structure is simple, constructed of saplings covered with blankets and sometimes animal skins. The ceremony performed in the lodge is the "purification ceremony," or simply a "sweat." Used by the Americas' Indigenous peoples, the ritual is intended as a religious ceremony for prayer and healing. The ceremony is led by elders who know the language, songs, and traditions and are well aware of safety protocols. In the bracing cold prairie weather, we sat in a steaming lodge while the elders sang and chanted to the rhythmic beat of drums and prayed to the spirits for total healing of all that ails us. At the end of the ceremony, I felt amazingly revived in vitality and mentally and spiritually refreshed. The place of psycho-spiritual healing in modern health care practices has been given short shrift, despite studies indicating the vital role of psychic and spiritual healing dimensions.

I remember similar shared experiences obtained with the Maori people of New Zealand in later years.

One senior participant and organizer of the conference was Susan, a nurse educator who had considerable experience in global health issues. She had participated in the McMaster–AKU Nursing School project partnership in its early years and had spent some time in Pakistan. An unexpected but propitious corollary to my participation in the conference was meeting Susan at the conference and our shared passion for training human resources for health and community development.

Susan cornered me one evening over dinner. She mentioned her current role in an organization that promoted a healthier world. She struck me as someone deeply committed to advancing health equity and facilitating the sharing of Canadian knowledge and technology to that end. In our conversations, she invited me to consider a nomination to the Canadian Society for International Health (CSIH) board, a national NGO that works domestically and internationally to reduce global health inequalities and strengthen health systems. As a current member of the board of that organization, she proposed to put forward my name to the board. She urged me to participate in the multi-sectoral Canadian efforts to aid international health developments, primarily funded by CIDA (Canadian International Development Agency), Canada's government agency for development aid. I agreed to consider accepting that appointment if offered to me.

A few weeks later, I received a letter from the CSIH office in Ottawa, informing and congratulating me on my board appointment. Over the next few years, I attended the board meetings in Ottawa. I learnt a great deal about Canada's mission to convene stakeholders and exchange knowledge on global health and capacity building. The organization also acted as the Canadian representative office of the Pan American Health Organization (PAHO), the Americas' WHO regional division. The CSIH also convened and sponsored an annual World Health Forum, bringing together diverse participants and practitioners in global health. I remained active in the affairs of the CSIH for several years.

Introspective Moods: Re-creating Clinical Practice Base

While walking one evening in the leafy environs of a pleasant suburb of Vancouver, an elderly lady approached me. She had evidently seen me walk there occasionally and somehow knew I was a physician. She was quite direct and asked if I was a doctor and new to the area. I said yes to both of those questions. She said, "Doctor, look around you. There are quite a few residential complexes around here, but we do not have a doctor here. Why don't you consider opening a medical office here? I'm sure people here would welcome that very much."

She pointed to a half-tucked-away, small low-rise shopping plaza, where the only thing I could see was signage of a pizza shop and a convenience store. It did not seem like the ideal location to establish a medical practice. However, I could see several tucked-away housing complexes, although there was hardly any road or pedestrian traffic. There was a pretty little elementary school facing the road and a small park.

I mentioned to Nilu my meeting with this lady and her suggestion for a medical practice in the area. The next day, we walked over to the quiet little plaza and looked around. It looked charming, and there were one or two empty spaces available for lease. Surrounding it was a small multi-residential apartment complex. One or two residents peeked out of the windows or tiny terraces and watched us.

I was getting reasonably busy now, adding some occasional locum work for doctors practising out of the British Columbia Children's Hospital (BCCH) and the Women's Hospital in Vancouver, both UBC-affiliated hospitals. This wide-ranging work offered opportunities for continuing medical education and refreshing my knowledge of Canadian medicine and systems, which had undergone noticeable change since I had finished practising in Alberta five years before.

Simultaneously, I strove to deal with the far-reaching effects of my ill-advised investments and attempted to put our much-battered family finances on a healthier footing. The cold, damp climate of Vancouver had affected Nilu's health and required attention. The girls were beginning to find that their years of travels and experiences abroad gave them an edge in their education, and their popularity rose. In the way of the young, they began to adapt to their new life and soon had made new friends.

Interestingly, I found that the multiple and disparate challenges associated with our resettlement we met with equanimity and optimism, since the past years' challenges and experiences had only deepened a sense of confidence, resilience, and hope. But questions of values and meaning and purpose in medicine loomed large in my quest to re-establish my personal and professional life in the altered conditions of my life, outside the sheltering embrace of a nurturing organization I had grown accustomed to.

In periods of an introspective mood, I reflected on the career prospects for a mid-career generalist physician. Most of my peers were well-established in successful careers, content with their seemingly staid occupations. At the same time, my restless quest for meaning and fulfillment led to uncertainties and new mountains to climb. In my more rooted moments, I grasped that medicine was a calling full of potentialities. An agile and adaptable generalist, perhaps a disappearing breed of practitioners, had some unique value.

I remained convinced that a generalist physician, motivated by love and passion for medicine, still held a meaningful place in a world increasingly controlled by narrowly trained practitioners in all fields of human endeavour. I saw medicine as a profession with almost limitless frontiers, and one which afforded an unparalleled panorama of the human condition – its riches, frailties, hubris, and potentials.

After considerable deliberation, we decided to establish our practice in the little mountainside village and called it Mountainside Medical Clinic. The surrounding community gradually started seeking medical care at the clinic. Before long, I no longer needed to seek locum or temporary positions, although I continued maintaining some visits to long-term care facilities and calls on the frail elderly. For over a decade, this office served as the central hub for my restless forays into widening my range of professional activities driven by my manifold professional and intellectual interests honed over the past years in diverse settings and conditions.

As expected, the routine of general medical practice – with its care of the walking wounded, the young, the distressed, the elderly, the sick, and occasionally the very ill – shaped the foundation of my re-established professional life, reminiscent of my earlier practice in Alberta. It had its moments of reward and gratification, a level of fulfilment, and a modicum of material comfort and stability. But I missed the excitement of grappling with immense challenges, complex systems, and resource issues demanding creativity to address questions of values, ethics, equity, and mission.

A Bold Foray: Addressing Mental Health

One day I got a note from Nathan, a physician in town for whom I had done a short locum. Aware of my broad interests in medicine, he suggested I call the manager of a community mental health centre, looking for a capable part-time physician to provide consultations on people suffering from major mental disorders. I had an academic interest in mental health and psychiatry, mainly due to efforts to address this neglected area of medical care and training in developing countries like Pakistan. Still, I did not consider myself sufficiently proficient at acting as a community health consultant in a specialized setting. Nevertheless, I called the manager to express my interest in considering applying for this position. He invited me to visit and meet with the staff of his centre.

Bob McDonald was a slightly portly, tall, balding gentleman who received me warmly in his office in Delta, a distant working-class suburb of Vancouver. He seemed quite impressed by my professional life and activities. He described the local mental health system's organization, the role the community mental health centres played, the clients they dealt with, and their medical and psychiatric care processes. He mentioned regional and provincial committees involved in reorienting community mental health to be made more equitable, accessible, and practical. He was involved in many committees and studies. Their work was at a critical juncture since the central psychiatric facility in the province, the Riverview Hospital, was being downsized, resulting in many people with major mental illnesses unserved. The remaining general hospitals' capacities for managing severe psychiatric conditions were deemed inadequate; hence, the community mental health required increased capacity and effectiveness.

He introduced me to several of the centre's senior staff members, including two psychologists, nurses, community mental health workers, and the office staff. There was also a part-time psychiatrist, a fiery Irish lady, who appeared overworked. She was very encouraging and said the mental health system needed new people and ideas, and there were many opportunities to contribute to rationalizing community mental health care.

The next day I received a call from Bob, stating he wished to offer me a position as a consulting mental health physician and hoped I would accept since his team felt I had the background to contribute to the system. I accepted the position, making it clear that I had my own medical practice and could only give so much time to mental health.

The Delta Mental Health Centre comprised two centres several miles apart that were located quite far from my home and office. Nevertheless, I felt re-energized by the possibility of contributing to community-care system development in a highly challenging area of health care. Over the next four or five years, care of people suffering from significant mental illnesses, improving continuing care, and supporting social support mechanisms became a fulfilling part of my professional life.

Psychiatric care in Canada and North America in general in recent years had been transformed by several key developments in the clinical sciences and health care systems. Rapid advances in understanding the underlying biology of mental illnesses led to many new drugs and therapies being brought to bear in the battle against chronic mental health disorders. Some of these drug treatments meant that large numbers of patients hospitalized in psychiatric hospitals and asylums could be de-institutionalized, a degree of human dignity and independence restored, providing adequate infrastructure for their continuing care in community settings existed. Thus, capacity building in mental health was the crux of the challenge. Outside of the specialized psychiatric facilities, there was a significant shortage of skilled human resources and competent facilities. Communal integration of de-institutionalized patients is a long and complicated process.

I found this engagement in mental health stimulating and demanding. Perhaps in no other field of medicine were the scientific advances as consequential as studies in brain biology, the mechanisms of mental and neurological disorders and drug therapy in the closing years of the twentieth century. Opportunities for acquiring new knowledge and competencies abounded, and I partook of these hungrily. As part of my community mental health appointment, I often attended medical rounds at the Riverview Hospital in Vancouver.

In 1913, this hospital, set on a thousand acres in Coquitlam, then a rural district outside Vancouver, was established. It traces its pedigree as a new "Provincial Asylum for the Insane" to the opening of the first asylum in 1878 in Victoria. The Victoria facility faced overcrowding, and a large tract of land was purchased in Coquitlam in the lower mainland. It was surrounded by a beautiful arboretum, a nursery, and botanical gardens, built with patients' assistance, in the belief that nature was of therapeutic value. Its beautiful grounds included wildlife, and over eighty species of birds have been identified. Yet, the hospital carried the stigma of mental illness and a sense of tragedy and trepidation evoked by psychiatric hospitals.

Its several character buildings housed the most psychiatrically disturbed patients and long-term residents. It has endured a long and difficult history. At its peak, it housed over a thousand patients in different wards; many had lost contact with their families. By the 1980s, the patient numbers had dropped significantly after the provincial government gradually started closing the facility. Some of the old wards and buildings were later used as backdrop for movies.

Nevertheless, the hospital was a repository of scientific knowledge and an affiliated training facility of the University of British Columbia. As I learnt of new advances in diagnosis and treatment, I was reminded of the crucial need to permeate knowledge of mental illnesses more widely in the medical community globally, especially to community physicians.

One morning over coffee, following a grand round discussing fascinating trials of a new approach to treating treatment-resistant psychotic illnesses, I was approached by Dr. Mike Kemke, a staff general practitioner. Mike, who had spent many years working in hospital psychiatry, asked me if I would be interested in taking a role in advancing the Riverview Hospital's and UBC's efforts in continuing mental health education for family physicians. He was aware of my work in establishing continuing medical education programs with AKU, as the staff appointment process required a detailed resumé on file for the application process. He and a hospital staff psychiatrist had spearheaded an effort over the past one or two years to develop a series of CME programs. Still, they needed additional experienced physician educators interested in this effort.

Mike looked after a Riverview Hospital ward, where I sometimes attended patients designated to receive continuing care from our mental health centre, or those we admitted from our centre for stabilization. I agreed to assist in this project. This involvement led to an exciting endeavour, reminiscent of our projects in Pakistan and Africa, to engage community-based physicians in applying advanced knowledge to their patients' clinical care closer to home.

Over the next several months, I developed a discussion document, "Clinical Teaching Unit (CTU)," with Mike and the Clinical Education Committee of the Riverview Hospital. Later, I shared with UBC and the Riverview Hospital committee a more detailed version of this endeavour to integrate and enhance mental health and primary care. I termed the concept document "Clinical Education Centre," which could function as an overarching coordinating system for individualized and modular psychiatric and behavioural medicine training for health professionals.

The CTU was conceived to act as an interface between psychiatry and primary and community care. It offered a comprehensive, interdisciplinary academic environment that modelled contemporary evidence-based psychiatric care. Its goal was to provide opportunities for practising clinicians to obtain enhanced mental health skills and apply them in their communities. The Riverview Hospital already had an academic arrangement with the Division of Geriatric Medicine at UBC. It enabled geriatricians and family physicians interested in geriatric psychiatry to obtain additional training and experience in this field. The unit also offered a deeper appreciation of relevant legislations, such as the *Mental Health Act*, and the social and human rights implications of these legislations.

Between 30 and 40 percent of primary care visits have a direct or contributory underlying mental health issue. Yet, many practitioners feel unqualified or unprepared to deal with these problems adequately. Community mental health centres are overburdened and short of qualified staff. The unit proposed to offer family physicians and other interested health professionals' short placements in acquiring more in-depth training and experience in mental health and psychiatry. It enabled them to better manage patients in their clinics and share their knowledge and expertise with their colleagues.

I approached Robert Woolard, the head of the Department of Family Practice at UBC. I proposed a joint training initiative to enhance mental health education for UBC trainees and practising primary care physicians. The department was responsive and led to future collaborations in teaching and research.

Bob McDonald frequently invited me to task forces and committee meetings dealing with the challenges of redesigning mental health services in the lower mainland of British Columbia. The substantial unmet needs in mental health and addiction became an important part of my clinical work and enabled efforts to strengthen community mental health foundations.

My work with the Delta Mental Health Centre drew me into providing care to other mental health centres and facilities in Vancouver. In particular, care for the elderly with mental health problems, including dementia, was a difficult and complex engagement area. Another rapidly growing problem I encountered was that of substance abuse and addiction.

Some exceptional people worked at the centres. A person who encouraged, inspired, supported, befriended, and readily assisted me was a nurse working at the Delta Mental Health Centre when I joined. I remember Doreen Littlejohn, a bubbly, highly energetic and competent mental health nurse, generous to a fault, as a friend and colleague and a source of inspiration. Doreen and I often shared care of patients from our respective disciplines – hers the harder of the two fields. We often made house calls together, shared concerns about difficult or non-compliant patients, and coordinated management plans. She unswervingly followed and advocated for patients with primary psychiatric problems and their diverse needs, never giving up, never losing her sense of humour, compassion, and humanity.

I remember one day when Doreen asked me to see Ruby, a woman in her sixties. Ruby was oddly dressed, with pins in her dishevelled hair and bright lipstick that was slightly smudged, smudged further as she hugged Doreen. Her clothes were curiously mismatched but proudly worn. She eyed me suspiciously as I walked into Doreen's office. Doreen introduced me to her. Ruby extended her hand to me; as I shook it, I noticed bright, multicoloured nail varnishes on her fingernails.

Doreen had briefed me on Ruby's history, about her difficult transition to community care since being discharged from Riverview Hospital more than six months before. She had been in the hospital with a difficult-to-stabilize bipolar disorder, a major psychiatric disorder requiring long-term treatment. Ruby refused to take her medications as directed and tended to have flights of grandeur and other behavioural issues, making it hard for her to be accepted and function in the community. She was fairly typical of the types of patients we saw in the centre. As her assigned mental health nurse, Doreen's job was to ensure she remained safe, stable, and compliant with the treatments.

I gently talked to Ruby, who became coquettish after the initial suspicion and smiled knowingly at me. While speaking to her, I formed a mental health assessment of her condition in my mind, as was the medical consultant's role, and silently formulated a treatment plan for her.

Back in my office, I thoroughly reviewed her course in the hospital and her discharge notes, including the treatments tried and proven helpful, and her behavioural issues. But while in the hospital, her treatments could be monitored closely and modified as needed; in the community, she was independent and often did not take medications as prescribed or keep her follow-up appointments with the mental health centre. Nurses like Doreen and home care workers did the heavy lifting of maintaining care connection between the patient and the health system.

I followed Ruby, with Doreen, on many occasions. She clearly was in the manic phase of bipolar disorder, with poor insight into her condition. I started her on a different antipsychotic drug cocktail, one drug delivered by monthly injections, and Doreen and I frequently monitored the effects and carefully watched for any adverse effects. Over the coming few months, she appeared to become stable and more compliant.

Like other nurses and staff at the centre, Doreen had a full roster of patients they followed, and it was challenging to attend to every contingency. One morning, Doreen asked me to accompany her to see Ruby at her home. Doreen had received a frantic call from Ruby's neighbour. As we approached Ruby's apartment, we saw her lying naked on her bed on a roof terrace, blissfully unaware of the commotion her behaviour was causing. Doreen gently bundled her into a bathrobe and led her into the apartment. I joined in. We talked to Ruby, who cheerfully denied she had done anything scandalous or disturbing. She did not meet the criteria for involuntary admission to a hospital's psychiatric unit and was not a danger to herself or others. Over the next few weeks, we patiently worked to restabilize her and followed her closely. But she was one of many who required intense clinical and social vigilance.

I recall Robert, a man suffering from intensely troubling delusions. A fiftyish man, prematurely aging and a chain smoker, he was disturbed by an unshakable conviction that his brain was wired and tapped by the CIA, who could "hear" his thoughts and who implanted troubling ideas in his head. A harmless, pleasant, rather shy man, he politely, and on more than one occasion, asked me to operate on him and remove the "wiring" in his head. He had been in and out of psychiatric wards and now lived with his heavy-smoking and dependent girlfriend. When he missed his appointments at the centre, Doreen and I would visit his messy, smoke-filled one-bedroom apartment to check on him. He would take his medications because he "liked Doreen and me," but he remained convinced his real problem was someone "messing with his head." Like many others we saw at the clinic, he had chronic paranoid schizophrenia, a serious brain disorder. We put him on a newer class of antipsychotic medications, in this case, a drug called clozapine, which required close follow-up care and periodic tests. Robert remained quite harmless for years, eventually developing lung cancer, which we discovered on close follow-up.

The mental health centre's typical session entailed assessing new patients referred to the centre; following, evaluating, and treating long-term patients; attending staff conferences centred around individual patients and their multidisciplinary meetings; and firefighting multiple problems around patient-centred care for severely ill patients. But there were other patients with less distressing disorders who also needed help from the centre. We saw many patients suffering from depression, severe anxiety disorders, or disorders of personality or conduct. A problem we commonly saw was alcohol and substance abuse and drug addiction. In the years to come, this became an increasingly troubling public health concern.

The DSM-5, a current version of the diagnostic manual of mental illnesses published by the American Psychiatric Association, lists and classified hundreds of disorders. This controversial classification system is a common but not universally adopted version of labelling mental health disorders. For various reasons, it is necessary to give labels to patients presenting with mental health problems.

I worked for several years at the mental health centre. In later years, Doreen moved to play a prominent role in health care for Indigenous people through the Native Health Society organization. The Native Health Clinic became an advocate for the rights and care of people suffering from mental health problems, HIV/AIDS, chronic illnesses, and the consequences of urban poverty. On a few occasions, I helped out at the clinic, bringing to bear what little knowledge and experience I had acquired over the years. Doreen remains a friend and an inspiring figure to me.

Enlarging Clinical Practice: Rewarding Diversity

My own practice was quite busy now. I admitted several of my elderly patients requiring institutional care to long-term care facilities. One I notably used was a well-kept and well-managed centre called Royal City Manor. It had a specialized unit that looked after patients with dementia. Given my involvement in managing some complex patients, the management asked me if I would take on the role of medical director of the centre. As I often visited the centre, I agreed to accept this role. It added to my knowledge but also placed added responsibilities on me. I continued in this role for a few years, and it required me to draw upon all my institutional capacity-building experience.

By now, I had served as a member of the board of directors of the Alzheimer's Society of British Columbia for several years. Hence, I was aware of the developments in this devastating disorder's clinical, research, and social dimensions. Over the previous few years, my care of patients with degenerative neurological and psychiatric diseases had been part of my practice. I was often called to make public and professional presentations on these important and growing public health concerns.

My family medicine practice dealt with run-of-the-mill general practice problems: coughs and colds, allergies, arthritis, chronic diseases like diabetes and high blood pressure, cancers, heart and lung disease, accidents and injuries, and emotional distress, including anxiety and depression. The ages ranged from newborn children to people in their eighties and nineties; people of all races and religious persuasion and political and social convictions enriched the practice. They represented the cross-section of the communities I strove to serve. All were, almost without exception, appreciative and pleasant and loyal. Christmas cards and gifts and greetings of Eid, Diwali, and Hanukkah cheered the ambience of the practice.

In this rewarding environment, I embarked on a short-lived public and community enterprise in the form of a practice newsletter. It became surprisingly and gratifyingly popular, circulating widely even outside my catchment area. I had always felt that public health education laid the foundation for a healthier and more participatory community. On many occasions, I had given talks at the local school and community centres when invited to do so.

There were many memorable characters and events that filled those days. One family I remember well was the Khayu family. Recently emigrated from Syria – in the late eighties, well before the devastating civil war – this large and gregarious family of three generations, headed by an engaging Mr. Khayu, the very warm and loquacious Mrs. Mariam Khayu, and their eldest son, Robert, were typical of some of the users of the medical clinic. The adult children and several grandchildren were a joy to care for, advise, and guide to the unfamiliar health care system of British Columbia. In later years, Mr. Khayu died of advanced prostate cancer, but his lovely family expressed their gratitude for the care he had received until the end.

I recall an almost blind, homebound, and wheelchair-bound gentleman with severely swollen legs from advanced diabetes, heart failure, and kidney disease. He refused hospitalization and advanced care. I frequently made a home visit to his home, and he invariably had me make a cup of tea for him to share with me. My many efforts to recruit his estranged family into his care were mostly unsuccessful, but we managed a home care program for him.

I remember vividly a charming elderly Irishman, George Murphy, with advanced lung disease and failing vision from an inherited form of blindness. A scholarly man, who would often quote Milton, Shakespeare, and other great writers, he had spent his younger years working and supervising a plantation in the Philippines and had regaled my office staff with his stories and jokes. Amazingly, I saw him almost twenty years later at another clinic where I was filling in for a friend. He was brought in by his daughter. Now blind and breathless but still alert and talkative, he recognized me by my voice and the name his daughter addressed me by. Excitedly, he asked me if I had operated the Mountainside Medical Clinic. I said yes. He announced excitedly, "You were my doctor." He wanted to know what had occupied me over the previous almost two decades.

There were, undoubtedly, moments and times of failure, errors in judgment, frustration, and shared pain in that period. I recall receiving a call from the local hospital one day, informing me that one of my patients was admitted for spinal paralysis resulting from prostate cancer spread to his spine. I remember this trusting elderly gentleman, whom I had cared for over several years and had followed his cancer with cancer specialists for some time. Had I missed some change in his condition that could have prevented this tragic development?

Busman's Holidays: Labour of Love

I sought professional and personal fulfillment from diverse activities. Since my return from Pakistan, I had filled my time with various professional activities, perhaps seeking to re-create a multidimensional professional life reminiscent of my multiple roles in my previous position with AKU. My urge to look beyond the horizon never left me. Not infrequently, I travelled abroad. In particular, I visited regions of Africa, for which I harboured a nostalgic attachment.

On one sojourn in Kenya, I got drawn into discussions relating to upgrading certain high-needs services in an old, established private hospital in Mombasa. The hospital board was concerned that many hospital patients could not access pain relief or palliation services in cancer care, as there were no specific palliative care programs in the region. There was also no access to chemotherapy or radiation therapy for patients with treatable malignant disease. The closest service was in Nairobi, more than 300 miles away, and that too was a very basic service.

I offered to help establish manageable symptom management and palliative care service at the hospital, recalling my earlier short training immersion in medical oncology at the Tom Baker Cancer Centre in Calgary years ago. I maintained some interest in cancer patients' ambulatory care, which the cancer agencies in Canada encouraged and supported among primary care physicians. Over that visit and a subsequent visit to Mombasa, I worked with a range of physicians and surgeons and the hospital laboratory and pharmacy in Mombasa to introduce a rudimentary evidence-based pain and palliation program and a standardized chemotherapy service to address some common cancer presentations. In this endeavour, the Alberta Cancer Society and other professional organizations assisted greatly by providing access to treatment protocols and guidelines.

My travels in Africa enabled me to visit some sophisticated health care and training facilities in South Africa. From advanced tertiary care university hospitals to community-based services, South Africa – despite its historical baggage of apartheid and inequality – had established a reasonably practical health care system that mirrored our efforts to promote an effective health care system in Pakistan. In the years to come, this accumulating experience and worldview would significantly inform my future endeavours to foster effective health services development in low-income countries, particularly in Africa.

One day, back in Vancouver, I was examining a patient with severe mutilation of his leg. His lovely wife got into a conversation with me. I learnt she was an Iraqi physician who had sought refuge in Canada with her family. She struggled to pass the Canadian licensing medical examinations, and she found it difficult to cross that hurdle for several reasons. She mentioned that several other doctors were in the same situation. Over the next few visits, I got to know her better. I offered to coach her for her examinations, which she accepted with great alacrity. I asked her to invite her friends and colleagues to attend as well. We set a time to meet in the evenings twice a week, after the regular office hours.

The following Tuesday, as I finished with my last patient of the day, I found six men and women sitting in the waiting room. I got to know them; they were from Russia, Ukraine, Iran, Iraq, and Afghanistan. In the later sessions, two more joined the group: one from Germany, another from Romania. They formed a study group, assisting each other with preparations for the demanding Canadian licensing examinations. I worked with them for several months until three passed the first and second parts of the three-part test. Three others, for complicated family and personal conditions, gave up trying to fulfill the requirements. I thoroughly enjoyed our exhausting two-hour sessions, as I loved teaching and mentoring. The students expressed their gratitude prolifically, but for me, the joy was to learn that three of them successfully completed their exams and the course of study required. Years later, I received notes from several of them informing me of their productive career advancement, which gave me immense joy and satisfaction.

Echoes of the Past: Physician Leader

I had a visit from my old friend, Mahmoud Mitha, who several years ago had spent some time under my supervision in Karachi for his master's in public health degree from Columbia University. Mahmoud, a smart and energetic lad, was now in a senior position as director of community development with a Christian hospital and health care group in Vancouver. Mahmoud was enthusiastic about his work, which recalled some work we had done in Pakistan and Asia. At that time, I served as the associate medical director of the Aga Khan University Medical Centre. Part of my work involved linking community health care with hospital-level secondary and tertiary care. Mahmoud strongly encouraged me to consider applying for the medical director position with this progressive hospital group in Vancouver.

I had a fair bit going on in my life, but I agreed to apply since this position was advertised. Soon, I was called for an interview.

The interview was held at Mount Saint Joseph Hospital (MSJH) in Vancouver. The hospital is an acute and chronic care facility of CHARA, one of the three Catholic groups, each with its distinct long history of service in medicine and health care. The founding organizations were now in the process of amalgamation and rationalizing their services to form an overarching Vancouver Catholic Health Care Group (VCHCG). The merger would bring together three acute care hospitals and several chronic and long-term facilities and community health programs under one management and brand. The strategy of the VCHCG was now to focus on the quality of patient care and achieve cost efficiency through the integration of support and corporate services. The planning exercise also included a new care delivery model that complemented clinical programs and population services.

The regional governmental health authority was also in the process of conducting reviews of acute care and other services, including mental health, home care, and alcohol and drug abuse services. A number of these services were provided by the group's facilities, including kidney dialysis, care of children and the elderly, joint surgery, heart surgery, and many other specialized services.

Joanne, the CEO of the MSJH, and Diane, the CEO of Saint Vincent Hospital (SVH), another acute and rehabilitation hospital of the network, headed the interview team. Also present were Frank, head of medicine; Robert Taylor, head of surgery; Marilyn, head of nursing; and several other department heads. The position of medical director of acute and community care called for an individual with wide-ranging clinical, planning, quality development, and supervisory skills.

The interview was thorough and wide-ranging. My former roles and responsibilities were carefully probed. My previous medical administration experience and linking hospital care with community-based care with the AKUMC and the AKHS evidently proved satisfactory to the interviewers.

I was appointed part-time medical director (later called physician leader) for the organization. The position required participation in many committees and groups involved in medical staff affairs and quality development, harmonizing and rationalizing the spectrum of services across the group. Central committees included the Medical Executive Committee (MEC), Joint Staff Committee (JSC), and several other committees to set direction and monitoring goals at the extensive network's executive levels. At least fourteen program streams were proposed with the intention that these be critically examined for their prospect of improved service delivery and quality. The interface between hospital care and primary care also needed further improvement and seamless continuity.

The joining institutions had their particular histories, culture, and traditions, which, not surprisingly, led to some tensions in the amalgamation process. A new group CEO was appointed, as was a new board. Many moving pieces in the puzzle required calm and far-sighted leadership, especially in clinical affairs.

Mahmoud and I often conferred on the common ground between our respective portfolios. We realized that hospitals' traditional role was evolving, and ambulatory care and community care were increasingly filling in the hospital's many functions. The MSJH and SVH served as community hospitals, while Saint Paul's Hospital (SPH) was a reputed centre for teaching and research and a high-technology hub. Therefore, we jointly developed a concept paper for discussion at the senior levels, fully aware of sensitive territories that each system cherished and wished to preserve.

Our document, titled "*Refining the Role of Hospitals in Primary and Secondary Care*," was presented to the planning committee.

The proposal called for a Centre of Excellence in Acute Community Health in the Vancouver Catholic Health Care Group. There were very few examples of hospitals extending a range of services directly into the community; we drew from our experience of Aga Khan University and its affiliation with the Aga Khan Health Services community health program. The proposal, one of several put forward by working groups, later grew into a comprehensive program of essential services over time. For instance, rapid-access breast clinics, formed at the MSJH; ambulatory diabetes care; psychiatric care for the elderly; and several others became well-functioning comprehensive programs.

My role also called for oversight of clinical care in acute services and involved a periodic review of departmental performance and challenges. Working closely with nursing services and other professional services, I found this role quite exhilarating and challenging. The extensive health care network functioned within the broader provincial health strategy; hence, there were periods of challenges of cooperation, coordination, and priorities. A relatively recently formed association of British Columbia hospital medical directors invited me to join the group. Headed by the vice president of medicine of the Vancouver General Hospital, the largest hospital in B.C., it served to support, share, and advance medical administration and clinical quality issues. I found the group's mission and interaction very supportive and helpful.

Doctor at Sea: Riding the Waves

It was still the early hours of the morning one day as Nilu and I gazed excitedly at the verdant forest around us. The ship, *MS Ryndam*, passed under the arches of the magnificent Bridge of the Americas at Balboa on the Gulf of Panama on the Pacific Ocean. We could see Panama City in the distance. The ship was about to enter the eighty-two kilometres of Panama Canal, the conduit across the Isthmus of Panama that connects the Pacific Ocean to the Atlantic Ocean. We felt the thrill of anticipation as the ship entered the locks of the canal. We were told it would take about ten to twelve hours to complete the canal crossing, passing through multiple locks and lakes. The two rows of locks operate by the gravity flow of water lakes. We watched in fascination as the towing locomotives moved the ship in the canal's narrow passage, traversing the changing panorama of nature and human activity. We finally emerged at Colon on the Caribbean Sea and thus to the Atlantic.

As the ship's physician, I was up early to hold a short morning clinic at the ship's medical centre and then was free to spend the day, available to handle any medical problems that may arise. Then there was a short evening clinic to attend. There were almost two thousand souls on board the fifty-six-thousand-tonne luxury cruise ship with the passengers and crew.

It had started when I received a call weeks earlier from Dr. John Carter, the Seattle-based medical director of the Holland America Cruise Lines. A month earlier, a physician friend in Vancouver suggested I apply for the ship's medical officer position, a position he held, which allowed him periodic breaks from the stressful job as an emergency room physician at a local hospital in Vancouver. He assured me that the large, American cruise company preferred experienced Canadian physicians over their American counterparts. I did not think there was much chance of landing such a position. Nevertheless, I wrote to Dr. Carter outlining my background and interest.

One afternoon, I received a call from Dr. Carter saying that the company's medical board had approved my credentials. I was eligible for periodic postings on cruises on their luxury liners. Surprisingly, he then went on to say that there was an urgent posting that needed to be filled on a voyage from Vancouver and across the Panama Canal and sailing around the continent of South America. He asked if I could fill that position for a three-week cruise due to depart Vancouver in about three weeks. He said it would also allow them to evaluate my professional conduct. Also, the physician assigned for that cruise was unable to fill that role for personal reasons. He said he would forward the medical manuals for marine medicine, regulations, and other background documents. He also directed me to online training and continuing education resources for physicians conducted by the Marine Medicine Institute of America and similar organizations.

I was thrilled by this early offer. I had always loved the sea and had taken several cruises in the past. As a young student, I had dreamt of being a ship's doctor after reading Richard Gordon's hilarious book, *Doctor at Sea*. But this offer came at an unplanned moment; I had a growing practice and an assortment of professional activities built over the few years since my return to Canada after my work abroad. On the other hand, I had worked almost unceasingly over the previous three or four years reconstructing my life – almost without a holiday – and was feeling the strain. After consulting Nilu, I accepted the assignment. Fortunately, a semi-retired physician was available to work in my office as a locum physician during my absence.

The trip had, however, been a baptism by fire in medical care at sea, and that suddenly called for all my clinical acumen in the very first hours after an evening departure from Vancouver on my first assignment as the ship's physician. I had boarded the vessel in Vancouver early in the day as required. I had spent several hours in thorough orientation to the ship's layout, safety procedures, emergency drill, and much else. I was shown the medical centre and introduced to two experienced nurses on board, Wendy and Linda.

The medical centre was surprisingly well equipped. There was a doctor's consultation room; two beds for observation, monitoring and stabilization; an X-ray machine; and a small, compact laboratory unit. An area for emergency surgical procedures with an operating table was tucked on the side. It also had a dedicated area for a kidney dialysis unit and a dental suite. There was a dentist on board as well. The centre was well stocked with standard drugs, various intravenous fluids, surgical equipment, plasters for treating fractures, and a range of other medical and surgical paraphernalia. There were some emergency medical and surgical reference books and journals.

Wendy, the senior nurse, assured me that "she had seen it all" at sea, and I need have no trepidations. The lovely second nurse, Linda, minded the medical centre as Wendy invited me to dinner in the ship's ornate dining room. It had been little more than an hour or two since we departed from the Vancouver cruise terminal. Everybody was in a holiday mood.

The dinner consisted of a buffet of a wide selection of mouth-watering choices, to which we helped ourselves. Wendy was filling me in on shipboard procedures and protocols and said the nurses would take care of minor illnesses, such as seasickness and coughs and colds, and minor injuries. I had been handed a pager to carry with me all the time. The next day was going to be a big celebration and party for the start of the cruise. While digging into my steak, my pager buzzed. So did Wendy's.

Wendy directed me to the nearest staff telephone. She answered her page as well. My caller asked me to report immediately to the bridge, as they had a medical emergency. Wendy took me to the restricted bridge deck and knocked on the door. I was let in by a middle-aged, bearded gentleman dressed in casual uniform.

He asked if I was the doctor. I said yes. He did not introduce himself. I assumed him to be a bridge officer on duty.

He showed me into a small cabin and said, "There's your patient, doctor. He has been complaining of pain in his abdomen. He has vomited a few times."

I saw a youngish man in his undershirt lying curled in a bed. There was an odour in the cabin. I bent over him, gently straightening him, and asked a few questions, while feeling his pulse. Wendy walked in with a blood pressure measuring machine, a stethoscope, and a medical bag. The man was perspiring slightly and looked pale, and he had a fast pulse. I quickly checked his chest and heart and took his blood pressure; it was a bit low. I put my hand on his abdomen; he winced slightly. I gently but carefully felt the whole belly and found a slight resistance to my probing hand in his right lower abdomen. As I released my hand, he winced. I tried again, with the same effect. This did not look good. The history and the signs seemed to suggest appendicitis, an inflammation in the abdominal cavity.

The bearded gentlemen asked what I thought was the problem. To my questions, he said the patient was a harbour pilot who had joined them in Vancouver. He had felt unwell since boarding, and soon after vomited once or twice. The bearded gentleman had laid him on the bed.

I told him I suspected an acute inflammation of the appendix as the most likely problem. It is a surgical problem. I felt some apprehension; I had little intention of handling a critical surgical situation in a ship at sea.

He asked if the patient may require evacuation. I said yes; we were in no position to handle such an emergency on board. He said that we were in the Strait of Georgia and close to Victoria on Vancouver Island. He asked if I would like to speak to the emergency medical services at the port. Soon I was talking to the emergency call centre, who transferred my call to the hospital in Victoria. I discussed the case and my impressions with the emergency physician at the other end of the line; he concurred with my decision to transfer the patient.

Over the next two hours, we proceeded to evacuate the patient, putting in an intravenous fluid line, controlling his pain, and carefully recording his status. The evacuation boat arrived, and we hoisted him in a special stretcher and transferred him to the hospital in Victoria.

The bearded gentleman said, "Good work, doctor." It was then that I realized he was the captain of the ship. During the rest of the cruise, I was not an infrequent visitor to the bridge. My unquenchable lifelong curiosity led me to ask endless questions about various arcane maritime procedures, equipment, and functions.

Later that night, a call was put through to my suite. The hospital called to say they had operated on the pilot and found a ruptured appendix. How he had managed to go through the previous few hours carrying on with his job remains a mystery.

That was my introduction to shipboard medicine. Nilu joined me on the ship at San Francisco, having missed the earlier excitement. We enjoyed the rest of the cruises with few life-threatening events, although there were the usual chest infections, blood pressure problems, and minor illnesses.

The passengers were generally quite elderly, with many medical problems. Some had heart disease, cancers, chronic arthritis, and other illnesses, and they carried huge supplies of medications. They loved to talk about their histories and the dramatic medical and surgical procedures they had gone through. They eagerly sought my opinion on various techniques and treatments. They were pleasantly surprised when I took the time to listen to their stories, often when cornered in the coffee bar or dining rooms, although I kept my counsel to myself whenever possible. Many grateful patients sent over bottles of wine to our dinner table, and on one or two occasions, Nilu received flowers.

The ship's officers were mainly American or Dutch; the rest of the crew were mostly Indonesians and Filipinos, all of them invariably pleasant. Their health problems were quite different. There was a degree of loneliness, anxiety, fatigue, and stress. The ship's hotel manager, a pleasant young dutchman, occasionally sought me out to talk about his anxiety and work stress impacting his job performance. He seemed to appreciate some reassurance and counselling.

One unexpected, but ultimately pleasant duty assigned to the ship's physician was to host a "Doctor's Table" on certain days on the cruise. The hotel department of the cruise company invited selected passengers to be "guests" at the table. Everyone has heard of the "Captain's Table," but the chief engineer and the doctor as ranking officers were also accorded that "privilege." Naturally, the idea of "hosting" these tables, where free wine and fine food lubricated nuanced conversations, camaraderie, and happy memories of the cruise and the company, was a friendly marketing tool. Nevertheless, I remember meeting some fascinating people at my tables. I remember meeting a retired United States Supreme Court justice and an aged nuclear physicist who recalled taking part in the "Manhattan Project" to develop the American atomic bomb and remembered some well-known names associated with that project. He had some remorse over the consequences and the subsequent trajectory of nuclear arms developments. There were other memorable characters as well. While some of these functions left me slightly perturbed, I believe these casual contacts continued to enlighten me on the realities of the diversity of the one world we inhabit.

My curiosity of all things marine got the chief engineer, a Scotsman, to invite me to his cavernous, noisy domain in the ship's bowels. I loved the engine room, with its stifling heat, deafening noise, smell of oil, clutter, rotating shafts of powerful diesel-electric engines, and all manners of equipment for everything from water treatment to electronics and guidance systems. We often had drinks in the staff room below, where I was greeted by the crew I had seen or treated. I got to appreciate their particular range of health problems, an area of medicine I had had little to do with in the past.

The ship rounded the stormy Cape Horn, surrounded by wild seas off the southern tip of South America where the Pacific and the Atlantic Oceans meet. The Straits of Magellan, considered the most dangerous natural passage between the Atlantic and the Pacific, allowed views of albatross and other seabirds. The ship docked at Ushuaia, Punta Arenas, and other fascinating ports along the way. Finally, Nilu and I disembarked in Valparaiso in Chile. After a day of enjoying that city, we drove to Santiago and flew back to Vancouver. It had been an illuminating foray into a different world of medicine.

In the years to come, we took many short trips covering virtually every ocean and many seas in the world. They were working holidays – not very lucrative, but a refreshing change from my packed regular work routine. But these assignments were often very demanding and unpredictable in their course, but almost always culturally broadening and educational.

Much was expected of the ship's physician. The doctor was encouraged and required to monitor, record, verify, and certify the ship's health and medical care status; assess the port health facilities of the ports visited; emergency evacuation and transportation procedures; and liaise with the ship's central medical authorities and programs. He or she was also required to perform periodic physical and occupational health assessments of the crew, certify the hygiene standards onboard, and sign numerous port authority documents necessary to allow the ship to dock at ports. We sailed on most of the Holland America fleet of ships, and on at least two occasions, their smaller luxury ships, the Windstar cruises. Each vessel was slightly different, and the supporting staff were diverse; the work and the demands varied. In later voyages, the company employed a doctor to look after the crew; however, you were still expected to be the supervising physician. I missed seeing the crew members and learning more about their backgrounds, families and communities, and the economic imperatives that distanced them from their families for months at a time.

After docking and clearing the port procedures one day, Wendy asked me to accompany her to visit a private medical facility that the cruise line was considering as their backup medical centre. St. Petersburg, a fascinating Russian port on the Baltic Sea, a city of palaces, museums, and culture, was a key stop on the itinerary with two or three days at port. The port agent had arranged transport and appointment for Wendy and me to visit a new private hospital, owned and operated by an Austrian health care group. It catered to the expatriate community, well-heeled locals and tourists.

The hospital director proudly showed us the new facility and modern Western-made equipment. Wendy was making copious notes; I went along, having seen many private for-profit centres of this sort. Little did I know I would soon be needing the backup of a hospital like this.

Soon after the ship departed one evening, I received a call from the nurse from the ship's medical centre. I walked into the observation room to see two nurses attending a young man in the bed. He was very agitated and seemed not fully aware of his surroundings. I learned that the young man, Jason, had spent the whole day partying with some friends and bar-hopping. His parents had just managed to bundle him back on board before the ship's departure. I examined seventeen-year-old Jason. He was obviously intoxicated, and signs were suggesting alcohol poisoning. His heart and blood pressure were unstable. I asked the nurses to do some blood tests on him and started intravenous fluids and medications.

The senior nurse, Wendy, strongly recommended that he be evacuated, since the company could not be held responsible for an adverse outcome.

I called his anxious father into the doctor's consultation room and explained the seriousness of his son's medical condition and that he may need to be evacuated. His father said that after a long time, the family had finally got together for their holiday cruise. He pleaded with me not to disembark him and promised he would ensure his son did not drink for the rest of the cruise. On the other hand, Wendy was quite convinced he was a high-risk patient, challenging to monitor continuously, and she urged me to authorize evacuation to the nearest hospital.

The decision was mine to make. I concluded that we could manage Jason on board, and I made up my mind to visit him frequently in the night. His family was incredibly relieved. I carefully watched his clinical condition for the night and the next day. His consciousness level fluctuated, but his heart, blood pressure, and nervous system findings continued to improve. The day after, when I entered the medical centre, he was sitting in a chair, fully awake and greatly chagrined. His grateful parents thanked me profusely and led him out. I believe this incident served as a wake-up call for the young man, since on final disembarkation, they assured me Jason had learnt his lesson and had not taken a drink since his incident. I gave them final instructions and suggested a follow-up visit with his family doctor.

Late one evening, while enjoying an onboard cabaret show, I was called to the medical centre. The nurse informed me that an older man had been brought in by his family, stating that he choked on his food that evening. The pleasant elderly gentleman was in significant discomfort, saying he could not swallow a piece of meat he had at dinner. He said he had been having increasing difficulty swallowing over the preceding few weeks.

I found him to be pale but stable. The symptom worried me because it suggested a blockage of his upper digestive tract. His elderly wife and his daughter were very anxious. We still had over a week to get back to the American port that was the cruise's final destination. I suggested that we transfer him to the nearest hospital to perform a procedure to look inside his esophagus. I called a hospital in Russia that could take him. We arranged the transfer.

Two days later, I received a fax stating they had done the necessary procedure and found considerable cancerous growth in his esophagus, causing the obstruction. The family was in the process of transferring him to his home in the U.S. I later received a nice thank you note from them.

There were also moments of trial of confidence, faith, and courage. I recall once when in the Caribbean when our ship was caught in a Category 4 to 5 hurricane. The vessel had failed to dock at a private island in the Bahamas because a gathering storm, high waves, and winds had made it impossible to do so safely. Sailing on towards Fort Lauderdale in Florida, the storm picked up more power, and winds howled and raged as the hurricane flung the giant cruise ship about like a toy. I had just attended an older woman who had been tossed about in her bathroom, hitting her head against the sink. I barely made it to my cabin; the ship's rocking and rolling made it almost impossible to walk up to the room where Nilu was anxiously waiting for me. The sky was completely dark. The loud, continuous grind of the ship's hydraulic stabilizers added to the din of the storm. Soon the waves were crashing against the cabin's windows, which was located on the ninth deck, above the bridge. The storm went on for hours, only getting worse by the hour. It seemed the ship had little chance of surviving the enormous battering of the waves and wind buffeting it from all sides. The bridge had announced several hours prior for all passengers to remain in their suites and keep their life jackets close. Yet, Nilu and I experienced a strange sense of peace and comfort as we slipped into bed holding each other. We thought of our children, our loved ones, of the wonderful life we had been blessed to live.

It was a rough night, but in the morning, the sun shone, and the sea was calmer. The ship had taken a considerable battering yet seemed to be relatively unscathed. We later learnt that the storm had caused hundreds of millions of dollars in damage and taken over forty lives in the Floridian coastal communities. Fort Lauderdale was our disembarkation port; we disembarked with mixed emotions.

I visited the medical centre, attended a few patients needing immediate care, and arranged for disembarking patients to be attended at the local hospitals. The storm damage was visible on land, almost palpable in its raw savagery and its potential power as a force of nature.

Back home, my days were again filled with the routine I had now grown accustomed to back on dry land. That is until something new and compelling came along!

> I realize that it is not my role to transform either the world or man: I have neither sufficient virtue nor insight for that. But it may be to serve, in my place, those few values without which even a transformed world would not be worth living in, and man, even if "new," would not deserve to be respected.
>
> *Albert Camus*

CHAPTER 10

TRAINING DOCTORS FOR TOMORROW:
MAKING MEDICAL EDUCATION RELEVANT TO SOCIETIES

The large, white Toyota 4×4 dropped me at the entrance of the New Africa Hotel. At the hotel's elegant, expansive lobby, my driver, Hamisi, handed me an envelope containing a note from Lawrence Hamilton, the chief executive of Aga Khan Health Services, Tanzania (AKHST), who had invited me for the interview.

I glanced around and saw a busy street in front of the tall hotel, crowded with people, old cars, blaring trucks, and overloaded Suzuki wagons. There was an elegant church with a clocktower at the crossroad on the hotel's side, with a front garden brimming with bright red hibiscus flowers and several big trees. This was my first time in Dar-es-Salaam, the bustling commercial capital of Tanzania. I had looked forward to this visit for a month since receiving an e-mail from Lawrence inviting me to meet with Aga Khan Health Services and Aga Khan University's Search Committee.

The long KLM flight from Vancouver via Amsterdam had been smooth. As the aircraft circled the wide bay and multi-hued blue waters of the Indian Ocean lapping the shores, I noted the reddish fertile soil, innumerable palm trees, and lush vegetation. A wide swath of countless rusty tin-roofed buildings – interspersed with small farms on the city's fringes – came into view. I caught a momentary sight of the city centre's few distant towers, congested roads, and numerous small fishing boats in the azure waters. The picture certainly was different from Nairobi in neighbouring Kenya, in and out of which I had flown dozens of times.

At the desk, I was met by the hotel's assistant manager, who welcomed me on behalf of Shabir Abji, one of the owners of the hotel. At that time, I was unaware that Shabir Abji, the chairman of the board of Aga Khan Health Services, Tanzania (AKHST), was the attractive hotel's owner. I was shown to an upper-level suite, out of which I got a fantastic view of the Dar-es-Salaam harbour. The church I had noticed earlier was across the street from my window; behind the church, I saw the city's expanse and its crowded waterfront.

The interview was arranged for the following morning. While tired from the long flight and the time difference, I was too excited to rest. I showered, briefly checked the hotel facilities, and walked out to the entrance. The blast of hot, humid November air struck me; before long, I would be sweating. I rejected the advances of the taxi drivers and decided to take a short walk. The African city was undoubtedly captivating, not unlike Karachi, but greener and dotted with several white, colonial-era, two- or three-storey buildings lining the streets facing the sea. I saw several roadside stalls selling roasted corn-on-the-cob, various fruits, and everything from sunglasses and cellphones to shirts and shoes. I rested a little in the afternoon, but later received a phone call from Dorothy, Lawrence Hamilton's secretary. She welcomed me to Tanzania and asked if everything had worked out fine with me. She reminded me that the committee would meet with me at ten o'clock the following morning.

Renewed Excitement: Daunting Challenges

The events that led to this visit to Tanzania in November 2002 had started a few months earlier at a dinner in Vancouver, hosted by well-wishers of AKU, Dr. Rahim and Roshan Thomas, for Shamsh Kassim-Lakha, my old friend and mentor, and the accompanying visiting delegation from Karachi. Shamsh briefed the guests on the progress and future development plans of AKU.

It was more than eleven years since I had left Pakistan to settle back in Canada. Shamsh explained that AKU was now at a stage where the Faculty of Health Sciences (AKU-FHS) was partnering with the Aga Khan Health Services (AKHS) hospitals of Kenya, Uganda, and Tanzania to establish postgraduate medical education (PGME) programs in Kenya and Tanzania. Advanced nursing education programs in all three East African countries were also under development.

Shamsh said that AKU and AKHS had decided to centre the first residency programs – in medicine, surgery, pediatrics, radiology, and pathology – at the Aga Khan Hospital, Nairobi (AKHN), and the family medicine residency program would be at the Aga Khan Hospital, Dar-es-Salaam (AKHD). The larger Nairobi hospital was a long-established secondary-care hospital with some specialized tertiary-care programs. It was slated to go through significant enlargement and upgrading, while the smaller Dar-es-Salaam hospital was considered more suited for family medicine training.

After dinner, Shamsh took me aside and said, "Azim, when you left Karachi, I said we'd call on you again. I think the leadership of the PGME program in family medicine is something you should strongly consider, given your experience. There is a lot to do in Africa. I suggest you contact Lawrence Hamilton in Dar-es-Salaam and Dr. Roger Sutton, the associate dean for PGME for East Africa."

I was well-established in Vancouver at that time. Among other things, I was running a busy medical practice, serving as a medical director of a large hospital group in Vancouver, and holding a faculty position at the University of British Columbia.

I recalled Roger Sutton very well. A former dean of medicine at the University of British Columbia, he had joined AKUMC Karachi as the professor and chair of the Department of Medicine. He later served as the dean of the faculty of Health Sciences (AKU-FHS) for several years. After completing his term in Pakistan, he was appointed associate dean to initiate postgraduate medical education for East Africa.

I was aware of some consultant reports relating to Aga Khan hospitals' and health centres' sub-optimal functions in East Africa. His Highness, the Aga Khan, had deliberated on this detailed analysis and other reports on East Africa's health services. The reports appeared to paint a somewhat bleak picture of some health care facilities in East Africa and recommended the closure of many underutilized or inefficient centres. The Aga Khan, a sagacious, benevolent, and visionary leader in global development, had directed that the Aga Khan health facilities instead be substantially upgraded and improved. He had also recommended that embedding health sciences education, particularly medical and nursing education, could boost the quality of service, clinical competence, and management of these long-established facilities, which had served communities where they operated for many decades.

Significant financial resources were committed to this endeavour. I was thrilled by the challenges posed by these fresh initiatives; they echoed our efforts in Pakistan and other parts of Asia that I had been part of. These bold new initiatives prompted me to reflect on my past experiences and draw on the literature surrounding Africa's social and economic dynamics. I wrote a concept paper entitled "*Towards Excellence in Primary Care Medicine in Africa: The Role of the Aga Khan University.*"

I wrote to Lawrence Hamilton and Roger Sutton, stating my interest in assisting in the development of medical education and improving health systems in East Africa under the AKU and AKHS aegis. I attached my paper with my letters. Their prompt response gratified me. The position now called for a chair and professor to develop the concept and high-quality family medicine training program at a specialist level.

The concept and specialty of family medicine were largely unknown and undeveloped in most countries of Africa. Lawrence asked for an early interview, to be held in Dar, for this position. As Roger was then in Vancouver, he suggested I meet with him there. I met with Roger, who had read the document I had written and appeared impressed. He interviewed me at his house and forwarded his evaluation to the Search Committee, which he and Lawrence jointly chaired.

The following morning, I was shown into a small hotel meeting room by Dorothy, Lawrence's secretary. She was a charming, local, young woman who had greeted me with a warm smile earlier after breakfast. As I entered, Lawrence walked over to me and greeted me. He introduced me to Shabir Abji, the chairman of AKHST; Dr. Ambrose Chanji, the medical director of the Aga Khan Hospital; the directors of nursing and human resources; Dr. Riaz Rattansi, an AKU-trained family physician running the Outpatients Clinic; and Dr. Riaz Quereshi. I recognized Riaz Quereshi, professor and chair of the Department of Family Medicine at AKU Pakistan. Years before, when I was in Pakistan, Riaz, a well-qualified family physician, had approached me to seek a position at the Community Health Centre. A few years later, he served as the head of the CHC, the initial appointment I had held in Karachi in 1986. In the years to come, he led the further development of family medicine that I had worked hard to embed into the AKU and AKHS education and service paradigm. He led the formal establishment of the Postgraduate residency program in Family Medicine at AKU in Karachi.

The interview was probing and wide-ranging and lasted several hours. I believe my vision, experience, and knowledge relating to program development issues, medical education, and encountered challenges informed my answers and added confidence to my responses. I was much later to learn that the committee had previously narrowed their search to a senior British academic, but appeared to prefer my candidacy for this position at the end of my interview.

Senior-level appointment within the Aga Khan Development Network is a long and complicated process. Traditionally, it goes through various levels of rigorous and impartial screening and consultations, the ultimate deciding criteria being the candidate's merit.

The next day I was shown around the Aga Khan Hospital and its surrounding areas. The area included a few grand colonial-style buildings across a narrow, busy street, one of which housed the AKU's Advanced Nursing Program (ANS) school. The hospital faced the stunning blue-green sea and a palm-fringed beach separated by a road that curved around a bay leading to the city's diplomatic enclave. The Indian Ocean's tranquil views and a few small mangrove trees decorated the cove, and several gigantic baobab trees lined the inner road of the exclusive area. The grand residences of the British, Swiss, German, Japanese, and other embassies were visible from the upper floor of the four-storey hospital complex.

The AKHD was really made of two main buildings: the old two-storey hospital and the "Phase 2" building, a newer four-storey white building with a sea-blue border and roof. The buildings were linked by two covered broad walkways, one of which was elevated. A gorgeous well-tended garden with several palm trees, flowering plants, and fragrant shrubs filled the grounds between the buildings and the parking lot.

Lawrence introduced me to several senior medical staff as we walked around the complex. He was rather vague in his answers to my many questions concerning the postgraduate medical education facility's location and readiness. The hospital was indeed a charming place, with quite a modern laboratory, an Outpatients Department, a pharmacy, and inpatient wards, situated at a gorgeous location. The old hospital had been serving the community for over five decades.

Lawrence had arranged for me to be taken around the city to feel the bustling, crowded city. The population of this busy seaport was estimated at around four million inhabitants. Dar's original name was Bender-Salaam, which in Arabic means "harbour of peace." The town was built from a harbour on the magnificent shores of Mzizima, which was then no more than a fishing village. In 1866, Sultan Majid of Zanzibar started building his palace, which he called Dar-es-Salaam, meaning the "abode of peace."

With its superb harbour and fresh water supply, the town soon prospered, drawing business away from Kilwa and Bagamoyo on the coast. The Germans made it the capital of German East Africa. The British took it over in 1920, after the First World War. Today, Dar-es-Salaam buzzes with industrial, commercial, diplomatic, and political activity. The port gives sea access to several landlocked east and central African countries and has its own import and export market.

I could understand AKU and AKHS's interest in positioning its expansion into advanced education and health care service in this rapidly developing region. AKHS has a long history in the provision of primary and clinical care, having a network of health centres and clinics scattered across the mainland of Tanzania and the archipelago of the islands of Zanzibar. The Aga Khan Hospital in Dar-es-Salaam served as the secondary-level referral hospital to the network. Many of these centres had deteriorated in their service quality, reach, and management during the preceding few decades due to a host of factors. These included population migration and transformation, governmental socialist policies of nationalization, and the unavailability of supplies and qualified staff.

~⸎~

After a few days enjoying Dar's tropical environs, I returned to Vancouver, thrilled at the potential prospects of resuming the development of medical education, impacting health care, and contributing to the redevelopment and upgrading of the AKHS health facilities in East Africa. These were my passions and lived experiences. Lawrence and Shabir had informed me that they would contact me with the Search Committee's final recommendation and the ensuing process. He did indicate that there could likely be some urgency in filling this position, as consultations with the Higher Education Accreditation Commission (HEAC) of Tanzania, a division of the Ministry of Higher Education, Science and Technology was at a delicate stage; the leader of the PGME initiative would be required to play a crucial role in the process. Potentially, that could mean a quick decision on my part – once again – and the challenge that might pose to my diverse range of established professional activities in Canada.

Early in January, I received a letter informing me that the Search Committee had unanimously endorsed my candidacy as the head of PGME. Nilu and I had to decide on the offer that potentially held significant ramifications. It would mean winding up our settled life in Canada once more. The girls were both attending university now and were quite independent. Lawrence stayed in frequent communication with me. The family concurred that this was a worthwhile transition, but it could potentially involve considerable personal cost, risks, and upheaval.

However, Nilu and I decided to accept the offer. Little did I realize at that time that this would be the most challenging professional endeavour of my life. The move this time could be significantly more complicated than the original move to Pakistan. I was now busy in academic work with the University of British Columbia, contributing at the Riverview Hospital (a provincial psychiatric facility), providing clinical consultations with a community mental health centre, and serving as medical director of an extensive public hospital network, as well as attending my busy private medical practice.

Education for Healthier Societies:
Framework for Postgraduate Medical Education

A few weeks later, I received an urgent note from Lawrence requesting my presence for the AKU/AKHS's meeting with HEAC in Dar-es-Salaam. It appeared there were some pressing issues relating to the registration of AKU and the approval of the PGME program in Tanzania. The HEAC had asked for a substantially more detailed plan for the conduct of PGME centred at the Aga Khan Hospital, including details for physical and clinical facilities, teaching and faculty development process, detailed curriculum, and a host of other data before they would grant approval for the addition of medical education to AKU's Tanzania Institute of Higher Education (TIHE).

In its earlier submissions to the HEAC and the ministry for approval and registration of the Advanced Nursing Studies (ANS) program, AKU had established the Tanzania Institute of Higher Education. It proposed that the PGME program would be administered under this umbrella. However, at this stage, the HEAC required considerably more details for the four-year advanced degree in medicine that the current PGME submission had applied for. The meeting was scheduled for early March. Lawrence understood that it would be difficult for me to move to Dar in that short period of time; however, I agreed to attend the Dar meeting with the HEAC team. I left Nilu to continue our preparations for departure to Tanzania.

Mr. William Sabaya, a veteran educator, administrator, and senior official of the HEAC, was in charge of the registration and approval process of new higher education programs in Tanzania. Two other senior university administrators accompanied him. I met with them, accompanied by Dr. Chanji, Lawrence Hamilton, and Amin Kurji, the resident representative of the Aga Khan Development Network (AKDN) in Tanzania. Amin Kurji, a businessman and a competent diplomat, was well-versed in the tangled, sometimes convoluted bureaucracy of Tanzania. He was involved in the early stages of the ANS program registration application with the AKU officials. He was, hence, well-acquainted with the early history of the provisional registration process of the AKU-TIHE in Tanzania.

Lawrence introduced me to the team of reviewers and outlined my role in developing and heading the PGME efforts of AKU and AKHS. I found Mr. Sabaya, an elegant middle-aged gentleman, to be sophisticated, highly canny, well-informed, and determined in his efforts to uphold the recently established higher standards for new academic programs enjoined by the government of Tanzania, and indeed of neighbouring countries of Kenya and Uganda. He was forthright, yet appreciated the need to enhance capacity for specialized education in science and medicine and our efforts in that direction. His associates I found to be discerning and self-assured, a new breed of technocrats committed to uncompromising standards for a progressive Tanzania. In their view, some earlier private and public initiatives in the social development arena had failed to deliver notable benefits, and newly established regional agreements called for much stricter oversight and approval mechanisms. They also raised some issues of "irregularities" with the track followed previously in the AKU registration process – an international university – in Tanzania at the time of the approval of the Advanced Nursing Studies (ANS) program two years earlier.

The HEAC team had made a detailed study of our submission, including reviewing the curriculum for the advanced degree program in family medicine that we proposed. The curriculum presented was based on AKU's Pakistan-based family medicine residency training model. Mr. Sabaya and his team did not think it was directly transposable to the conditions of Tanzania and the broader East Africa region. They also wondered why our program was four years, where Tanzania's norm for specialist programs was three years. They also pointed out many other requirements that needed to be satisfied, including upgrading the hospital's clinical training and service capacity, to approve our plan.

We had a long and, I believe, productive meeting. Amin Kurji reviewed the long history of the many Aga Khan programs and institutions in Tanzania's socio-economic development and the wider East Africa region. The AKDN now envisioned a progressive enlargement of commitments to engage further in human development regionally. We assured them of AKU's commitment to follow the prescribed path to approval and registration according to Tanzania's laws and pre-scribed procedures and the East Africa Universities Commission guidelines.

The HEAC team accepted our request for additional time to meet their strict requirements as we worked through the many steps towards structuring the PGME endeavour of AKU.

I departed Dar with a much clearer understanding of the considerable barriers and challenges that were faced in introducing advanced medical education in the East Africa region. Ours was the first private institution to initiate a PGME in Tanzania and Kenya, a region with an obvious high need for well-trained special-ists. A handful of public universities and hospitals conducted the existing pro-grams of PGME in the East Africa region, and there were no specialized training programs in family medicine and primary care, a specialty of high need.

～⁊～

A month later, Nilu and I moved to Dar-es-Salaam. It had been a hasty and com-plicated departure, with a few loose ends unfinished. But it was essential for me to plunge into preparing for the next HEAC meeting, planned for July or August.

We were most fortunate to settle into a charming, old bungalow, with a vast garden backing onto the ocean. A balustraded rooftop terrace allowed stunning star-studded panoramic views of the night sky on clear African nights. The rustle of leaves of massive fig and eucalyptus trees in the garden competed with the scent of jasmine, jacaranda, and hibiscus to soothe the senses in this idyllic setting. In the walled garden roamed crested cranes, secretary birds and four lesser flamingos. A dry swimming pool was home to a family of tortoises, and a large cage held eight colourful parrots. A large mesh-wired pen held about a dozen geese and ducks, although on many occasions, we would see them walking freely about the large garden during the day. There were also a few white rabbits. Our dog, Sasha, loved gambolling around the extensive lot, mingling and occasionally quarrelling with the menagerie of creatures that shared and enriched our lives. At least two pairs of African eagles nested in the higher reaches of the tall eucalyptus trees. At nights we were lulled to sleep by the crash of waves against the back wall.

The house belonged to some family friends; Mr. Sadru Virani, a successful businessman, was generous to a fault, and he and his family did everything they could to see us settled in. They lived in a modern house on the large, shared plot and were a source of constant support and friendship throughout our time in Tanzania. We soon found a used, rugged, small Suzuki 4×4 vehicle, perfect for Tanzania's roads and conditions. Mr. Virani found us a reliable and faithful driver, Ramzan, who knew his way around Dar's labyrinthine and congested streets. While Nilu, with the help of the neighbourly family, attended to our new domestic situation, I concentrated my time and energy on the issues at hand.

Appraising Internal Dynamics: Building Capacity for Medical Education

First, I had to take stock of the assets – material, space, and professional – that we could use to strengthen our case for offering advanced medical education. Lawrence and Ambrose Chanji worked closely with me in this elaborate exercise. I also needed to intimately understand the normative practices, infrastructure, and fault lines that may pose obstacles to improving standards in the hospital's relaxed environment.

Lawrence, a boyish-looking Englishman, had considerable health care experience, acquired in his work with the British National Health Service. Several years before, he had been commissioned to undertake a consulting role with Aga Khan Health Services, Tanzania (AKHST), a critical study, and was, therefore, well-versed in its protean issues. Later, he was appointed CEO of the AKHST, the role he now played. He was acquainted with the numerous NGOs and aid and development agencies and foreign missions based in Tanzania. His contacts proved very helpful to me later, as I worked assiduously to build a network of health and social agencies, both foreign and local, supportive of health care training and service innovation relevant to underserved societies in Tanzania and beyond.

Ambrose was a late middle-aged Tanzanian national. A British-educated gynecologist, he served as the medical director of the AKHD. In Ambrose, I found an elegant, seasoned, and compassionate physician, well-respected by the medical staff and patients alike. He epitomized the gentle nature and civility of the people of Tanzania. He was also exceptionally well-connected with governmental agencies and departments, and he facilitated my many meetings over the coming months and years with a host of influential officials and academics. He was consistently supportive of the PGME enterprise and worked closely with me in our meetings with the HEAC and other public bureaucracies concerned with higher education and health services.

I soon discovered that the AKU-AKHS's PGME initiative, at this stage, was rather loosely conceived and structured. There were sound arguments advanced for the introduction of medical and nursing education within the East African health network, including its potential to upgrade the quality and range of care within the AKHS facilities and beyond. The planners also foresaw the need for a health care paradigm that was relevant, humane, equitable, and cost-effective in a region experiencing a rapid economic and social change, but which lacked replicable models of cost-effective health delivery and proficiency.

While aware that there would be significant challenges in developing and promoting innovation in comprehensive clinical care, the degree of disruption of the status quo and its creative reconstruction to enable the paradigm's actualization was perhaps less thoroughly explored. The questions of resources – both human and technical – commitments, planning, and management were domains less thoroughly examined. As in Pakistan, the thinking was to develop a prototype model of competent medical care, resolutely hammered on the anvil of critical population health imperative and progressively diffused widely, with the premise that it could ultimately impact the quality of health care in the region.

The founder and planners always understood that AKU and AKHS, given their size and resource limitations, could only have a limited direct impact on health outcomes. Their influence, mission, and vision revolved around the eventual widespread acceptance and adoption of a progressive care model in both public and private health care systems. However, unlike the AKU and AKUH in Pakistan, which were conceived and freshly born with a clear mission, vision, and goals, the East African Aga Khan health network – with its long tradition, culture, and history dating back decades – was in dire need of revitalization, reorientation, and restructuring to address the altered conditions and modern challenges in health care and medical education.

As I worked to marshal all the facts and data that could advance our proposal to the government accreditation bodies, I also realized there were indications of significant disaffection and limited buy-in from the hospital's clinical staff, who were wary of the impact PGME could potentially have on their practices and status. I started a series of meetings and collegial consultations with the full-time and part-time medical staff of the AKHD. Over the coming weeks and months, issues relating to the inadequacies of the clinical standards, working conditions, staffing, and competitive forces in medical practice began to surface. Rather than quality, expediency was seen increasingly as the driver of the clinical services delivery and care model at the AKHD. Many felt disconnected from the development of clinical services and the planning of the hospital.

It became clear that the organization's clinical and departmental leadership was inconsistent, ineffectual, and unsatisfactory. There was also limited capability, resources, or pathway for the continuing professional growth of the medical practitioners and other health professionals such as nurses, pharmacists, and laboratory technicians. Hence, it was essential to consolidate structure and leadership in the medical staff and provide a vision of progressive change.

Over the coming weeks and months, I emphatically underlined these concerns to Lawrence, Ambrose, and Shabir Abji, laying out a report detailing my findings and the critical steps required for the way forward. The report detailed the strengths, weaknesses, opportunities, and threats with respect to the institution.

In the context of the place and time, there indeed were significant strengths: a long tradition of care; the availability of certain rarely available services, such as several major medical and surgical procedures; advanced diagnostic imaging; a consulting medical staff in many major medical and surgical areas; an excellent physical structure; and a roster of corporate users. But there were also apparent weaknesses: low staff motivation, morale, and accountability; few guidelines on expectations and vague reporting structures; unsophisticated quality-control mechanisms; tensions between full-time and part-time medical staff; the recruitment and retention of well-qualified staff; few role models and educators; and oversight weakness in management and operational processes. Many of these issues echoed my past experiences in institutional leadership capacities in Pakistan and Canada.

The AKHD's clinical competence, range of essential services, medical staff motivation and commitment, diagnostic standards, and care-process management needed urgent improvement before we could expect the HEAC to accredit the hospital as a centre for medical education. The AKHST board, under Shabir's leadership, invited me to brief them on my perceptions about a way forward to transform care quality to acceptable standards that enabled the introduction of formal postgraduate medical education.

A detailed presentation underlined the need to improve clinical governance, establish scope and facilities for a broader range of ambulatory care, upgrade surgical suites, and enhance laboratory standards, among other pressing needs. It underscored the shortage of high-demand specialty areas, such as chest diseases, infectious diseases, kidney diseases, neurological disorders, and pathology. Well-planned long-term clinical services and a physician resources development plan were, thus, of prime importance. The clinical and educational services needed to be synergistic, harmonized, and mutually supportive.

Embracing Family Medicine: Making the Case; Interlocking Pieces

At a follow-up meeting of the AKHS board and senior management, I presented a document entitled *"Aga Khan Hospital, Dar-es-Salaam: Reconfiguring Clinical Services: Embracing Family Medicine."*

An important observation of the document underlined was the current practice of primary-care medicine provided by various specialists, who had little grounding in the core principles of evidence-based primary medical care. They tended to focus their patient management from the perspective of their specialty, rather than the well-founded approach of trained generalists. For instance, many patients experiencing chest pain – regardless of age or how vague the symptom – often dropped in to see a heart specialist. In most cases, the cardiologist, having excluded heart disease, would discharge the patient from their care without adequately considering or addressing the numerous other causes of non-cardiac chest pain. The patient, thus, often suffered unnecessary referrals, costly tests, and unsatisfactory contact with the health care system. An initial presentation to a well-trained generalist would likely have resulted in comprehensively evaluating the patient, referring to an appropriate specialist if and when warranted.

A presentation at a later date to the Aga Khan Hospital Nairobi stimulated the hospital to define the role of family medicine more clearly and to implant family medicine firmly as an essential service within the hospital and the Kenya AKHS network more broadly.

～♀～

The AKHD had not set aside a site for housing the PGME program. Initially, I worked out of borrowed office space while considering the future allocation of suitable areas for this critical new program. Lawrence suggested possible locations in the lesser-used areas of the upper floor of the old hospital wing, some that would require pretty extensive renovations. I was not too keen on a long, drawn-out process that could further delay the program's approval.

In the meantime, my energy was primarily directed at that time to substantially revise and detail the four-year residency program curriculum to make it more relevant in the context and accepted framework of postgraduate medical education in Tanzania and the neighbouring region. Simultaneously, I sedulously attempted to collaborate, motivate, and structure the clinical practice and medical staff for improved efficiency and training. I directed my initial efforts to enlist the heads of departments and senior medical staff to collaborate to improve efficiency and enhance the clinical care spectrum. My approach was to offer inducements of providing individualized continuing medical education, faculty affiliations, resource commitments, and an improved work environment. This method was generally received with gratifying enthusiasm and support. I outlined a vision for transforming the institution simultaneously into a "teaching" and "learning" organization.

I realized that the key to motivation internally lay in the clear and compelling articulation of the vision, goals, and impact of PGME on enhanced practice standards, professional satisfaction levels, the organization's and staff's profile, and the elevated prestige associated with a university affiliation. This need to articulate a coherent vision was more imperative since the first PGME program we planned to introduce in Tanzania was family medicine, an unknown and poorly understood specialty in a region where the band of recognized specialties was narrow and traditional. A compelling case to the HEAC and the ministry and the medical community at large called for a model of cost-effective care and training to impact health outcomes of populations most marginalized, neglected, or trapped in cycles of poverty and exclusion.

These multiple strands of actions urgently needed to be interwoven into a comprehensive action plan. One crucial strand revolved around creating an enabling environment conducive to optimal education and research, another strand around clinical care by upgrading, professionalizing, and regulating medical care. Simultaneously motivating and incentivizing medical and health care staff at the putative hospital training centre was essential. Concurrently, another strand required a compelling proposal to develop a medical specialist training program and curriculum that was relevant, effective, efficient, and acceptable to the concerned authorities charged with accrediting higher education initiatives. Achieving this objective required establishing suitable training sites and facilities and ensuring qualified faculty, educators, management, and administration. It also necessitated the formal establishment of the academic Department of Family Medicine in the institution. Yet another strand called for ensuring the long-term commitment of appropriate material, space, and human resources to the bold new venture. None of these critical elements were substantively in place in the early stages of the program.

~ ⌒ ~

The institutional planners' thinking was that higher education in nursing, medicine, and auxiliary health sciences in the East African countries of Uganda, Kenya, and Tanzania would be mostly autonomous but coordinated and supported by Nairobi, where the office of the dean for PGME would be located. AKU's main site in Karachi played an advisory and supportive role.

The ANS programs in nursing had already been registered and approved in all three former British colonies, which were now independent countries, each with its own regulatory framework. However, the HEAC in Kenya and Tanzania now set a much higher bar for approval of the PGME initiatives. As in Tanzania, the Kenyan HEAC placed demanding barriers to the approval process of the proposed suite of PGME programs centred at the Aga Khan Hospital, Nairobi.

At our following meeting with Mr. Sabaya and his team, I was by then on much firmer ground. Developed with some consultative input from Karachi and local and experienced overseas physicians, I put forward a revised curriculum for our program and a detailed plan for the reorganization and strengthening of the clinical services and training environment of the AKHD and linked health centres. Ambrose Chanji and Lawrence were with me to echo and amplify our revised position and requisite resource commitments. I had requested, obtained, and reviewed AKU's initial registration process and experience with Tanzania's Ministry of Science, Technology and Higher Education and was conversant with the HEAC's previously expressed concerns with the past cycle. At our request, the senior legal representative from AKU's Karachi office arrived to participate in our meeting with the HEAC.

Our submission made a strong case for the value of family medicine in the context of developing countries like Tanzania.

The thrust of our justification for the proposed program in family medicine was to review the current state of health care in severely resource-constrained developing countries in Africa, where a large majority of people had little or no access to adequate medical care. There was one doctor for over twenty thousand people, and those doctors were usually practising in urban centres. Rates of infant mortality, maternal deaths, and preventable deaths from inappropriate treatment or neglect were staggering. Disease patterns were also in transition; non-communicable diseases such as hypertension, diabetes, and heart disease were rising rapidly, taking an increasing toll of life, side by side with the common infectious diseases such as malaria, childhood pneumonia, measles, and diarrhoeal diseases. New diseases such as HIV/AIDS were emerging and devastating the health and economic futures of vast populations.

Non-physicians provided most of the health care, particularly in rural areas and peri-urban areas. Faith healers, traditional healers, traditional midwives, and government-trained clinical assistants provided most of the service but were poorly trained to provide comprehensive and competent care, and they lacked supervision, further training, and facilities. The few qualified physicians available tended to practise in the larger cities, and some chose to specialize in the few narrow specialties that were more lucrative. The training of doctors did not adequately prepare them to meet the range of needs of the population. The few general practitioners in practice lacked the necessary breadth and depth to handle complex cases and to mentor, supervise, plan, and effectively lead health care for large populations.

The program we proposed was a prototype for a well-trained physician who is a competent practitioner of all the essential medicine domains, an educator, and a health care team and health initiatives leader. Hence, a rigorous four-year additional broad-based training of doctors imparting enhanced clinical skills, preventive medicine, and planning and leadership skills leading to an advanced degree of Master of Medicine (M.Med.) was proposed by AKU and AKHS.

I also handed them several documents I had developed that detailed the place and scope of this specialty. We advocated and encouraged the replication of accumulating international experience of family medicine in developed and rapidly developing countries in Asia, Latin America, and Africa, including Egypt, Zimbabwe, and South Africa. I produced studies supported by the WHO, UNICEF, WONCA (World Organization of Family Doctors), and other reputable academic centres.

We left the two days of intense meetings feeling encouraged. Our team had put forward a cogent case for AKU's proposed international structure, leadership, governance, and funding, and we addressed all legal and logistical requirements in accordance with the national laws.

Crossing the Quality Gulf in Health Care: Advocacy and Confronting Complex Realities

I perceived a need to expound further on the place and scope of a broadly trained generalist physician who could provide clinical leadership and oversight in the fragmented and underdeveloped health care system in Tanzania. We assessed that there remained a significant gap in providing and overseeing competent medical care at the primary- and secondary-care levels, impacting outcomes. Therefore, we needed the buy-in and support of politicians, health planners, bureaucrats, and national health care funders.

I discussed this crucial need with Ambrose and Amin Kurji, who were well-respected in the government circles. Amin Kurji suggested we meet with the Tanzanian minister of health, whom he knew quite well.

A few days later, accompanied by Amin, I was shown into the office of the minister of health. He was a perceptive, pleasant gentleman and received us cordially. Amin outlined the purpose of our visit once again after he had introduced me to the minister. The minister listened with great interest as I attempted to diplomatically express our desire to help improve health care in Tanzania and the region through the carefully considered advancement of medical and health care education and its potential role in uplifting population health if adopted widely by the government of Tanzania. I underlined the advantages of placing broadly trained competent generalist physicians, whom we call family physicians, in clinical and management positions, particularly at the primary-care and district-level hospitals. I underscored the fact that our proposed curriculum not only strengthened clinical competencies but also provided a sound understanding of the principles of epidemiology, community health, and the vital integration of preventive and curative health care.

After reflecting for a while, he called in an assistant from the outer office and asked him to bring a copy of the national five-year plan for Tanzania's social and health care development. He said he was well aware of the need to significantly transform the way health care was delivered in Tanzania and the organization of health care in economically more advantaged countries, including the place of family and community physicians in health care. He went on to outline how the current system had evolved and been structured in Tanzania, more along the lines of vertical programs, such as HIV/AIDS, malaria control, immunization, maternal health, nutritional support for children, and central drug policies. Many of these programs were funded explicitly by development partners and overseas funders. He appreciated our contention for the desirability of horizontally integrating health care, particularly at the primary and district levels. He encouraged continuing exploration of initiatives that took into account the harsh economic and social, cultural, and demographic realities of Tanzania and neighbouring countries.

He recommended I meet with several regional and district medical officers of health and get their perspectives as well. He gave me a copy of Tanzania's health care and social development plan. Clearly, Tanzania, like many recently independent countries, was dependent on significant external budget and technical support from multilateral, bilateral agencies and NGOs for its development, each with its own specific interest and requirement. This reality added an extra layer of complexity to significant transformation efforts in locally conceived health and social development.

Ambrose knew the chief provincial medical officer of health for the large Dar-es-Salaam and surrounding region. I met with Dr. Mutesa in his busy office at the regional health head office. This meeting proved to be a signal advancement in our endeavours to promote the notion of positioning a well-trained clinical leader into primary- and secondary-care networks. Dr. Mutesa, a soft-spoken man, proved to be a highly sapient and dedicated public health specialist with a firm grasp of public health care's realities and challenges in Tanzania. He noted that there was considerable room to improve effective care delivery, noting the scarcity of qualified leaders in this area. He immediately appreciated the advantages of a broadly trained physician leader to oversee and integrate clinical care and public health at all health system levels. He was supportive of the notion of training generalist clinicians with a sound grounding in preventive care to lead the transformation of health systems in the country. He indicated his willingness to share his perspective and support more broadly with his colleagues in public health bureaucracy.

In my several meetings with him over the coming weeks and months, I got a deeper insight into the extant training programs in public and community health, as well as specialist programs in Tanzania, each distinct in its scope of training and application, and none that could provide the critical bridge to integrate the health needs of populations.

My next port of call was to meet with Professor Charles Mkony, the dean of the School of Medicine at the Muhimbili College of Health Sciences, University of Dar-es-Salaam. Charles proved to be another strong ally to our program. I learned a great deal about the challenges facing medical education, some archaic university norms, entrenched departmental fiefdoms, inflexible curricula, and out-of-date modes of education and training, dearth of facilities, equipment, and learning resources. All this echoed my experience in parts of Asia, where I had engaged in familiar battles for modernization and relevance.

There were other ports of call to solicit support for our program. The WHO country office for Tanzania readily encouraged and endorsed our initiative. The country director was well-versed in the principles that underpin effectively linking health care levels from primary to secondary to tertiary care and the need to search for effective leadership models that enable and support that process. He supported our vision for a transformative medical education model, developing human resources for health, innovative health services and solutions, and community participation.

Another organization with widespread reach, influence, and reputation in the region was the African Medical Research and Education Foundation (AMREF). They focused principally on the areas of HIV testing, TB, malaria, training of local health care providers, and safe motherhood initiatives. The organization was also interested in strengthening health systems and developing appropriate training materials.

Fond Reminiscences: Inspiring Role Models

AMREF was founded in 1957 by three doctors in Kenya as the "Flying Doctors of East Africa." I have a fond recollection of meeting one of the founders, Sir Michael Wood, a renowned plastic surgeon. During my vacations from Makerere Medical School to my home in Nairobi, I occasionally spent time at the local hospitals. One afternoon I observed a surgical operation at the Gertrude Garden Children's Hospital being conducted on a young African child who had extensive burns on her arms and chest. The affable surgeon was performing a "Z-plasty" to release contractures that severely hindered the arm's movement. He explained the procedure and stages of treatment required to restore normal function semblance to the arms.

I was very fortunate that the surgeon operating that day was Dr. Michael Wood. We later got to talking in the surgeons' changing room. From him, I learnt about AMREF and its Flying Doctors service that he was heading. Conversationally, he asked if I would like to take a trip with the service on their next flight. I eagerly accepted the invitation.

It wasn't long before I received a call the following afternoon to meet at the Wilson Airport, where a Cessna 402B awaited, ready for takeoff. The flight destination was the northern part of Kenya in the Samburu district to transport two injured people to a hospital for emergency treatment. The Cessna, piloted by an experienced bush pilot, flew over dry scrubland to a remote location and landed on a cleared patch of a dusty makeshift runway. I saw two or three people standing around a crude stretcher. In the distance, a few goats were grazing. The pilot and a male nurse jumped out of the plane; I followed them onto the dusty, hot African savannah grassland. The pilot and the nurse quickly examined a child lying on the stretcher and then gently transferred him to the aircraft, securing him in the back of the plane. I was told the child had suffered a severe head injury and needed transfer to Nairobi for urgent treatment. Transport by road was out of the question. But there was one more patient to be picked up. We took off again, flew for about half an hour, and made another landing. An elderly man was helped into the back seat of the Cessna. The flight back to Nairobi touched down at the small aerodrome late in the evening; the two patients were transferred to waiting vehicles. It was one of the most thrilling experiences for me, and it profoundly ingrained respect for pioneers like Michael Wood and others who care, share, teach, and give selflessly of their knowledge and passion. He and many others became beacons of light that lit the path of my own career in the years ahead.

The AMREF's Tanzania director was an amiable gentleman and endorsed further support for our educational endeavour. He offered us liberal use of their training literature, which was mostly directed towards non-physician health workers.

Overcoming Hurdles: Housing Postgraduate Medical Education

The HEAC reverted to us in a few weeks stating they had requested external reviews of our curriculum and program proposal from external several organizations, which included the Royal College of General Practitioners in the U.K., several universities in South Africa and Zimbabwe, the University of Dar-es-Salaam College of Medicine, and the venerable Makerere University, Kampala. In the months and years to come, I later had collegial interactions with all these institutions. We shared knowledge and experience in our early efforts to entrench sound family medicine principles and practice in education and service in health care in Africa and beyond.

A few months later, we received the welcome news that the Ministry of Higher Education, Science and Technology had granted us provisional registration and approval. It appeared that the external organizations had endorsed our proposal, standards, and methods quite readily, with some minor suggested changes. We were now authorized to begin our recruitment of eligible students and staff. It came with a set of challenging requirements to be met in the future. We were informed there would be a mandated review in a year of the program's progress, the academic structure and organization, learning resources, faculty, quality development, and space allocations.

We had overcome the first hurdle; much more remained to be done. In the meantime, I moved my office and the PGME administration to an imposing old two-storey building across the street from the hospital, close to the ANS program's location. I cajoled the hospital's in-house maintenance department to expeditiously make minor internal modifications and furnish and equip the space. This space then served as the initial nucleus for the PGME office, separated by a garden and gated wall from the ANS complex. It had a beautiful view of the palm-fringed emerald ocean.

We now had two approved programs under the umbrella of AKU-TIHE. The beautiful building was formally termed the "Doctors Plaza" because it previously housed several private physicians who admitted their patients to the Aga Khan Hospital. The lower floor of the building was used as tutorial rooms by the ANS program. On the upper floor, one corner space was occupied by a private practitioner, a surgeon. Dr. Sylvester Faya, a general and orthopedic surgeon, conducted most of his surgical practice through the facilities of AKHD. He was a scholarly man with a cosmopolitan outlook, well-trained and well-respected, and committed to enhancing Tanzania's medical education opportunities. He proved to be a strong ally for me in my struggles to develop a competent and committed faculty and broaden the appeal of family medicine in the context of Tanzania.

I had widened the support staff in the department. I appointed Riaz Rattansi to serve as the interim program director for the residency program. Quiet and self-effacing and an excellent general clinician, Riaz had been through the rigours of a demanding family medicine residency training at AKU Karachi. He worked hard with me to set the professional standards for the learners and faculty. His insights into the norms of bureaucracy and medical practice in Tanzania proved invaluable.

I was fortunate to hire Fatma Mawji as my secretary, who made outstanding contributions to the daily running of the PGME office. Small-framed, passionate, and energetic, Fatma had previously worked in administration with the Aga Khan schools in Dar. Her dedication and understanding of the value and complexity of our embryonic venture, her meticulous attention to detail, her loyalty and hard work, and her easy rapport with the medical and hospital staff gained the trust of all she interacted with. I deeply valued her unstinted faith, encouragement, and support on days when the pressures seemed unrelenting. Assisted by Joseph Masome, a mature, well-connected gentleman and a graduate of the University of Dar-es-Salaam, who greatly assisted in progressively developing the library and learning resources we needed, we were now in a position to launch our program.

Humanizing Medicine: Optimizing Medical Education

It was time to draw ideas, talents, and resources from around the country to support the novel medical education enterprise. I organized a national symposium titled "Humanizing Medicine: Optimizing Medical Education."

This well-attended symposium proved to be a point of departure for the program and drew attendees from a broad section of medical practitioners, medical students, educators, health care planners, universities, and local and foreign aid agencies. The symposium laid bare the critical questions of quality, accessibility, affordability, relevance in health systems, training and education, and public policy. It lent further encouragement and impetus to our initiative to disrupt outmoded practices and procedures and envision a bolder, more inclusive and equitable perspective to address gross disparities in global health.

In my presentation, I drew on the WHO's *World Health Report 2003: Shaping the Future*. The report stated that the stark disparities in health status and outcomes were a result of multiple factors. Amongst them, the way a country organizes and staffs its primary health care and whether medical education and medical practice are closely linked to people's needs. The report further stated that effective education required ethical positions as well as technical skills, and that we have to be clear about values as well as our science. Fundamental changes were needed in the education institutions, in the medical schools, in the health care systems, and in public policies and priorities. These recommendations were in consonance with the thrust of the AKDN, particularly the AKHS, AKU, and AKF, which worked synergistically to alleviate poverty, aid civil society development, and realign services and education to uplift the quality of life. Presentations by Ambrose Chanji, Charles Mkony, Silvester Faya, and others outlined the local scene in medical education and health care, daily challenges, and resource constraints that practitioners and the health system faced on a daily basis. The symposium appeared to have made a common cause of the necessity to comprehensively reorient and reinvigorate health care in the country on a more enlightened plane.

Pluralism and Regional Integration: Audacious Vision, Building Bridges

In the meantime, the Nairobi-based PGME programs had not yet been approved. At the associate dean's request, I flew to Nairobi to assist in refining and submitting their programs to the Kenyan HEAC.

Mushtaq Ahmed, the associate dean for postgraduate medical education, was a former chair of the Department of Surgery at AKU Karachi. We had a close working relationship in Pakistan and now in East Africa. Each residency program was conceived as a regional program, and hence, the department chair's mandate was to develop and represent his or her specialty regionwide. This regional approach became actualized when we started the recruitment of qualified applicants to the family medicine residency, which attracted applications from all three regional bloc countries. We drew on the Tanzania approval and registration experience, contributing to the Kenya-based program's eventual acceptance several months later.

Our many discussions also included integrating program oversight, sharing learning resources, offering clinical conferences, standardizing examination formats between the AKU PGME programs, and establishing a family medicine training centre at AKUH Nairobi. Accessing AKUH Nairobi's many specialist clinics gave a significant boost to the Tanzania-based PGME.

I travelled to several hospitals and health centres in Tanzania and Kenya to explain and promote family medicine's concept and its scope and value to the practitioners and health care systems in the region. There was, understandably, some hesitancy in accepting a novel approach to medical and health care by many practitioners and administrators who considered it a "foreign" model of training and care. Yet, the large public hospitals that I visited in major cities like Mombasa, Kisumu, Moshi, and Mwanza, with crowded Casualty and Outpatients Departments and overflowing wards, testified to the crying need for a model of care that underscored the imperative for primary care closer to home. Community-based medical care, disease prevention, early diagnosis, and appropriate treatment of the vast majority of presenting problems are principles that lie at the heart of family medicine.

My presentations were always welcomed and politely received, and on many occasions, they generated the much-needed debates on the normative and often inefficient model of current care provision. I was not surprised by the skepticism towards formalizing principles and practice of family medicine broadly into the deeply entrenched modes of health care; it was a step too far and transformative for easy adoption on a large scale. Many regarded the concept of training as a "super-specialist generalist" physician, an elitist model in Africa's harsh realities.

I was not disheartened, but it would be disingenuous to state that I did not feel the pressure of the multiple simultaneous challenges weighing on me. First, there was a paramount concern to substantially boost the competence, quality, capability, ethics, and psychology of the Aga Khan Hospital and its health network, in order to function effectively as a reputable academic medical centre. Second, introducing and embedding the highly demanding postgraduate medical education standards was a challenge, with its associated rigour, multiple controls, processes, and discipline. A third challenge involved the question of introducing a novel and little understood specialty of family medicine into the institution and the country as an essential and impactful innovation into public health care, where a demonstrable track record was lacking. Finally, the extant operating conditions in the country, with its severe dearth of qualified and committed human resources and supporting facilities, hampered the efforts to create an enabling environment for transformative PGME.

The Nairobi-based specialty programs faced somewhat similar challenges, particularly the decades-long hospital traditions of practice, staff tensions, entrenched interests, and quality concerns. However, they were initiating PGME in traditional high-demand specialties such as medicine, surgery, gynecology, and child health. Unlike the Tanzania-based family medicine program, they did not have to promote or extol the values of these recognized and much sought-after specialties.

In April 2004, following a rigorous examination and evaluation process, the family medicine residency program formally started with six residents. Three of the cohort were from outside Tanzania; three were women. A similar profile of the applicants followed in subsequent years.

Our initial steps included an entrance examination to test basic scholastic and problem-solving abilities and a test of basic clinical knowledge. We set up a panel of interviewers to screen the applicants' suitability for the demanding postgraduate training and to rank the applicants – entirely on their merit. By this time, we had established the infrastructure and framework of the PGME project, including instruments and procedures to oversee, guide, and assess progress. I had submitted to the HEAC a detailed outline and plan of the faculty structure. It detailed the qualifications, experience, proposed faculty rank, and their clinical specialty and input into the residency training.

Over the period of the previous several months, the AKHD medical staff had progressively supported and embraced the PGME project; many of their concerns had or were energetically being addressed, and their work environment visibly improved. There was yet much to be done to address earlier identified deficiencies and inefficiencies in hospital operations and services. The AKHS leadership redoubled their efforts to realign practice, efficiency, and education synergistically with the PGME program.

Faculty Development: Context and Challenges

One of the most significant challenges facing the training program is developing a competent, motivated, and trained faculty well-versed in modern medical education principles. A severe shortage of physicians with the necessary credentials and commitment to training and mentoring residents of AKU and AKHS was a major impediment in the program's early phase. Most practicing hospital clinicians had little direct experience in teaching and research. Many saw education as unrewarding financially and often in conflict with service priorities. Some perceived it as a threat to personal and professional freedom. Given the clinical and methodological range of learning in family medicine, specialists in various specialties are required to be drawn into teaching and imparting the necessary skills to the residents. The specialists need to appreciate the educational objectives of the program as it relates to the content of their specific discipline, since family medicine is not simply a sum of knowledge of disparate medical and surgical specialties but a discipline with its own distinct body of knowledge, skills, and attitudes – and a unique art of holistic patient care.

The faculty's appointment and development were a demanding exercise, requiring unwavering impartiality, tact, sensitive negotiation, and fine balance. I offered a faculty position and incentives to each attending physician on the AKHD, following a thorough review of their professional proficiency, service record, and conduct. With each, we agreed on individualized teaching and a personal professional development plan that elaborated on the expectations and commitments of both parties. I was gratified and encouraged that all the AKHD physicians accepted appointments as lecturers or senior lecturers in the nascent AKU's academic Department of Family Medicine. The AKU's regional Appointment and Promotions Committee in Nairobi later formally approved the appointments.

There remained knowledge and skills gaps that needed to be filled. Wide consultation enabled me to recruit several prominent or consulting visiting specialists in the program. I connected with several experienced senior clinicians and educators from the University of Dar-es-Salaam's Muhimbili Medical School, including Professor Charles Mkony, the dean of the school. Other committed teachers and mentors were Dr. Mohammed Aziz, a professor of surgery at Muhimbili. Dr. Sylvester Faya was an avid teacher, mentor, and contributor to the program's advancement.

Dr. Rajesh Vyas, the service head of medicine at the AKHD, a gentle and compassionate general physician, accommodated the students into teaching rounds as I had requested, as did Dr. Nuruddin Lakhani, a young pediatrician, an early graduate of the AKU Medical College. Dr. Ilum Lars, a Danish surgeon who spent more than two years heading the surgical service at the AKHD, made exemplary efforts at imparting basic surgical knowledge and skills to the family medicine residents. Dr. Nicole Speiker, a geneticist and laboratory medicine specialist from Holland, contributed to education in the locally hard-to-access special areas of knowledge in her field. Dr. Hitesh Vyas, an Indian ophthalmologist and educator, then on the staff of the AKHD, contributed generously to the program's quality development. Professor Zul Premji, a researcher in infectious diseases with special research experience in malaria, was among those who filled in essential skill gaps.

Going forward, the faculty body expanded with the addition of visiting professors, honorary professors, and short-term visiting consultants; most were from the U.K., U.S., and Europe. Over the coming years, this mixed model of teaching staff paid notable dividends. Dr. Gijs Walraven, the director of Aga Khan Health Services at the Secretariat in Paris, who had considerable experience in tropical medicine and health care problems in developing countries, accepted the position as honorary professor. He was generous with his contributions of expertise and counsel.

Our critical need was for well-trained and committed family physicians to teach, supervise, mentor, and guide the family medicine trainees. Initially, Riaz Rattansi and I filled this role. Dr. Ed Perry, a British-trained general practitioner, joined us from Zimbabwe, where he had spent several years. He remained on the Department of Family Medicine staff for almost two years before returning to the U.K. to take up a medical school faculty position in the U.K.

We upgraded the Family Medicine Centre (FMC) education capacity to demonstrate skilled, comprehensive, and continuing care for people of all ages, regardless of their health problem, who presented to the FMC.

～～⁓

The FMC led to many memorable encounters. One day, my resident asked me to see a young child, brought in from Tanzania's hinterland. This emaciated child had a large swelling in the abdomen and pale eyes. We found the child had an enlarged liver and spleen, raising the possibility of chronic malaria. The child had been treated several times with medications, including the usual malaria drugs, but continued to have bouts of fever and a failure to thrive. Laboratory tests confirmed malaria, but it seemed the parasite was resistant to the commonly available malaria medications that had been administered, an increasingly common problem caused by improper use of medications. Overuse or improper use of medications was causing many parasites and bacteria to become resistant to the first-line medications, an increasingly worrisome development in Africa and in other parts of the world. This problem called for educational, policy, and supply responses at all levels. We admitted the child and were able to obtain a combination of drugs, which over time cleared the parasites from the bloodstream and infected organs. Later follow-ups confirmed that the child had indeed recovered and was beginning to grow well.

One morning, a middle-aged couple entered my consultation room in the FMC. The woman poured out her concerns that her husband was getting increasingly weak and was short of breath. I reviewed the previous consultation and test results they had brought with them, including consultations obtained in England several years before. Our assessment of the man, a well-established local businessman, revealed an enlarged heart and interesting heart murmurs. It seemed that this gentleman had heart valve disease caused by childhood rheumatic fever, a common condition in sub-Saharan Africa. I advised the need for specialist consultations and possible surgical correction of the damaged heart valves. But he adamantly refused to consider surgical treatment. I saw this gentleman on several further occasions. I asked him if he would consent to be examined by my students, who were at that point doing their M. Med Part 1 practical examination. He very willingly consented and gamely sat through the examination process in the next few weeks. For the residents, it was a test of their clinical diagnostic skills. We continued to care for him, eventually arranging surgical treatment at the AKUH Nairobi.

The hospital dealt with some preventable problems as well. One sad case was that of an American tourist, who was transferred to our hospital in a comatose state, brought in from a wildlife game reserve. He had not been taking his malaria prevention tablets as directed. At the time of admission, he had severe malaria in his brain and regrettably did not survive despite our best efforts.

Our new PGME initiative had not escaped the notice of many national and international organizations and universities.

I received requests for curricular electives for students wishing to experience medical challenges in the developing countries from several medical schools in Canada, Australia, the U.K., and the U.S. With our limited capacity for supervision, we could place only a few senior medical students in our program. Fortuitously, there was also interest expressed by experienced generalist clinicians who wished to spend sabbaticals of up to three months or longer connected to our program. This interest was a most welcome evolution since it instilled a fresh and external unbiased perspective on the program's strengths and weaknesses by those who partook by their presence and rigour. I recall the feedback and penetrating perspectives offered by the visiting short-term clinician teachers. Dr. Anne Forrester and Dr. Neil Ferguson from Scotland come to mind for their outstanding contributions to the program's maturation. A young and active family medicine specialist and researcher who made notable contributions to the program was Dr.

Stephanie Tache from the University of California, San Francisco (UCSF). In the days ahead, we developed a special relationship and education partnership with the UCSF, an initiative that immensely helped strengthen our education and research capacity. The U.S. Aga Khan Health Board was generous in offering material and technical expertise in several high-needs areas such as laboratory medicine, critical care, and infection control.

❧

The postgraduate family medicine residency program is designed to impart skills, attitudes, essential clinical knowledge, and skills in the major medical disciplines, as well as an understanding of the determinants of health and disease. It fosters critical thinking, problem-solving and leadership skills, self-directed lifelong learning, and an ethical outlook. It encourages the acquisition of broad humanistic, pluralistic, and cultural values, as well as compassion and respect for basic human rights. It is science-based but contextual and relevant to the needs of populations.

The curriculum calls for progressive responsibility, case-based learning, practical experience, facility and field-based learning, and intense learning exercises. It mandates research into pressing clinical and health concerns impacting the quality of life. The two-part curriculum is divided into two periods of two years each, separated by a successful Part 1 examination. The final Part 2 exam is written at the end of completion of the competent defence of a requisite research paper and a demanding review of the satisfactory completion of all assessments conducted by local, regional, and external examiners.

Our first cohort of residents was made up of six eager doctors, with distinctly different backgrounds. Llywaywe Hussein was a bright, personable, and optimistic young woman whose family hailed from Zanzibar. A relatively fresh graduate, she had one or two years of formal internship training. In the years to come, she went on to become an assistant professor in AKU's Department of Family Medicine in Dar. She later joined the U.S. Aid program in health in Tanzania in a responsible clinical and planning position. Wilfred Kaizerege was a more mature physician with several years of experience working in public health services, mainly in women's health and child health. He eventually headed a large health centre owned and operated by a large gold mining conglomerate on Lake Victoria's shores. Aswila Sood was an eager young Kenyan doctor with an entrepreneurial bent who became a successful private practitioner and an educator in the U.K.

Jacob Shabani, another brilliant Kenyan, held a consultant position in the Family Medicine Centre at the AKHU Nairobi and continued to contribute to medical education. John Rwegasha, a Tanzanian who had spent several years working at the Aga Khan Health Centre in Morogoro, went on to become a consultant physician and head of the department at the Muhimbili University Medical Center in Dar-es-Salaam. A few residents moved on to more immediately lucrative careers before completion of their gruelling four-year training program in family medicine. Even those residents who had not completed their entire program were deemed well-qualified and were recruited for a variety of clinical, administrative, and planning positions in Tanzania and elsewhere, signifying testimony to the holistic skillsets the program espoused.

The launch of a highly complex, multifarious enterprise in advanced education and health care in the untilled soil that existed at the time cannot be expected to unfold unimpeded. There were instances of resistance to change, regulatory obstacles, and antiquated systems of care processes. It required steely determination, the conviction of purpose, reasoned course-correction, considered compromises, and a clear vision to till the soil – to plant the seeds, to harmonize, to win acceptance and trust. In the first year, we had constituted a syncretic faculty body, set the course for the hospital's continuing functional upgrading and broadening of services and suitability as a teaching unit, obtained provisional registration of AKU's first PGME program in Tanzania, framed an ethical foundation of critical human resource development, and harmonized the crucial strands to enable quality education and service. We had instituted tentative steps to position the specialty and principles of family medicine within the health care system in the country and region. We had fashioned some alliances and supportive co-operation among teaching institutions conducive to improving population health in the country.

The training program continued to progress, to evolve and take into account lessons learnt, evidence-based medical education, and the evolving nature of the science of medical education methodologies.

> *No pessimist ever discovered the secrets of the stars, or sailed to an uncharted land, or opened a new heaven to the human spirit.*
>
> *Helen Keller*

CHAPTER 11

BRIDGING ACADEMIC MEDICINE
AND POPULATION HEALTH

Africa, the second largest continent, made up of fifty-three countries, has a population of over 1.2 billion.

In antiquity, the Greeks are said to have called it Libya and the Romans to have called it Africa, perhaps from the Latin *aprica* ("sunny") or the Greeks *aphrike* ("without cold"). Africa can be considered a vast plateau, slightly tilted, with the highest portion in the southwest, sloping towards the northwest. There are imposing mountain ranges and dramatic geological landmarks. The East African Rift System is the most remarkable geological feature, which lies between 30 degrees and 40 degrees E. The four-thousand-mile Rift begins northeast of the continent's limits and extends southwards from the Ethiopian Red Sea coast to the Zambezi River basin. Its course is marked by many of the lakes of East Africa. Associated with its formation was the volcanic activity responsible for most of East Africa's highest peaks, including Kilimanjaro.

Africa is widely recognized as the birthplace of the *Hominidae*, the taxonomic family to which modern humans belong. Fossils of *Australopithecus afrensis,* affectionately called "Lucy" – considered the mother of all humans – was discovered almost 3.2 million years ago in Ethiopia. Modern humans are believed to have appeared as early as two hundred thousand years ago in the eastern region of sub-Saharan Africa. Somewhat later, those early humans spread into northern Africa and the Middle East and, ultimately, to the rest of the world.

Africa is the most tropical of all the continents; some four-fifths of its territory rests between the Tropics of Cancer and Capricorn. It has the most physically varied populations in the world, from the tallest people to the shortest; body forms and facial and other morphological features also vary widely. It is the continent with the greatest human genetic variation, reflecting its evolutionary role as the source of all human DNA.

Throughout human history, movements of people have occurred within, into, and out of Africa along its northern coasts, across the Sinai Peninsula, along the Red Sea, and especially in the Horn of Africa and coastal areas as far south as southern Africa. Along the east coast, trading cities arose and fell, cities that had overseas contacts during the past two millennia with peoples of southern Arabia and as far east as India and Indonesia. Internal movements during that time contributed to the heterogeneity and complexity of the native African societies. Pre-colonial Africa possessed perhaps as many as ten thousand different states and polities. Many great kingdoms and states left their mark on Africa's early history, such as Ghana, Gao, the Mali Empire, Kwa Zulu, and Zimbabwe.

Sub-Saharan Africa, home to more than one billion people, half of whom will be under twenty-five years old by 2050, is a diverse region of the vast continent. It offers human and natural resources that have the potential to yield inclusive growth and wipe out poverty, enabling Africans across the continent to live healthier and more prosperous lives.

The economy of most of Africa can be characterized as underdeveloped. Much of its economy is predominantly agricultural, and subsistence farming still engages more than 60 percent of the population. Africa experienced considerable economic growth during the twentieth century and is continuing a rapid transition to a more diverse economy. As part of the colonial legacy, however, for some countries, the export of two or three major agricultural products or minerals – such as peanuts, cocoa, petroleum, or copper – has come to provide most of the foreign exchange. Fluctuations in the prices of these commodities have made the economies of these countries vulnerable and fragile. Vigorous promotion of industrial development in the last few decades with foreign aid has saddled most African countries with enormous foreign debt. Economic growth is complicated by rapid population growth, geopolitical tensions, regional rivalries, boundary disputes, tribal and ethnic strife, and internecine civil and political contests. Added to these transportation and communication challenges, large-scale deforestation, cycles of droughts and climate-related displacements, and movements of migrant workers seeking opportunities in the few better off or resource-rich countries adds another layer of obstacles to progressive civil society and stable growth.

Yet, progress on many fronts, such as regional trading and economic blocks and continent-wide cooperation through the African Union and other bodies, is discernible. Development financing through transcontinental institutions such as the African Development Bank enhances multilateral and bilateral development and investment schemes. Hence, wide variations exist in the level of sophistication of its development institutions, particularly in education and health care. Egypt in the north and South Africa at the southern end of the continent, given their particular histories, demonstrated higher levels of organization and refinement; both countries I had occasions to study and interact with in the days ahead.

The former British colonies and territories in East Africa – Kenya, Uganda, and Tanganyika – obtained independence in the early 1960s. Tanganyika, under socialist president Dr. Julius Nyerere, took a turn leftward towards egalitarianism and self-reliance. Tanganyika and Zanzibar united into a union in 1964, and the nation took the name Tanzania. It is ethnically, linguistically, and religiously diverse, with a population of over fifty-six million.

Many important hominid fossils have been found in Tanzania, such as six-million-year-old Pliocene fossils. The genus *Australopithecus* ranged all over Africa two to four million years ago, and the oldest remains of the genus *Homo* are found near Lake Olduvai on mainland Tanzania. The country attracts archaeological, cultural, and wildlife viewing; tourism, mining, and agriculture are considered primary economic activities.

Tanzania has made some progress towards reducing extreme hunger and malnutrition. Approximately 65 percent of the population live below the poverty line; 30 percent are considered malnourished. Tanzania's economy is heavily based on agriculture; industry and construction form a major and growing component of the economy. Tourism contributes to around 18 percent of the nation's gross domestic product (GDP).

The broad span of historical, cultural, and socio-economic milieu made it necessary to obtain a general understanding of the interrelated forces shaping socio-economic progress in Tanzania and other African countries in the region. I revelled in the fundamental study of cultures, traditions, arts, history, and geography of this large, diverse, and congenial country; its many attractions; and its atavistic sociably simple life. My travels and studies allowed me to comprehend the state and the evolution of education and health care in the country more deeply. Professional education has tended to be narrow and utilitarian, with bare grounding in the humanities, social and cultural anthropology, and the history of medicine. This educational deficit, I believe, has tended to constrict the space for contextual responses and integration of critical factors in improving large populations' quality of life. Social, economic, and environmental determinants of health get short shrift in the curricula of medical education in most East and Central Africa countries, subordinated to the imparting of the traditional clinical and curative skills, considered by many the essential core of medical education.

Making Medical Education Responsive to Needs

Medical education is a complex, demanding, and continuous process. Thus, the challenge was to shift professional development in medicine and health care towards sound appreciation and creative integration of the manifold determinants impacting societies' health and well-being. To be relevant and impactful, the advanced medical education in family and community medicine we were promoting, therefore, needed to be inclusive, problem-based, evidence-based, intellectually rigorous, and innovative. Most of all, it was imperative that the graduate of this program was armed with critical problem-solving, clinical, preventive, planning, and leadership skills; accepted within the pantheon of medical specialists in the country; and widely welcomed and employable in public- and private-sector enterprises in health care.

Therefore, to advance this project, it was imperative not only to establish the program but to advocate tirelessly its place and utility within the health care system. One approach we took was to organize a national and regional symposium on medical education that could disseminate the science and evidence supporting such an educational innovation, debate its applicability in Tanzania, and seek to build bridges, enabling the development of networks locally and regionally. I entitled the symposium "Training Doctors for Tomorrow: Making Medical Education Responsive to Societies."

The symposium proved to be the point of inflection for AKU's PGME endeavours. Many delegates and officials from Tanzania's medical schools and universities and private and public health facilities attended the symposium. It enabled us to consider the wide range of opinions and sentiments concerning the challenge of shifting the normative discourse on medical education in the context of national underdevelopment and the daunting scale of the population's health care needs. But it also strengthened our resolve to demonstrate and disseminate the concept more widely and the crucial need for broad participation of organizations involved in health care planning, education, and delivery.

We discerned that many established practitioners and trainees chose a path to obtain professional fulfillment and material compensation that revolved around seeking opportunities in wealthy countries of the West and the oil-rich Middle East, thus aggravating the detrimental national brain drain of the last few decades. Few saw realistic prospects of substantive change in the infrastructure for health, training, and opportunity. We intuited a sense of fatalism in some and a low sense of morale and hope for personal progress in an inflexible system.

Ambition and Resolve: Crystallizing Context

It became abundantly clear that to pioneer an innovative training and career pathway in medicine in the context of East Africa's realities was a more daunting undertaking than a small, private, non-profit development organization had anticipated. However, it did crystallize and increase our resolve and commitment to fundamentally alter the conditions prevailing on the ground incrementally for the long-term impact on the population's health and quality of life. Civil society needed to be strengthened and supported, economic opportunities widened, social and cultural assets renewed and revitalized. In this, the Aga Khan Development Network agencies, including AKU and AKHS, moved further to support the public sector's efforts in development. The pressing need to foster partnerships and linkages, seeking commonalities in goals and synergy in advancing the crucial agendas in health and education, underscored our enterprise.

Proposing Strategic Health Innovations and Research

A clear picture began to form: health innovations that offer the potential of public good through wide dissemination and application in public and private health care services are needed in most countries in sub-Saharan Africa if they are to leap forward in their ability to cope with the huge unmet needs of their populations. Strategies for improving population health require locally applicable clinical and health services, research, disseminating knowledge and research findings, and the integration and application of knowledge to impact health status. Very little population health research takes place in universities and academic health centres. Existing and advancing clinical knowledge relating to common disorders is unavailable to most health care providers; out of date or inaccurate information often forms the basis of clinical care in under-resourced health centres staffed by under-trained health workers. As a result, there are serious gaps between what the health systems provide and their full potential – indeed, their expectation from a trusting public.

Health care is among the best endowed of all industries in the richness of its science base. Major gaps in knowledge exist, but clinical science progresses, often providing a rational basis for choosing the best drug, surgery, and diagnostic strategies, as well as other care elements. Yet, an enormous amount of that scientific knowledge remains unused. Failure to use available science is costly and harmful; it leads to overuse of unhelpful treatments, underuse of effective care, or improper use of therapies for common medical conditions. Hence, there was an urgent need to galvanize the public and private health sectors and the concerned professions to build a better and safer health care system. Placing patient safety at the centre of the health system's principal concern and wide-scale adoption of tried and tested therapies and clinical protocols in delivering medical care for the most prevalent conditions seemed a crucial need of the time.

Diffusion of innovations and effective care pathways is a significant challenge globally, not particular to developing countries. Drugs and technologies researched and developed in the advanced industrialized societies are not always the most appropriate or acceptable solutions in underdeveloped countries. Therefore, there is a need to seek proven, easily available, cost-effective, and culturally acceptable solutions.

I put forward a preliminary proposal to AKU and AKHS to establish a "Centre for Strategic Health Innovations and Research."

The concept paper called for dedicating a research centre that could converge knowledge and available research on local geographical and environmental factors, disease distribution, and anthropological, cultural, and traditional practices to further research and advance scientifically sound solutions to some of the most pressing health problems affecting populations. Addressing health is, therefore, a quest for the most appropriate health interventions, health policy, health systems, health financing, and health resources. Within it, a "Health Technology

Assessment" unit is suggested since uncritical importation of burgeoning expensive technologies in medical care can impair rather than advance health care for large populations through the diversion of scant resources away from the most critical needs of societies. More than a decade later, AKU established a Centre for Education Innovation and Research in Karachi with a similar mandate.

Advancing the Role of Family Medicine Regionally

At my request, Ambrose Chanji put me in touch with health care leaders in some significant regions of the country where there were some established medical schools and affiliated teaching hospitals.

Kilimanjaro Christian Medical College (KCMC) was established in 1997, a constituent college of Tumaini University located in Moshi in northeastern Tanzania. Moshi is situated on the lower slopes of Mount Kilimanjaro, a dormant volcano and the highest mountain in Africa. Moshi was established as a military camp by the Germans in 1893, and the word "Moshi" refers to smoke that emanates from the nearby mountain. The KCMC started as a Christian-centred institution with the faculty of medicine, later incorporated more faculties, institutes, and directorates. Hence, it was a young institution, but my meetings with the university's leadership helped me understand the conviction of their vision and commitment to developing human resources for health through the more conventional training routes and specialties. However, my discussions with them planted the seeds of a new, more general medical specialty, better suited to provide comprehensive clinical and community care and health care leadership. In years to come, I believe, the notion of advanced generalist training gained traction with the addition of postgraduate education in the Faculty of Medicine.

Bugando Medical Centre (BMC), a secondary- and tertiary-care teaching hospital located in the city of Mwanza, along the southern shores of Lake Victoria, is affiliated with the Catholic University of Health and Allied Sciences. It was built by the Catholic Church in Tanzania between 1968 and 1977. Over time, its particular service focus on cancer care and treatment made it only the second public cancer treatment centre after the Ocean Road Cancer Institute in Dar-es-Salaam. Once again, I found a sincere welcome to my friendly overtures and sharing with the organization about the Aga Khan University's and Aga Khan Health Services' mission and vision in Tanzania.

There were several commonalities in our mission and goals; however, both the BMC and the KCMC were public hospitals, each supported by large external donor pools. I again disseminated the notion of embedding medical care principles inherent in the practice of family medicine and community health in undergraduate and postgraduate medical education to make a meaningful impact on population health in the long run. The two universities saw this enterprise as a path of innovation in medical education less travelled and unexplored in the country. However, my presentations on the concept of a "generalist" with advanced training – armed with broad skills, knowledge, and attitudes – did receive support from the more foresighted faculty and administrators.

There were indications of a gradual acceptance of the concept of family and community health as a new specialty in Kenya and Uganda. The Kenya Ministry of Health identified family medicine as a priority for the development of capacity in health care. In Kenya, policy and strategic documents, as part of the Second National Health Strategic Plan, were under deliberation. It expressly recognized that the most appropriate person to respond to the health sector challenges was a well-trained family practitioner. By invitation, I had the privilege to attend at least two meetings of the task force constituted by the ministry, academia, and the private sector to advance its finalization.

In Kenya, Moi University School of Medicine (MUSOM) in Eldoret, established in 1988, embraced the concept. Their program was spurred by a report that underscored the barriers to equitable health care, inefficient health care systems, rising costs, inappropriate emphasis on narrow specialties rather than generalist training, and maldistribution of the physician workforce. The report stated that more than 80 percent of the population had very limited resources to pay for health care and emphasized the value of integrating curative with preventive care.

Accompanied by a respected Kenyan Health Sciences education and policy consultant and Mushtaq Ahmed, the AKU associate dean for PGME, I visited the Moi University in Eldoret. We shared our vision and philosophy in health sciences education with the Moi University leaders and were pleased with their acknowledgement of the need to foster regional training and support networks in promoting the new specialty of family medicine in the East Africa region. Moi University was then attracting the interest of one or two foreign universities, training programs, and aid agencies, who saw the potential for research and development in the region.

I recalled Uasin Gishu Hospital's old ramshackle buildings in Eldoret from my childhood school days, now transformed into a teaching hospital with modern equipment and programs. Eldoret, a small city in the Kenya Highlands, catering to the large dairy farming community in colonial times, had by now grown into a large metropolitan area with a diverse population and economy. I dropped in for a quick and nostalgic visit to my old high school, where I had spent a short and happy year long ago. To my astonishment, the old classroom and my desk were still there as I remembered them.

At this time, the venerable Makerere University School of Medicine in Kampala, Uganda, my alma mater, also explored positioning family medicine and health as a crucial piece in enhancing population health through advanced graduate education of physicians. With its long and distinguished history and its ventures into innovative programs, the university was well-placed to venture into unfamiliar territory. The university also received technical and research support from several foreign universities. Dr. Amorto Atai, a highly dedicated community health practitioner, had recently assumed the position to head the development of this program.

Dr. Atai, an unassuming, middle-aged general physician, obtained her under-graduate medical education in India. A single mother, she had experienced the travails of professional struggles in a male-dominated academic world. She chose to advance her passion for accessible good medical care through community-based education endeavours. In the days ahead, she served as an examiner in AKU's M. Med examinations. She was committed to regional partnerships and support; we found common ground in our endeavours to influence policymakers and the bureaucracy in steering the course of education and health care for substantive transformation and reorientation. My meetings with her, the dean, and senior educational planners of the university proved fruitful and mutually supportive. Soon after, Mbarara University in Uganda also launched a postgraduate training program founded on Makerere's principles. Several years later, I found myself drawn into assisting Makerere University's Department of Family Medicine to review its curriculum.

Moi University in Kenya and Makerere University in Uganda were both public universities that had boldly embraced the idea of a new specialty in Africa's particular context. Our program in Tanzania, AKU and AKHS, was a private initiative built on a decades-long history of service, preventive, and community health, delivered through a wide network of health facilities, including hospitals. The three East African family medicine programs strove to establish cooperation and support, which in the months and years to come, blossomed into an extensive network in East, Central, and Southern Africa.

Fostering Regional, Transcontinental Linkages

The opportunity to expand our message's reach came when I received a letter from professor Jan de Maeseneer, head of family medicine and primary care at the University of Ghent in Belgium. In his letter, Jan de Maeseneer described a project initiated by a consortium of several Flemish Belgian universities and led by Ghent University. It was funded by the Belgian government's University Development Co-operation to "Develop and Support Quality Assurance of Postgraduate Medical Training in Family Medicine and Primary Health Care in Southern and Eastern Africa through South–South Cooperation." He invited the nascent AKU's Family Medicine Residency Program's participation – the only program of its type in Tanzania – into the project. This communication was a welcome development for our program since garnering support and resources and creating a conducive environment proved to be a gruelling and lonely exercise, particularly in Tanzania.

The project, eventually funded by the European Union, sought to further cooperation and shared experiences between different faculties of medicine involved in developing this essential specialty in Africa, based on an encouraging earlier experience in supporting an eight-member South African university consortium. The plan was to encourage and enlist leading universities in East and Central Africa to partner with the South African consortium so that accumulating knowledge and experience could be shared, and best practices could be embedded into new initiatives. The proposal was an exciting development since it rooted the validity of our own initiative on demonstrable proof of concept. Furthermore, it drew on the pilot experience obtained in Africa's conditions to foster wider diffusion of a vision we wrestled with positioning in the pivotal health systems realignment in Tanzania and the region.

In January 2005, I attended a meeting in Pretoria, South Africa, held at the venerable halls of the University of Pretoria, to confer with the organizers and putative partners for an East and Southern Africa consortium to strengthen family medicine training. Apart from Jan de Maeseneer and his team, there were representatives of public universities from Ghana, Sudan, Zimbabwe, Kenya, and Mozambique. AKU joined as a founding member of the collaboration, the only private university participating in the pan-Africa network. I found Jan de Maeseneer to be urbane, generous, empathetic, and well-versed in the issues relating to sub-Saharan Africa's development. At later dates, we shared experiences and challenges and partnered in Kampala's and Pretoria's future conferences.

The South African academic leaders presented a thorough review of the South African consortium experience. Successes, setbacks, lessons learnt, and missed opportunities were aired and debated freely. Each invited university from the African countries described their program's state of development and organization, including its challenges and readiness to participate in the wider enterprise. AKU's program and its forward-looking plan received heartening plaudits and support.

Dr. Julia Blix, head of family medicine at the University of Pretoria, the host institution, was a dynamic and passionate proponent of primary care medicine. Like other heads of family medicine departments in South Africa, she organized the practice and training in family medicine in rural as well as urban health facilities, a few of which we had the opportunity to visit. Their well-planned training path included progressive clinical, management, and leadership responsibilities and skills in the integration of all levels of medical and community care. The placing of primary care and family medicine at the heart of the health care system in South Africa had the endorsement and support of South Africa's government. In future visits to South Africa, I witnessed the clinical and training programs in Cape Town and Johannesburg. In the coming years, Julia Blix served as an external examiner in AKU's final examination leading to AKU's Master of Medicine degree.

In the years ahead, this supportive African network grew significantly, with the addition of Uganda and Zambia universities. The network held several scientific conferences over time as it gathered momentum. My several meetings with Jan and his colleagues impressed me with the goodwill and backing extended by established universities in Europe, including Maastricht University, Ghent University, and many others. Opportunities for curriculum and faculty development and family medicine training complexes materialized in the coming years.

Leveraging Collaborations and Partnerships

The AKHD, a seventy-bed secondary-level hospital, lacked both the numbers and range of patient problems to train doctors at a postgraduate level effectively.

Its trajectory to attain an improved quality of care and to add clinical services and enhanced oversight and professional development was an ongoing exercise, but progress was slow and hesitant at times. It lacked particular critical clinical education material and specialists in areas such as dermatology, plastic surgery, eye diseases, neurosurgery, psychiatry, and cancer diagnosis and care. Its clinical laboratory was inadequate or not well-equipped to perform some tests essential in diagnosis and patient management. Therefore, I needed to link my students with other facilities that could fill some gaps for the present time.

Simultaneously, I continued to apply the heft and prestige of the PGME project to the best of my ability to uplift the hospital's performance and staffing in crucial areas such as the clinical laboratory, pharmacy, and medical records. I advised or participated in working groups or committees striving to improve functions in these vital areas of hospital services. One concern was to rationalize the acquisition and use of medications within the AKHS facilities. We established a Pharmacy and Therapeutics Committee (P&T) charged with the responsibility for streamlining drug acquisition requests and developing an in-house formulary that guided the cost-effective use of drugs, driven by the WHO list of essential drugs. One objective was to resist pharmaceutical companies' marketing pressures to stock their expensive and newer medications in the hospital pharmacy, where generic and evidence-based alternatives are available.

I engaged in meeting with many external specialists and facilities that could provide the services and educational experience that the AKHD could not currently provide adequately.

The Ocean Road Cancer Institute (ORCI) is one of the oldest health institutions in Tanzania, having been founded in 1895 by the German colonial government. Set in stately arcaded colonial buildings facing the azure blue Indian Ocean, initially it served exclusively as a hospital for the German community. The British reserved it for the use of European communities when they took over Tanganyika after the First World War. Later, in 1996, under the ministry's direct control, it proceeded to provide integrated, accessible, and affordable cancer care. It collaborated with several international organizations and received clinical and technical input from the International Atomic Energy Commission, University of Copenhagen, and other reputable institutions.

The family medicine trainees needed to understand the changing epidemiology of cancer in the developing world, its relationship to HIV/AIDS and infections, and changing lifestyle and preventive measures to reduce its prevalence through appropriate preventive measures. The students needed to grasp the natural history of cancer; its early detection, diagnosis, and treatment; and public health policies to reduce its prevalence. One vital element was the relief of pain and suffering from this devastating illness. Cancer claimed over ten million lives worldwide at the end of the millennium. International research claimed rates of cancer would double in the next twenty years in Africa. Yet, most patients did not have access even to basic cancer care in developing societies of Africa.

The chief executive and the medical director of the hospital received me kindly when I approached them for cooperation in the essential core education in cancer medicine for my students. I shared with them the mission and vision of AKU and AKHS in developing training programs that have the potential to alleviate the health status of people in the region, with specific anticipated roles that well-trained primary-care physicians might play in health systems in the future.

They immediately grasped the critical role those frontline physicians had to play in the prevention, early detection, treatment, and referral of patients with this large group of life-threatening diseases. They showed me their clinical, research, laboratory, and learning facilities, which were quite impressive.

Following approval by the ORCI board, we were able to rotate our students through this progressive organization.

Many forms of cancer are known to be preventable or treatable if detected in the early stages. Cancers like cervical cancer in women, Burkitt's lymphoma in children, and bladder, liver, and stomach cancers were common in the region but usually presented at advanced stages, making treatment much more complicated, expensive, and palliative rather than curative. A few malignant diseases are easy to detect early by simple tests, such as cervical cancer in women, provided screening services are widely made available. The problems were compounded by a dearth of trained practitioners and facilities to diagnose cases in early stages, make appropriate referrals, and provide continuing care closer to home. Lack of drugs, supplies, cancer pain medications such as opioids, and radiation therapy made it even more imperative that disease be prevented to the extent possible, risk factors modified, and myriad complications of malignant disease be mitigated in disadvantaged populations.

This illustrates just one neglected medical training area we sought to change through enhanced training in family medicine and contextual primary care. Our educational and research engagement with the ORCI was fruitful; it afforded our trainees an essential educational opportunity. But our program also required additional training sites to impart special skills in other domains of medicine. We bridged this academic gap by enlisting departments of several other hospitals. Temeke District Hospital, a facility of the local health authority of Dar-es-Salaam, extended the courtesy of welcoming our students to their clinics and wards. Muhimbili Referral Hospital and a private non-profit orthopedic hospital, CCBRT, allowed similar courtesy and cooperation to the program. In return, AKU facilitated nursing upgrading education to some of these hospitals' staff through the university's advanced nursing program.

We felt that some experiential gaps still existed in our residents' training, particularly in areas of maternal and child care, HIV/AIDS, malaria, tuberculosis, infectious diseases, nutritional disorders, and mental health. These were large concerns in public health, where a few hospitals and health centres were charged with providing the bulk of care. The Aga Khan Foundation in Tanzania had partnered with and supported one such facility. This was the Raha Leo Health Centre in Zanzibar, which served a largely rural and semi-urban population on the main island of Unguja. This centre had the ideal demographics and clinical mix of cases crucial for comprehensive family medicine education. I found the centre, staffed by nurses and clinical officers but no medical doctor, to be a prototypical public health centre. What it lacked in sophistication, it made up with staff dedicated to making a difference. Our consultations with the district leaders, facilitated by the AKF, saw the benefit of collaboration for both organizations in adding value to community care of the served population.

Soon we developed a mutually beneficial collaboration agreement, in which the PGME students – who were qualified physicians with increasing levels of experience and breadth of knowledge – would be placed for blocks of time to provide clinical care and help improve diagnosis, drug therapy, and quality of medical records at the health centre. The centre saw large numbers of patients, particularly women and children; it performed routine screening and immunizations and assessed individuals, families, and communities' nutritional status. It screened for malaria, TB, and HIV infections and provided counselling and appropriate referrals. Hence, it integrated preventive with clinical care and public health education for large populations, ideal conditions for broad-based clinical education, and research in efficient primary care principles.

While developing linkages with Raha Leo Health Centre, I was invited by the regional medical officer of health to visit the Mnazi Moja Hospital in Zanzibar. This sizable, busy public hospital serves as a secondary referral hospital and is proficient in maternal care and obstetrical problems.

After assessing the hospital's capabilities and standards of care and ethics, we decided to use the hospital's facility for training our residents. Our senior trainees could also contribute to upgrading several care standards at the hospital, such as infection control, pain management, and detailed patient evaluations and medical recordkeeping, which were some areas of weakness we perceived in the busy hospital. This partnership was a further step in keeping with AKU's and AKHS's commitment to share best practices in care with public and private institutions. An agreement with the large hospital enabled my students to rotate through the hospital to obtain additional skills in the operative aspects of obstetrics and gynecology, a much-underdeveloped area of health care in Africa's developing countries. Obstetrical complications of inexpert home deliveries are, unfortunately, a very significant problem in women's health.

Distributed medical education that was beginning to evolve posed a special problem for the project of PGME in family medicine: to recruit, train, mentor, and oversee appropriate faculty. While I had quite successfully attracted interested senior clinicians to train and supervise our students, this was not always the case in the busy, public health care facilities. I worked on a document that outlined professional standards for faculty and learners, which underlined competence, honesty, ethics, pluralism, confidentiality, responsibility, and professional development maintenance. The document also stated AKU's and AKHS's commitment to respecting their rights and freedoms and supporting their professional growth. Over time, this document served as a template for the recruitment, retention, and support of the faculty. We shared it with the Kenya-based PGME programs.

The AKUH Nairobi, a multispecialty hospital, now emerged as an additional training site for the family medicine residents in some key areas of medicine where we lacked sufficient training resources in Tanzania. These specialties included psychiatry, dermatology, and diseases of the eyes, ear, nose, and throat (ENT). The hospital had already oriented itself to postgraduate medical education, and hence, it proved to be a relatively painless exercise for my program. Simultaneously, with the hospital's management, we started developing the Family Medicine Centre at the AKUH Nairobi, which would also serve as another teaching unit in the Aga

Khan health network in the years to come.

A significant problem remained: faculty's shortage of trained family physicians that could serve as preceptors and role models. Riaz Rattansi and I filled that role to the extent possible. We were grateful for visiting family physicians who contributed significantly to filling this vital role.

Privileged Relationship: Global Reach

A fortuitous development led to further strengthening our program. I had an unexpected visitor to my office one morning. An elegant, youngish-looking gentleman was shown in by Fatma, who had booked him to see me. The man introduced himself as Chuck Smuckler, a senior program consultant for the prestigious University of California, San Francisco (UCSF) Global Health Sciences (GHS). Chuck, an affable and seasoned public health professional, and I became good friends over time. He told me of the endeavour by the UCSF's GHS project to partner with suitable academic institutions of health sciences education in Africa that could benefit from the considerable expertise and resources of the UCSF in teaching, research, and global development. He mentioned that the search for acceptable partnering institutions in Tanzania had not produced appropriate candidates. The existing universities he had visited and assessed did not appear to be suited at this time. He went on to say he had been directed to AKU's PGME project by some who had expressed the apparent merit of our initiative and its potential to impact health care in the country.

Over the coming days, we shared detailed information about each institution's history, missions, goals, and strategies. We probed for consonance in vision, compatibility of the respective organizations and resource commitments. We encapsulated each institution's mission, vision, and founding principles. The UCSF statement read:

> *The mission of the UCSF Global Health Sciences is improving health and reducing the burden of disease in the world's most vulnerable populations. It integrates UCSF expertise in all the health, social and biological sciences, focuses that expertise on pressing issues in global health, and works with partners in countries throughout the world to achieve these aims. The Department of Family and Community Medicine has a*

keen interest in promoting academic excellence through its research and teaching programs.

The background on the Aga Khan University and Health Services, East Africa read as follows:

The Aga Khan University will be an autonomous, international institution of distinction, primarily serving the developing world and Muslim societies in innovative and enduring ways. The AKU-EA envisions itself as a leading university in East Africa of quality and distinction, relevant to the local needs of the population. Its mission includes preparing individuals for constructive and exemplary roles and shaping public and private policies. AKU expresses its commitment to building an environment that fosters intellectual freedom, distinction in scholarship, pluralism, compassion and humanity's collective responsibility for a sustainable physical, social and cultural environment. The AKU expects to implement a diverse range of programs, develop distinct and diverse campuses, and to capitalize on the experience and knowledge it has gained, to strengthen its role as a change agent and catalyst in the Muslim and developing world. Its current commitment in East Africa is to develop programs of relevance in the field of nursing, medical education and educational development.

The Aga Khan Health Services - East Africa envisions making significant contributions to improving the effectiveness of the health care systems in the region. It seeks to be a self-sustaining health care system with entry points extended to the major centers of East Africa and to a broader socio-economic constituency. It will support major teaching and research programs.

The UCSF-GHS project was conceived originally by global health scientists headed by Dr. Halie Debas in 2003, the chancellor emeritus and a former dean of UCSF School of Medicine. An Eritrean by birth, he had gone on to become distinguished professor and chair of surgery at the UCSF. His familiarity with Africa and its challenges and pressing needs informed his vision and mission. In later years, he served on the board of Aga Khan University. In our discussions, Chuck kept in close contact with Dr. Debas, who was supportive of the progress of our consultations. Halie Debas requested Chuck to invite me to visit the UCSF and its vast network of clinical, educational, and research facilities.

Finding congenial and enabling conditions for collaboration, Chuck Smuckler and I developed a document outlining our partnership, which we forwarded to our respective leadership and governing boards for approval.

Chuck and Stephanie warmly received Nilu and me in San Francisco about a month later. Arrangements for our stay in San Francisco had been made at the sumptuous residential wing of the UCSF Faculty Club. Over the next week, I saw the university's various clinical and educational facilities, including international programs in health care, research, and education facilities and programs. The Medical Library and Learning Center housed a vast collection of print and digital resources, which the university most generously made available online to AKU. Their learning labs and surgical training suites were innovative, and in the years to come, they assisted in creating skills labs at AKU. Their cutting-edge research in molecular biology and immunology also aided AKU's own developments in coming years.

The UCSF-GHS had developed particular expertise in HIV/AIDS, infectious diseases, epidemiology, and health systems research. Their impressive clinical and teaching programs in mental health, cardiology, surgery, and cancer medicine were at the cutting edge of science and art. The new hospital was state of the art in most clinical specialties. The older San Francisco General Hospital and its satellite clinics cared for large numbers of disadvantaged and marginalized populations for a broad spectrum of clinical problems, including mental health, addiction, HIV/AIDS, and infectious diseases, the ideal training ground for family medicine training.

My next few days were a whirlwind of meetings and pleasant reacquaintance with the charming city. I met with Dr. Kevin Grumbach, chair and chief of service of the Department of Family and Community Medicine, who offered departmental support for AKU's family medicine training initiative in East Africa. Dr. James Kahn, the former head of the department, was most helpful and supportive in linking available learning resources and research to support AKU's education endeavours. I was privileged to hold discussions with many department heads and senior faculty, including the Departments of Medicine, Pediatrics, Cardiology, Psychiatry, Surgery, and Infectious Diseases. The cordial exchange of ideas and vision helped us find common cause in the search for excellence in medical education and domains of medical care.

At the UCSF faculty's request, I presented an overview of the mission and vision of Aga Khan University and the Aga Khan Development Network at a luncheon organized for the event. The ensuing discussions resulted in enhancing collaborations and linkages between the two institutions of higher learning and development.

Over the next few months, a detailed memorandum of cooperation between the two institutions was developed. In particular, it provided for faculty development for AKU, faculty exchange programs, research participation, and strengthening clinical collaboration in HIV/AIDS, malaria, and infectious disease management. The affiliation agreement elaborated areas of cooperation, including scientific and academic exchange, faculty development, training, joint research activities, placement of trainees of AKU and the UCSF, and staff appointments.

The UCSF Regents approved it. However, AKU wished to expand collaboration and partnership areas to include a broader range of relationships with the more expansive AKU programs internationally. Over time, an expanded agreement was arrived at by the leaders of the two institutions.

In the coming months, at the formal signing of the agreement between the institutions, the chancellor of AKU, His Highness the Aga Khan, was awarded the Gold Medal of the University of California, its highest honour. The Gold Medal was awarded in recognition of the AKU's and AKDN's wide-ranging multidimensional development enterprises to improve the quality of life in the developing societies of Asia and Africa.

For the PGME program in family medicine, the agreement immediately provided a well-qualified preceptor to the students, a significant addition to our faculty capability. Dr. Stephanie Tache, MD, MPH, joined us and aided in student teaching and supervision.

~৬~

As AKU's faculty numbers and teaching capability grew, we could further faculty development and formalization more rigorously. AKU's Nairobi-based PGME suite of programs was now stable and in high demand. The heads of the East Africa PGME, programs including the family medicine program centred in Tanzania, met monthly to share experience, coordination, faculty appointments, and exchanges and development, as well as set standards and processes for examinations.

The AKUH Nairobi was already making a significant investment in physical and programmatic growth. New diagnostic, training, and staff expansion were propelling the hospital to new heights. The Aga Khan Hospital in Nairobi was formally elevated to the status of university hospital, called the Aga Khan University Hospital, Nairobi (AKUH-N), the second university hospital in AKU's system after the AKUH in Karachi. The AKUH-N Heart and Cancer Centre was soon inaugurated, greatly expanding the high-end service capability and training in cardiology and cancer care. The rapid, carefully planned clinical services progression in Kenya greatly added to the PGME project's vitality.

During the numerous joint planning meetings between AKU and AKHS Kenya, attended by department heads and senior administration staff, the transformation of the Nairobi hospital to a tertiary-care facility and its effects on the remainder of the AKHS were thoroughly aired and harmonized for maximum efficiency and linkages. As in Tanzania, Kenya moved to position education and clinical services enhancement as co-equal missions of the teaching hospital and supporting health centres. At one gathering of the joint group in Nairobi, I presented a paper titled "Integrating Academic Medicine and Clinical Services: Medical Staff and Faculty Development Issues." The process of fostering cooperation between the academic staff and established clinicians in Nairobi – as in Dar-es-Salaam – of full-time faculty and honorary faculty was always fraught with complex challenges and tensions.

In Dar-es-Salaam, a foundation ceremony was held to inaugurate Phase 3 of the Aga Khan Hospital. The commitment to enlarge the hospital's bed capacity and enhance clinical services to address the growing demand in areas such as primary care, kidney dialysis, cancer, heart disease, trauma, neurology, intensive care, pediatrics, and minimally invasive surgery was timely and supportive to the PGME project. Our previous studies and deliberations and reports of local and visiting consultants informed the vision of building local capacity and competence in crucial fields of medical care.

In his remarks at the ceremony, His Highness the Aga Khan underscored the imperative for synergy and mutually supportive medical staff and service development to transform health care to the country's highest standards. In the days ahead, both the Nairobi and the Dar-es-Salaam hospitals worked strenuously towards obtaining Joint Commission International (JCI) accreditation. In the following years, they became the only hospitals in their respective countries to achieve this coveted high-quality recognition.

Enlarging Regional Health Care and Education Networks: Linking Network Levels of Care

The quality development that resulted from embedding postgraduate medical education resulted in a sustained momentum to enhance the quality, relevance, and responsiveness of other AKHS facilities in Kenya and Tanzania. The Aga Khan Hospitals in Mombasa and Kisumu were on the cusp of transforming their standards and scope of services to match their sister hospitals in Dar and Nairobi. At the request of AKHS, I made several visits to both community hospitals and participated in quality and service enhancement planning.

Noorali, the hospital's CEO, received me expectantly at the charming small community hospital entrance in Kisumu. Set in the lake region's hot and humid environment among bougainvillea and jacaranda shrubs, it had a pleasing ambience. In the few years since Noorali's arrival from the Prince Aly Khan Hospital in Bombay to take charge of the management of the hospital, he had streamlined and harmonized patient care processes. These upgraded information systems tracked practical utilization and management data. He strove to organize the medical staff into a progressive professional body.

In our discussions, I gathered that the hospital's main challenge was recruiting and retaining and motivating professional staff, improving physician performance through participation in medical audits, improving clinical practice standards through continuous professional development (CPD), and enhancing professional accountability. These challenges echoed our experiences in the other network hospitals in Dar-es-Salaam and Nairobi, where a concerted effort demonstrated an impact on medical care quality and effectiveness. I found the small medical staff body ready to commit to enhancing their professional competence and joint participation in uplifting the hospital's performance and profile. I assured them that the introduction of PGME programs in Nairobi and Dar-es-Salaam augmented AKU's and AKHS's vision of supporting quality improvement throughout the AKHS network by sharing knowledge and best practices. It enabled and enhanced professional engagements and satisfaction and promoted the development of an effective referral network.

The AKH, Kisumu, was initially opened in 1951 as a dispensary and maternity home. In 1952, inpatients were added, quickly growing to enlarge the hospital capacity, most recently to seventy-six beds. Located in Kisumu on Lake Victoria's shores in Kenya, it serves a large urban, semi-urban, and rural population.

Noorali arranged for me to visit a recently opened satellite clinic of the Kisumu Aga Khan Hospital in Kisii. Kisii town, now a bustling urban centre in the South Nyanza region close to Lake Victoria's humid shores, caters to agriculture, tourism, construction, and small-scale industry. The new Aga Khan Health Centre was well chosen and planned. It also had a few inpatient beds and undoubtedly had the potential to provide linked service with the AKH Kisumu.

While I was meeting with the clinical officer in charge of the centre, he asked if I could examine a young man who appeared to be very ill. "Yes," I said, "I'd be happy to."

A health centre attendant walked with me to a walled compound behind the centre and knocked on a single-storey home door. It was one unit in a housing complex of about eight or ten units. I noticed that the housing complex was located in a peaceful compound adjoining an imposing two-storey *Jamatkhanna*, a house of prayer of the local Ismaili community.

The door was opened by a tired-looking, middle-aged woman with streaks of grey hair, wearing a long traditional dress. The attendant said I was a visiting doctor and had come to see her son. The woman greeted me and looked somewhat surprised but appreciative. She took me into her small but clean flat and showed me into a small bedroom towards the house's back. I saw a young man lying in bed, partially covered by a light blanket.

At first glance, I could see he looked ill, thin, with a gaunt face and yellow eyes. I softly introduced myself, said I was a visiting physician, and asked if I could examine him. He nodded his emaciated face. I got some history from the anxious woman, his mother, who poured out the story of her thirty-year-old son's long illness over the last several months, and how he continued to get weaker, turned away food, and mostly lay in bed. She said she usually saw the clinical officer at the health centre; once, several months before, she had taken her son to see a doctor at the AKH Kisumu. Several tests had been done at that time, and he was given some pills.

As I examined the pale young man, I noticed all the characteristic signs of advanced liver disease: jaundice, distended abdomen full of fluid, all clinical signs suggesting liver failure. I checked his heart and lungs with the stethoscope I had borrowed from the centre. It was evident this young man had advanced liver disease, most probably caused by a viral infection, like the hepatitis B virus, common in the region. Specific vaccines and drugs for the treatment of hepatitis

B were emerging in the developed countries but were still prohibitively expensive for most developing countries. Viral infections of the liver also predispose to an increased risk of liver cancer.

I spent some time talking to the young man and his mother. I explained that the young man needed to have some more tests and be in a hospital. I said I would write a detailed note to a consulting physician in Kisumu, recommending transfer to the Aga Khan University Hospital in Nairobi for further tests and treatments. I gave her my letter and a copy for the health centre file.

As I was doing this, two women visited the flat. They had seen me enter the patient's flat from the *Jamatkhanna*, which they were diligently cleaning at that time. They were very kind and visited the mother frequently to support her and her sick son. They insisted on taking me to lunch at their nearby flat. I learned a good deal about the state of health and support of the communities in the Kisii region and was happy to know that the new health centre and the back-up support provided by the AKH Kisumu were responsive and growing.

I completed my work at the centre and returned to Kisumu late that evening. The following day, I met with Noorali to share with him my impressions and suggestions. We discussed the potentials the Kisii Health Centre offered in enhancing service and training in the district. Noorali suggested that I meet the medical director of Nyanza Regional Hospital to learn more about the Nyanza Region's health care challenges. The AKH had a good working relationship with the Nyanza Hospital.

The medical director of the hospital, Dr. Odhiambo, was an experienced general surgeon who greeted me cheerfully. He showed me the extensive facilities of the public hospital. Like most regional hospitals in the East Africa region, it was overcrowded and usually served as the hospital of last resort for the vast lake region of Kenya. Many cases presenting and admitted to the hospital were preventable diseases or treatable diseases, often showing late in an advanced state or improperly treated.

On the wards, I saw cases of severe hookworm anemia, pneumonia, and bilharzia – an infection caused by a burrowing parasite common in the lake region. The disease often affects the urinary bladder or the digestive system and liver, and in later stages, it results in severe damage to these systems. Very busy surgical, maternity, and children's clinics and wards characterized the hospital's work in confronting common diseases and surgical problems.

I outlined our family medicine training initiative and our desire to enroll suitable young physicians from the region into the program, which he recognized as an essential unmet training issue in medicine. Dr. Odhiambo was thrilled and supportive of this educational initiative and undertook to spread the word to his staff and colleagues.

I happened to mention that I was born in this hospital more than five decades ago. He was quite excited and took me to their records room. There were countless manila paper files on shelves and desks in the medical records room. He talked to one of the records clerks, who brought out a dusty, faded register from a back room and fingered her way down the names recorded for the month and year of my birth. I was astonished when she pointed to an entry with a name: father's name, mother's name, the attending doctor. There were my parents' names in faded but readable cursive script. The attending physician was noted as Dr. Wiseman, a missionary doctor, whose name I recall my father mentioning to me. I was moved by this visual notation of my birth and amazed at how well the old birth records had been preserved since colonial times. I was still very young when the family then moved to Nairobi, where I grew up.

In years to come, the Nyanza Regional Hospital became a partnering institution with Columbia University in the U.S. in a surgical training program, which still flourishes to the best of my knowledge.

~ ⁹⸳⁶ ~

The AKH Mombasa, located in the busy Indian Ocean port city, also has a long history of service to the community. It provides clinical care, advanced diagnostic services, and a comprehensive suite of general medical services. Mary McCluskey, an Englishwoman and a seasoned administrator, served as the CEO. She had previously worked with AKHS in Central Asia for several years.

An engaging lady, she had a progressive vision for the future of the AKH Mombasa and medical services priorities and community needs. Mary proudly showed me a recently renovated Doctor's Plaza, close to the hospital, which also housed some diagnostic facilities and services such as dietitian and physiotherapy. The hospital users were primarily private and corporate patients. However, it recently extended its satellite services into the less prosperous coastal area around Mombasa and engaged in some primary health care initiatives in partnership with the AKF. Dr. Salim Sohani, a CHS preceptor from my time at AKU Karachi, enthusiastically headed this initiative. He eagerly filled me in on challenges facing the AKHS health network in the area. Salim had obtained additional community health qualifications from a reputable public health school in the U.S.

The AKH, however, faced stiff competition from two or three other private hospitals that competed for similar groups of users.

Over lunch, at the old and famed and now somewhat dilapidated Mombasa Club, Mary described her vision and goals for the hospital's future development. She was eager that the AKH Mombasa be linked to AKU's PGME programs and teaching and learning resources. She was keen that professional development possibilities further energize the medical staff through AKU's regional presence. Over coffee, sitting on the faded and threadbare upholstery of the club on the veranda overlooking the sparklingly blue Indian Ocean, I re-enforced AKU's commitment to enhance education linkages, shared experience, and vision for the network CME efforts and staff development.

Later, I recounted the vision, goals, and objectives of the family medicine specialty program to the hospital's resident medical officers. Some of them appeared keen to follow that training and career pathway. Also, education exchanges with AKU's teaching hospitals took a significant centre stage in our conversations.

In my visits, I found an eagerness to modernize and transform care quality to the highest standards. The management and the medical staff accepted recommendations to establish regular continuing professional development, clinical audits, and outcomes research, as they worked to benchmark quality to international standards.

Both the AKH Kisumu and AKH Mombasa achieved the demanding ISO 9001 standards to recognize their processes and exacting standards of care outcomes. These hospitals were later linked in a referral system to the AKUH Nairobi for advanced care modalities and fruitful educational exchanges.

While in Mombasa, I took the opportunity of meeting with the medical staff of the Coast General Hospital, a massive public hospital. The Coast General Hospital is a teaching hospital and a regional hub of referral for complex medical problems from Kenya's Coast Region. Several young interns and junior doctors expressed interest in considering family medicine as a career choice and requested information on our program.

Initiating School Health Programs: Prototype for Service and Research

Mary had made arrangements for me to meet with the principal and senior administrative officers of the newly opened Aga Khan Academy (AKA) in Mombasa. The academy wished to establish high-quality school health services on the campus. They had sought some input from exclusive private U.S. academies for their school health development; Mary had suggested a consultation with the new AKU family medicine program as an alternative source of advice and guidance.

The academy was the first in a series of academies that the AKDN planned to establish in various cities in several countries in South Asia, Central Asia, the Middle East, and Africa. The academies were envisioned to be co-educational, non-denominational day and residential schools. The academies' vision was to develop ethical, public-minded students who possess a pluralistic outlook. Its curricular and co-curricular activities work to educate influential homegrown leaders who are engaged in their local communities and are aware of the implications of their actions. I met with the institution's leaders on the Mombasa Academy's stunning campus overlooking the Indian Ocean, previously a renowned Oceanic Hotel site.

I saw this as an opportunity to develop a high-quality school health program prototype since there were few models of excellence in comprehensive school health in developing countries. I realized the establishment of a program that served not only to cater to the school population's medical and health needs but also to extend its health education and school health research into its liberal curriculum would add value to such an endeavour.

A well-planned school health service could screen, stabilize, or treat pupils, thereby enabling some potentially well-qualified but medically disadvantaged applicants to enroll in the school. Pupils handicapped by treatable or modifiable disorders such as asthma, epilepsy, autism, visual or hearing problems, or other conditions could have a fair chance of entry into the progressive and prestigious educational institution if their condition is effectively controlled and managed. The academies purported to "financially needs-blind" and based their admission policy entirely on the applicant's merit. Besides, the academies' curriculum called for research projects and community outreach that promoted the public good in various ways.

A very productive series of meetings resulted in the Health and Wellness Centre's (HWC) eventual establishment at the Mombasa Academy and a long-term vision for health care and health education for the AKA network. In years to come, I served as a medical advisor and consultant to future academies established in Maputo, Mozambique, and Dacca, Bangladesh.

Integrating Service and Education: Closing the Circle

Back in Dar-es-Salaam, the continuing challenge of intertwining medical education and the development of quality health services continued.

Over the previous year, the AKH in Dar had made concerted and vigorous efforts at reforming its service and organizational plan. CEO Sulaiman Shahabuddin's initial priority was to staunch the financial losses, primarily incurred through deceitful or improper practices of a few hospital employees, irregular supplies and purchase contracts, and other questionable practices in several departments. An invigorated AKHS Tanzania board and an intensified regional AKHS cooperation and participation reinforced the oversight mechanism. Additionally, rationalizing clinical services development to better competitively position the hospital and health centres to serve its users' needs and support PGME programs were beginning to show positive results. The PGME project, with its considerable sway in demanding demonstrable quality improvement in clinical standards and practice, was an essential factor in uplifting and broadening clinical services. AKU and AKHS East Africa increasingly pursued a vigorous policy of linking, synergizing, and supporting regional development through programs like group purchasing, human resources training and exchanges, benchmarking quality standards, educational seminars and conferences, and networking in all areas of cooperation deemed beneficial.

In the early years of AKU in Pakistan, Sulaiman was a seasoned manager in AKU's Material Management Department. He was later seconded as the acting CEO of the AKH Nairobi. He was a thoughtful, amiable, and diligent manager who had worked his way up in the network. He was rigorously detail-oriented, cost-conscious, and dedicated to quality improvement in the system. He fully appreciated and supported the role of health sciences education in quality enhancement. In years to come, he became the regional CEO for AKHS East Africa as the network continued to expand.

The international Aga Khan University had also transferred the leadership at the highest level over the previous year. Shamsh Kassim-Lakha had served at the helm of the development of AKU for decades, lastly as president of the university.

His decision to step down from that role was accepted by the Aga Khan, AKU's founder and chancellor. Shamsh later assumed leadership of the University of Central Asia (UCA), another major AKDN enterprise. Firoz Rasul was appointed president of AKU.

Firoz, an engineer with advanced management training, a successful business-man, a savvy entrepreneur, and a community leader, brought a fresh impetus to the global development of AKU. His boundless energy, new insights, and unwavering commitment to quality, synergy, and impact set the university on an expansion trajectory. The university chancellor and a diverse international board continued to set high expectations and vision for the university. AKU's tempo of development was picking up pace in East Africa, particularly in health care and health sciences education. Detailed studies were underway to establish critical new programs, faculties, schools, and institutes.

I remember spending considerable time in meetings and discussions with visit-ing consultants and planners in my office on developing long-term vision and strategies to address the many needs and competing priorities in human resource development for the East Africa region. I fondly recall spending most of a pleasant day and a home dinner with David Fraser visiting from the U.S.

David had previously served in the Aga Khan Secretariat in France as the Social Welfare Department head. His Highness had now charged him with organizing a high-level panel of AKDN leaders under a higher education forum structure to harmonize and leverage the network's varied education programs. I was intrigued by this notion and shared my thoughts on developing countries' critical educa-tional needs, now and into the future.

Over the past year, I had succeeded in taking over a sizable two-storey building as the permanent Office of Postgraduate Medical Education. This substantial build-ing, previously occupied by a South African health insurance company, satisfied the growing and complex requirements of the PGME program. I had committed to the HEAC and the faculty and students a suitable physical space and presence in the myriad administrative, teaching, and support functions of PGME. I found our earlier space inadequate for the purpose. We needed lecture and seminar facilities, faculty meeting and common rooms, library and learning facilities, and offices. As part of the Phase 3 campus development plan, we had specified the growing requirements of the PGME programs in the years to come. For now, however, the PGME needed to have a credible presence and efficiency.

The latest addition to AKU's graduate education under the umbrella of the Tanzania Institute of Higher Education (TIHE) was the Institute of Education Development (IED), located at a distant larger facility. The IED's director, Gordon Clark, was a dynamic Australian who had previously worked at the IED in Pakistan. The IED's mission was to advance the training and management competence of education leaders, administrators, and teachers through a demanding training program that culminated in a master of education (M.Ed.) degree.

Both Gordon and the ANS director, Khairunissa Damani, had requested my department's input into the refinement and mentoring of the basic health sciences component of their respective programs' curricula. This was a pleasure since it enabled us to share knowledge and best practices in health sciences, teaching, and learning within the three units of the AKU-TIHE. AKU's presence was now building a firmer and visible presence in Tanzania and could collaborate more effectively with Kenya- and Uganda-based programs.

A Tradition of Service: Revitalizing Primary Medical Centres

A network of primary medical centres (PMC) has provided essential primary care in many Tanzania and Kenya centres for over seventy years. Over the past several years, efforts were made by the AKHS-T directed at improving the effectiveness of these centres.

In Tanzania, the major centres originally functioned as maternity homes and later expanded to provide preventive and curative services to children and adults of both genders and all age groups. Studies had underlined concerns about the costs, quality, effectiveness, management support, and relevance to the population's health. However, their long history of service, few local alternative sources of care, and long familiarity with the communities gave these centres a valuable role in the local health care scene. Also, interpreted correctly, they were close to home community care sites, first contact care for a wide range of undifferentiated clinical presentations, interventions like childhood immunizations and maternal and child care. Committed volunteers locally oversaw them. If reoriented and improved, the PMCs could serve as important sites for education in primary care medicine, for they bore witness to transitions in community health patterns, patterns of utilization and demands.

At the AKHS's and AKU's encouragement, I undertook several visits to the main centres located in Morogoro, Dodoma, Iringa, and Mwanza. The objective in mind was to provide a report on a paradigm and programmatic shift that better aligned AKHS facilities with modern, affordable health care delivery methods, aiming for standards of excellence in service and education.

AKHS had also enlisted Ismaili health management volunteers from Canada, the U.K., and the U.S. who were keen to contribute to improving health care and accountability in the PMCs. On one occasion, we visited at least two centres together.

The Dodoma local PMC committee's volunteer chairman was a middle-aged businessman, who received me enthusiastically and showed me the centre under his charge. He and his team were eager for the embryonic academic Department of Family Medicine's anticipated input to revitalize the health centre. My concern was the level of input that may be necessary to make a meaningful improvement in the quality of care.

The PMC was located in a sturdy old building on a busy street, not far from the local train and bus station. Dodoma was the designated capital of Tanzania and was in a rapid growth phase. One medical doctor, assisted by two clinical officers and two nurses, saw the bulk of patients gathered in the large, open waiting area. A small in-house pharmacy, a small laboratory, a space for childhood vaccinations, a four-bed inpatient unit, and an office for the manager and accountant constituted the PMC. This was the typical structure of the PMCs, except Mwanza and Iringa had small surgical operating suites as well, which were underused because of the unavailability of trained staff and shortage of equipment. Mwanza and Iringa centres had a more extensive but underutilized inpatient capacity.

The medical doctor at the Dodoma centre was a tired-looking, balding, middle-aged man who had worked with the PMC for over fifteen years. Previously, he worked for several years in a public hospital. I sat down with him and collegially discussed his work, his level of satisfaction, and the problems he faced in his daily medical work. He showed me the register of the types of clinical situations commonly encountered at the centre. He frankly expressed some frustrations he and his colleagues faced in their work, including a shortage of secondary-care public or private facilities to accept very sick patients, a chronic insufficiency of drugs and supplies, and the unavailability of access to up-to-date knowledge and guidelines in managing difficult medical problems.

It became clear to me that while the centre provided some commendable care for common conditions such as malaria, diarrhoeal diseases, and respiratory infections under difficult circumstances, its capacity to deal competently with a broad spectrum of other medical problems was severely limited by a multitude of factors, including knowledge gaps, inadequate diagnostic facilities, and insufficient support systems.

I saw an emaciated child with a distended abdomen, thin limbs, and thinning hair – all signs to support a diagnosis of malnutrition, a powerful corollary of poverty. The mother carrying the child sat patiently, waiting for her turn to consult the medical and nursing staff. I felt a twinge of sympathy, but also a sense of helplessness since this child was one of many testifying silently to the more significant underlying systemic failures of social and health care responses in resource-constrained countries. There appeared to be systemic inefficiencies at all levels of care – primary, secondary, and tertiary. The AKHS-PMCs operated in a milieu of social, economic, and policy environment outside their direct control.

My visits to Morogoro revealed similar findings. The Morogoro centre's medical officer, John Rwegahsha, a Makerere graduate, was a young physician several years into service as a general medical practitioner. I had considerable opportunity to watch him; I was impressed by his desire to learn and his attempts to apply modern knowledge to his practice. I discussed with him AKU's program in family medicine, and he was keen to apply. He applied to the PGME program. After going through the rigorous selection process consisting of an entrance examination and a series of interviews, he entered into the four-year postgraduate training program.

John qualified for a master of medicine degree (M. Med) in later years and was one of my most promising students. He went on to obtain further training in diseases of the digestive system in South Africa and, in later years, joined the faculty of Muhimbili University College of Health Sciences (MUCHS) in Dar-es-Salaam. He was amongst those of the family medicine residency program who went on to share their knowledge and leadership qualities with a range of organizations in health care in the years to come.

My visits to other PMCs were equally telling. The Mwanza PMC was perhaps more advanced in its organization and clinical capacity. The local health committee took considerable interest in the management and oversight of the centre. There existed a loose referral relationship to the regional hospital in Mwanza.

Following consultations with the local clinical staff, managers, committee members, and other health care facilities, I presented a detailed report to the AKHS administration and board titled *"Strategic Review of the Aga Khan Primary Medical Centers in Tanzania: In Search of an Effective Health Care and Education Model."*

I felt it incumbent upon me to press to bridge academic medicine with population health in Tanzania. The goal of the AKHS review was to serve more people well and meet more community needs. Numerous deficiencies were noted in our detailed review. These included levels of staff training, motivation, and supervision, poor recordkeeping, incomplete health data, weak drug and vaccine supply chains, repair or replacement of equipment, and inadequate financial accounting and management processes.

My report raised several critical questions: How can medicine be made more humane, patient-centred, effective, and widely available at low cost? Can the science, concepts, and essential family medicine values – safe, timely, effective, efficient, and equitable care – be applied on a wide scale in a resource-poor and fragmented health delivery system? How can medical education be redesigned to influence and reorient public health care?

At His Highness the Aga Khan's request, Gijs Walraven, the head of health at the Aga Khan Secretariat in Paris, established a small group of experts to comprehensively study and propose solutions to the myriad issues facing PMCs that impeded optimizing and reorienting the centres in Tanzania. Sulaiman obtained the assistance of a volunteer with experience and skills in finance, accounting, and management to determine some intractable problems that resulted in the less-than-optimum quality of care delivered at the PMCs. The three of us worked hard to review and compile studies and data that assessed the goals, strengths, weaknesses, opportunities, barriers to improvement, and relevance to the larger AKDN mission and strategy. We also wished to link future developments to the Tanzania National Health Sector Development Plan collaboratively. The report ultimately resulted in pilot projects at two PMCs and led to substantive uplift of service quality and professional practice at the PMCs.

Advancing International Partnerships: North Africa and the Middle East

My time in Tanzania afforded me many occasions to travel locally and internationally in the furtherance of the AKDN's mission of linking medical education with health systems development, improving population health and quality of life, and making medicine and health care more humane and compassionate, accessible, and equitable.

One day I received an invitation from the dean of medicine of Suez Canal University in Egypt to attend a conference on problem-based learning. Ismailia, a city in northeastern Egypt, is situated on the west bank of the Suez Canal. It is located halfway between Port Said to the north and Suez to the south. The canal widens at that point to include Lake Timsah, one of the Bitter Lakes linked by the canal. It was founded in 1863 during the Suez Canal construction by Khedive Ismail the Magnificent, after whom the city is named. From our hotel, we could see the shipping traffic traverse the famous landmark canal.

Suez Canal University, established in 1974, like Aga Khan University, had established special units for research, education, and community development. Its focus was to seek problem-based solutions to local problems and to engage communities in its search.

The conference allowed me to share experiences and program information with local educators, researchers, and faculty from several Egyptian and Sudanese universities attending the conference. There were remarkable similarities in the challenges facing higher education institutions in developing countries concerned about community development through contextual educational endeavours.

I remember well the few pleasant days spent in Port Said, a city at the northern end of the Suez Canal on the Mediterranean Sea. The city was established in 1859 during the building of the Suez Canal. It boasts numerous old houses with grand balconies, giving the city a distinctive look. Since its foundation, people of all nationalities and religions have been moving into the city, and each community brought in its own customs, cuisine, beliefs, and architecture. A concrete lighthouse dates from the canal's opening in 1869. On the waterfront was Simon Artzt, a former department store. Now disused, the art deco building offers a glimpse of the past, to when Port Said was a cosmopolitan trading hub. A visit to a local public health centre gave some idea of the Egyptian health care system, which has made significant advances by emphasizing primary care at all levels, especially for women and children.

Nilu and I took the opportunity to visit several historical sites in Egypt, especially the Al Azhar Park in Cairo developed by the Aga Khan Trust for Culture (AKTC). The lush urban park is located near the historic district of Darb al-Ahmar in east Cairo on the grounds of what was once a five-hundred-year-old garbage dump. The AKTC's enterprise resulted in the revival and upgrade of local artisan skills, area rehabilitation, microfinance, and health and education support. It generated employment and economic opportunities. The designers insisted on integrating Islamic landscape traditions in their design and greenery choices, hence preserving a historical legacy. The American University of Cairo offered its nursery for propagating the flora of the park. Archeological involvement included rehabilitating a twelfth-century Ayyubid wall and revitalizing the neighbouring Darb al-Ahmar area. The area's population, one of Cairo's poorest, lived under inadequate sanitation, insalubrious living conditions, and extreme poverty. They lacked education, hygiene, and access to basic health care. The AKTC's leadership in building partnerships and collaborations with public and private NGOs continues a trajectory towards socio-economic progress, including access to microfinance, education, and primary health care projects.

In Luxor and Aswan, we were privileged to see programs in other development sectors initiated by the AKDN.

There were calls for travel to other localities in the Middle East and Central Asia. Working holidays in Syria, Jordan, Lebanon, and Morocco reaffirmed the need for progressive and supportive knowledge-exchange partnerships and collaborations, with the view to augment the pool of expertise relevant to raising the quality of life in many developing societies confronted with enormous socio-economic challenges.

One memorable journey involved a visit to Salamiyah, an ancient city in Syria. It was known during Babylonian times as far back as 3500 BC. It is a city with a long history of connection with the family of the Aga Khan. The city is an agricultural centre, and before the Syrian Civil War, it was a centre of progressive agriculture-based economy and harmony. Our visit was warmly received by local leaders, who had organized themselves in various social and economic assistance programs. The city's Health Committee was pleased to brief me on their community's health issues and were keen to obtain assistance in professional education and health management strategies. After a couple of pleasant days spent with a warm and welcoming community, during which I shared some guidelines on community health screening and health education, we spent several days in the historic city of Damascus, the oldest continuously inhabited city in the world.

Mountains and Medicine: Observations and Tentative Steps

An invitation from the resident representatives of the AKDN in Kyrgyzstan and Tajikistan offered me an opportunity to comprehend development challenges confronting some isolated and mountainous regions of Central Asia. On learning of my planned visit to Central Asia, Gijs Walraven, the director of health at Aiglemont, requested me to provide independent observations and recommendations to AKHS in its plans for health advancement in these countries in which the AKDN was increasing its involvement.

Following spending a few pleasant days in Turkey, Nilu and I travelled to Bishkek in Kyrgyzstan. Bishkek is a city of wide boulevards and marble-faced public buildings, combined with numerous Soviet-style apartment blocks surrounding interior courtyards. Originally, it was a caravan rest stop on one of the Silk Road branches through the Tian Shan range.

The collapse of the former Soviet Union in 1991 accelerated a downward spiral of deterioration and underfunding of social networks in a number of ex-Soviet republics, amongst them the landlocked mountainous countries of Tajikistan and Kyrgyzstan. The social decline was compounded in Tajikistan by a bitter and prolonged civil war.

The AKDN diplomatic representative, Noorjehan Mawani, a Canadian, had arranged for me to visit and assess the public and private health facilities. The Aga Khan Foundation's CEO Shinan Kassam, another Canadian with considerable experience and training in development issues, invited my opinion and input into reviewing and strengthening the AKF's role in health sector development in Kyrgyzstan. Our long drives and an occasional helicopter flight into the rural districts revealed staggering vistas of mountain peaks and valleys, plateaus, bare grasslands, crystal-clear rivers and streams, and scattered villages. Tea and meal breaks at tiny tea houses introduced us to the local folks' warmth and generosity, many dressed in the region's traditional colourful attire. Poverty and privations of nomadic life were clear to see, as were the people's generally cheerful disposition. The surreal sights, scant bucolic populations, the occasional battered Soviet-era vehicles, yurts, and the pastoral animal husbandry evoked scenes from 1950s-era movies, except this was all too real and present.

The AKDN and the AKF worked to support the Ministry of Health's health sector reform efforts. They focused on three essential domains: rural development, public health initiatives, and early childhood development. The program objectives included village-level preventive and health promotive initiatives, enhancing health professional capacity within the ministry, and influencing policy, practice, and health metrics in the ministry's programs. The public health component focused primarily on health education, healthy schools, and maternal and child health. It also targeted the prevention of deficiency disorders, such as iodine deficiency, anemia, and nutritional disorders, and preventing and combating communicable diseases, such as brucellosis (acquired from goats and sheep) and diarrhoeal diseases due to poor sanitation.

A general survey of the AKF's pilot efforts to harmonize with and add to the government's efforts to address some critical public health concerns in rural areas was commendable. My observations harkened back to the experiences in Pakistan, India, Syria, and East Africa that were also characterized by poverty and poor infrastructures, but in vastly differing terrains.

Kyrgyzstan, a landlocked country with a population of over five million is rated as the second poorest country amongst WHO-Europe Office area of operation, with a GDP in 2000 of $1,870. It has a high infant mortality rate – around fifty per one thousand live births – and a life expectancy of approximately fifty-five years. Kyrgyzstan's history spans a variety of cultures and empires. It has been at the crossroads of several great civilizations as part of the Silk Road and other commercial routes. Soviet power was initially established in 1919. During the 1920s, Kyrgyzstan developed considerably in cultural, educational, and social life. A high degree of national literacy was attained and public health services were plentiful, based on the Soviet models. Today, 25 percent of the population lives below the poverty line.

Geographically, Kyrgyzstan is landlocked between Kazakhstan, China, Tajikistan, and Uzbekistan. The Tian Shan range's mountainous region covers over 80 percent of the country, leaving little available area for agriculture.

I initially visited several health and education institutions in Bishkek, where I was received politely and respectfully, if somewhat reservedly. From various leaders and stakeholders, I gathered the organizational and practice norms under which they operated – much of it inherited from the Soviet era – the challenges and professional concerns, and their hesitancy in proposing constructive reorientation to government authorities.

The organization of the health system had both strengths and weaknesses. On the positive side, the system was – and still is – organized by levels of care and intended to cover the entire population, including remote villages, through a progressive referral mechanism. However, the system was based on extensive networks of hospitals, "Polyclinics," and easy availability of human resources, especially physicians. Narrowly trained specialist physicians, who had a poor understanding, experience, and involvement in comprehensive clinical and primary care, served as principal primary medical care providers. Hence, medical care tended to be episodic and fragmented and lacked continuity.

Recently proclaimed health sector reform plans are intended to strengthen public health measures, such as immunization, maternal and child health, school health, and environmental sanitation. The National Health Reform strategy also encouraged public–private partnerships and a commitment to rationalizing hospital infrastructure and developing appropriately trained human resources. One significant component of human resources development involved retraining large numbers of unemployed or under-employed physician specialists in becoming family and primary care physicians. There is increasing recognition of the inherent need to provide preventive and curative care closer to the rural villages and townships that are home to over 70 percent of the population. Urban health care is delivered through a network of Polyclinics, staffed by medical and surgical specialists who seem to lack adequate facilities for their work. Increasingly, "Family Medicine Centres" are located within the Polyclinics in urban areas.

Several public and private organizations provided these physician reorientation and retraining efforts, but they were disjointed and uncoordinated in their actions and lacked overarching tactical and strategic guidelines. Some of these efforts were funded by foreign aid agencies and development financing from the Asian Development Bank, the Swiss government, and other multilateral funders.

Major cities like Bishkek are supplied with specialist public hospitals and a few private hospitals. I visited the Kyrgyzstan State Medical Academy and had an opportunity to observe its undergraduate and postgraduate education programs. The academy trains a large number of local and international students. The students have a choice of learning in Russian, Kyrghyz, or English. The library and learning resources in English are scant and out of date. There were students from India, Pakistan, Bangladesh, the Middle East, and, oddly, a few from Germany. The physical facilities are rambling and run-down, with long dimly lit corridors leading to classrooms and basic sciences laboratories.

The vice-rector for education was a balding, slightly portly, and friendly middle-aged man. We had a productive dialogue. He asked if I would consent to provide a lecture to the hospital and the academy staff. A couple of days later, I gave a presentation on "Advances in Preventive Cardiology," a topic I thought relevant given the burgeoning rise in cardiovascular disease in the region.

I later visited a second city in Kyrgyzstan, Osh, a town located in the Fergana Valley, a large triangular valley that spreads across Kyrgyzstan, Uzbekistan, and Tajikistan. Osh lies close to the Uzbekistan border and has a significant Uzbek population. It is the oldest city in the country, estimated to be over two thousand years. It was a major market along the Silk Road. In 1990, ethnic tensions between the Uzbeks and Kyrgyz led to many deaths.

After meeting some out-of-work doctors seeking further training and employment opportunities, I visited one or two health clinics. There is an excellent Aga Khan School in Osh, which had established programs to upgrade teacher training in modern teaching methods.

Our trip to Naryn was a happy one since it enabled us to see an important AKDN initiative's rapid progress. Naryn, a small town on the Naryn River banks, is also located on one of the Silk Road branches. It is the main transport link to the Torugart Pass to China. It was designated as the Kyrgyz campus of the University of Central Asia (UCA), then under construction.

The UCA, the first internationally chartered institution of higher education, was founded in 2000 by His Highness the Aga Khan and the governments of Tajikistan, Kyrgyzstan, and Kazakhstan. The UCA is a not-for-profit, secular institution under the sponsorship of the AKDN. The university was created to be a catalyst for social and economic development in the region's mountain societies. Among its schools and faculties, research institutes focus on mountain societies research, public policy and administration, civil society initiative, and cultural, heritage, and humanities units.

We flew from Bishkek to Dushanbe, the capital city of Tajikistan. It is close to the Fann Mountains, which have snow-capped peaks that rise to over five thousand metres. The landlocked country is bordered by Afghanistan, Uzbekistan, Kyrgyzstan, and China. It has a similar history to its neighbour Kyrgyzstan and has been ruled by numerous empires and dynasties. The region was later conquered by the Russian empire and subsequently by the Soviet Union. Independence in 1991 was followed immediately by a fierce civil war that raged from 1992 to 1997, resulting in a regression of civil order, authoritarian leadership, and political repression. It is estimated that over half a million people were displaced during the brutal war, and sixty thousand died, many of starvation.

More than 70 percent of the population is rural, and the population is young. It is among the poorest counties in the world, with a GDP of $1,260 in 2000.

Dushanbe has a population of ethnic Tajiks, Uzbeks, Kazaks, and Russians. Its population is served by many public general hospitals, specialty hospitals, numerous universities, and technical colleges. The AKDN and AKHS offices facilitated my visits and meetings with universities, hospitals, and health facilities.

I found a familiar pattern in social and health infrastructure to the one in Kyrgyzstan. The Tajik Medical Academy admitted a large number of local and high-paying private international students.

The patterns of health-related issues followed the trajectory of rapidly rising chronic diseases, side by side with the prevalent infectious and environmental disorders. There was a noticeable mismatch between the skills, attitudes, and knowledge of the health professionals and disease profiles and distribution, both in urban and rural areas. Projects to retrain and retool professionals and facilities were beginning to sprout in an uneven, poorly coordinated manner. Gynecologists, surgeons, pediatricians, and psychiatrists were undertaking intensive six- to twelve-month training in the essential concepts of family medicine and primary care.

My discussions with the director of a conversion program were fascinating. A passionate family physician, who obtained her family and community medicine training in Germany, led a small group of doctors who provided the education curriculum in primary care. She was convinced of the merit of their training methods. Still, she recognized the many inconsistencies and inadequacies and available resources in the inherited fossilized health care system, which was challenging to reorient to address the current needs and standards.

A postgraduate medical institute was charged with the overall responsibility to provide specialist medical education, including a recently added family medicine specialty. It was an old, sprawling complex of buildings, laboratories, classrooms, and dormitories. I did not get the opportunity to meet with the institute's leaders but obtained a general sense of the institute's work from some students and lecturers.

An area of particular interest for me is the Gorno-Badakhshan Autonomous Oblast (GBOA), dominated by mountain ranges, predominantly the Pamirs in the south. This area occupies about 45 percent of Tajikistan's total land area but accounts for only about 3 percent of Tajikistan's population. Only about 1 to 2 percent of the land is suitable for agricultural use. The large geography, low population density, harsh winter conditions, and limited transportation systems are challenging considerations in planning health services.

The AKDN arranged a special permit for us and rented a large Toyota 4WD to drive us from Dushanbe to Khorog. It was one of the most exhilarating and hair-raising drives of our lives. It was reminiscent of the drive from Islamabad to Gilgit we had taken many years ago in Pakistan.

The Pamir Highway, an ancient Silk Road route, was built during the Soviet era and connected Afghanistan, Uzbekistan, and Tajikistan to Osh in Kyrgyzstan. It is sometimes called the "cocaine highway" because it is a route for illegal drug trafficking. Some part of the road is paved, but most of the road is unpaved and gravelled, damaged and pot-holed by erosion, earthquakes, landslides, and avalanches. The landscape varies from dry plains bordered by high mountains to narrow roads hugging cliff ledges that dropped down hundreds of metres to turbulent rivers below. Small villages made interesting stops for lunch and tea. We could see the rocky landscape of Afghanistan on the other side of the Panj River. It took us over twelve hours to reach the stunning settings of Khorog bordered by peaks of the Pamirs.

The Serena Hotel in Khorog was an elegant and charming little hotel, designed in the manner of a traditional Pamiri home. It was a welcome sanctuary for the next few days. With views of the Ghunt River and breathtaking mountain landscapes bordering Afghanistan, it is an enterprise of the Aga Khan Fund for Economic Development (AKFED) to promote social and economic development through fostering sustainable tourism.

The town of Khorog has a population of about thirty thousand and sits at over 2,200 metres (6,560 feet) elevation in the Pamir mountains at the Ghunt and Panj Rivers' confluence. It is sometimes referred to as the "roof of the world." Several bridges, built by the AKDN, connect Tajikistan to the Afghanistan regions, as these areas are considered part of Badakhshan, with common histories and peoples.

The AKDN/AKHS offices in Khorog were established to support the large, isolated region's economic and social well-being through multiple mutually supportive enterprises, with an early emphasis on education and health. The two-storey office building housed the Health Professional Development Centre (HPDC), consisting of a computer laboratory, a modern library, meeting rooms, and staff offices displaying several GBAO and Tajikistan district maps. The maps were pock-marked with tiny coloured flags that indicated programmatic activities in primary health care and public health projects.

The manager of the AKHS, an Indian national with excellent community health credentials, provided an illuminating overview of their interest areas, areas of putative collaborations through active public–private partnerships or under development. He informed me of the Aga Khan Foundation and AKHS-driven health programs emphasizing preventive and primary care, a shift from normative hospital-based curative care of the Soviet era to community-based essential health services. Phase 2 of the plan was expected to expand the program to other remote valleys and shift the emphasis towards consolidating gains, providing training to change the attitudes and practices of health staff, and strengthening district health systems. It also established a research agenda to study key issues that concern health sector reform and enhance management skills.

I visited the central district hospital, the Khorog Oblast General Hospital (KOGH). The hospital shares the campus with three other specialist hospitals – Dermatology Hospital, Ophthalmology Hospital, and Cancer Hospital.

The KOGH, a five-hundred-bed inpatient facility, I learnt, operates on a minuscule budget, around $230,000 per year in 2006. The funding is based on an outmoded model of care and a formula for hospital funding based on the number of beds and the length of stay.

The hospital director, a rather taciturn, balding late-middle-aged surgeon, was polite but reserved. He gradually let out his frustrations relating to poor work conditions and salaries for the doctors as our dialogue proceeded. I understood the hospital doctors were paid about $30 per month. There was little motivation to work harder. Many well-qualified doctors left for better-paying neighbouring countries, especially Kazakhstan, Russia, or countries in the West. The remaining were handicapped by a chronic shortage of functioning equipment and a lack of steady supplies of drugs. The well-off went to Moscow or Almaty for treatment.

From his account and hospital records, I gathered most of the occasional admissions were for surgical emergencies, such as stomach ulcers, gallbladder disease, and severe injuries or accidents. There were very few elective (planned) operations done, and they were usually for hernias or other more straightforward surgical problems. The patients tended to stay in the hospital for many days, sometimes weeks, quite in contrast to the very short hospital stays adopted by most Western hospitals. Antibiotics and other medications were used quite freely, often before and after operation in surgical cases. The surgical techniques used were obsolete and generally superseded by more scientifically approved methods by most progressive hospitals globally. Attitudes and standards for infection control were rather casual and perfunctory. There were few medical admissions, and some children in the wards.

He walked me through dimly lit corridors to several dingy wards. Most hospital beds appeared unoccupied. The walk revealed poorly ventilated, isolated clinical units; unsanitary patient care areas; and dysfunctional patient-flow and access patterns. The hospital pharmacies were quite bare, and the laboratory was minimally equipped with old equipment and appeared to be little used. The operating theatres were dank and poorly ventilated, with minimal equipment.

We briefly discussed the partnership between AKHS and the district government through the Essential Hospital Services Unit initiative. He was supportive of this partnership, as it was beginning to bring much-needed improvement in knowledge, best practices in medical care, modern equipment, and linkage to the external medical fraternity.

The AKHS planned to substantially upgrade and rationalize hospital services at the KOGH and consolidate it with the three other adjacent specialty hospitals to create a functioning general hospital with shared material and human resources. Under the partnership, volunteer physicians and surgeons from the U.S., the U.K., and Canada recently had started to provide remote and on-site clinical consultation and mentorship, donated equipment, sponsored training, and worked to improve clinical practice standards and norms. This program was still in the early stages, but one or two nursing volunteers currently on-site had developed training and upgrading curricula and practice-based teaching for nurses.

The nearby Cardiology Hospital revealed a similar range of issues, lacking even essential equipment to diagnose and treat heart disease. Visits to a few family medicine centres indicated gradual progress towards more comprehensive outpatient care, prevention programs for breast cancer, and early detection of disease. These were initial and tentative steps, not yet fully understood or appreciated by the public or health planners.

While in Khorog, we visited the Aga Khan Lycée, a school operated by the Aga Khan Education Services (AKES). The Lycée strives to create a harmonious balance between academic demands, sporting and cultural activities, and community life.

Like other institutions of the AKDN, its goal is to instill critical-thinking skills and the ability to analyze conditions that enable creative solutions to local problems.

A visit to the site of the future Tajikistan campus of the University of Central Asia (UCA) showed a location backed by the Pamirs' spectacular vistas. As part of the first internationally chartered university in the world, this private, non-profit, innovative institution dedicated to the study of mountain societies will offer undergraduate and graduate programs. Its School of Professional and Continuing Education (SPCE) had already developed preliminary programs in Khorog and Dushanbe designed to recruit and develop local talent in human development regionally.

Upon departure from Central Asia, I strove to apprehend, intellectually and emotionally, the range of observations and impressions born of my short sojourn to this dazzling, isolated high-mountain region. There were apparent contradictions: On one hand, the inheritance of a Soviet-style social infrastructure, high levels of literacy and education, health care built on abundant trained medical human resources, and freely available tiered health care facilities in a referral network at no cost to the users; on the other hand, the present dilapidation of infrastructure, dated and below-par standards of health and socio-economic development over the last few decades. What were the political, economic, human, and global dynamics that led to the material deterioration in the quality of life and human development? The experience was entirely dissimilar to my previous experiences and impressions obtained in Africa and parts of Asia.

In the domain of health, my impressions, supported by some evidence, suggested a disconnect with global advancements in the science and practice of medicine and health care, in public policy and management, in the lack of political and cultural pluralism, and in apathy and a deficit in motivation to ignite a dynamic and progressive society. Yet the building blocks were evident: warm and caring people, latent scientific and management talent, and a growing thirst to re-engage with modernity on its own terms. What appeared to be needed was a spark to reignite the individual and collective enterprise, to reorder social and economic and human development. I discerned that too was taking a momentum of its own, sparked by individuals, organizations, and systems making their way into the region. The AKDN, I perceived, with its various agencies and programs, was one such catalyst. But there were other humanitarian and development organizations assisting the government efforts to spur development.

Upon my return to Dar-es-Salaam, I developed a detailed report of my observations, impressions, and conclusions. My report was not meant to be an expert or a comprehensive survey of facts and recommendations but rather an independent, impartial, and personal observation. In it, I summarized the existing and emerging health profile, the disparate services and initiatives with little apparent overarching vision and goals, resource constraints, and cooperation and coordination. Chronic diseases, such as hypertension, heart disease, diabetes, cancer, and mental illness – many preventable through the application of current knowledge and practices – were beginning to overwhelm limited resources and services. Communicable and environmental diseases, such as typhoid, cholera, hepatitis, and intestinal infections, were still highly prevalent. Urgent realigning the health sector towards rebalancing preventive and curative care, focusing on primary and community care, reorienting the skills, knowledge, and attitudes towards the health providers and planners appeared critical requirements and needs of the time. Strong public health measures appeared called for. Rationalizing hospital care to reduce wastage and inefficiency and to foster effective use of health care expertise and technology were critical imperatives.

My report to Gijs Walraven included suggested topics and modules for physicians and other health care professionals' continuing professional development.

Professional Growth: Benchmarking Best Standards

My academic and clinical leadership position encouraged, indeed required and supported, that I remain current in the art, science, and developments in protean aspects of medical care. Medical education that served to humanize medicine and health care in all its varied modes and stages continued to be my preoccupation. Medicine has been driven by science, technology, and economics, less so by art and compassion in the modern world.

I attended a program entitled "Leading Innovations in Health Care and Medical Education" organized by the Harvard Macy Institute (HMI), held under the Harvard Medical School's aegis, the Harvard Graduate School of Education, and the Harvard Business School.

Initiated in 1995, it was directed by Dr. Elizabeth Armstrong, a dedicated educator and advocate of global networking and sharing knowledge. This enriching, immersive program, held on the Harvard Medical School premises and other

Boston facilities, allowed me to compare and share experiences of senior leaders in medical schools, universities, and health care institutions. In the hallowed premises of Harvard University, a small, select group of leaders in medical education from all continents was represented, bringing diverse experiences, challenges, and perspectives. Strangely, at that conference, I seemed to be the only representative from Africa.

The meeting gave space and inspiration to focus on the relevance, context, innovation, and adaptive changes in education. While largely attended by educators and leaders from the developed West, a sprinkling of participants from Singapore, the Middle East, and Australia added spice and vim to the ensuing discussions. The question of adaptive and transformative medical education in Africa's severely resource-constrained conditions that I brought to the table evinced a gratifying empathetic and supportive reaction from the participants.

In the months to come, the HMI network contributed significantly to teach and to learn from the AKU-AKHS's enterprise in health professional's education in Africa and Asia.

Over five years, we were closer to instituting postgraduate medical education in primary care and family medicine on foundations of innovation, relevance, and global networking to support a more humane and equitable health care system.

> *People know what they do;*
> *They frequently know why they do what they do;*
> *But what they don't know*
> *Is what they do does,*

> *Michael Foucault,*
> *The Order of Things*

CHAPTER 12

CONTINUING ENGAGEMENT:
PERSPECTIVE ON FUTURE DEVELOPMENTS

The true meaning of life is to plant trees under whose shade you do not expect to sit.

Neil Henderson

The summer of 2008 was hectic. Nilu and I had just returned from Tanzania in July, a little earlier than planned, because of our beloved daughter Aliya's upcoming wedding. She was marrying her university sweetheart, Ameya, in a few days; there was frantic activity everywhere. Fortunately, my older daughter Nadya and the rest of the family had ably taken charge of all details, since we did not have anything with us except our suitcases, nor a home to call our own.

All went well, and over the next few days, we needed to resettle ourselves back in Canada yet again. The previous five years or more spent in Africa engaged with AKU and AKHS had been most satisfying, but a little draining. I now needed, once more, to think about re-establishing a fulfilling future professional life in Canada. I also had to rectify the consequences of trusting but injudicious financial decisions I had made previously.

In my last days with AKU in East Africa, the university president Firoz Rasul and dean Mushtaq Ahmed had asked that I consider continuing some formal or informal engagement with AKU and asked to suggest what roles I may wish to play. In the same vein, Sulaiman, the CEO of AKHS, offered an advisory role that I may want to play in the institution's further development as there were many new initiatives envisaged in the coming years. There was a memorable farewell dinner, and everyone said kind and warm things. Returning home had been a difficult decision to adhere to; nevertheless, I felt it was time to make a fresh start.

> *If we knew we were on the right road, having to leave it would mean endless despair. But we are on a road that only leads to a second one and then a third one and so forth. And the real highway will not be sighted for a long, long, long time, perhaps never. So, we drift in doubt. But also, in an unbelievable beautiful diversity. Thus, the accomplishment of hopes remains an always unexpected miracle. But in compensation, the miracle remains forever possible.*

These sententious words of Franz Kafka's have always served to sustain me when life's future direction appears unclear, and choices are murky and uncertain.

I soon began searching for job openings that could provide adequate compensation and be intellectually stimulating. I took up a few locum positions and started covering evenings and weekends for one or two clinics. A lot had changed in Canada in the years I had been away, and I tried to adapt to a very different health care system and way of practising medicine.

Still fresh from our beguiling time in Africa, I was reminded of a rather unexpected digression in Canada's resettlement plans. A close friend asked me if I would consent to accompany a senior Indonesian government official, a deputy minister, back to Indonesia following a recent heart attack he had suffered while attending a conference in Vancouver. The government officials were keen that the recovering patient be accompanied by a physician and a nurse for the deputy minister's safe transport. Of course, they would cover all expenses for this process and take care of the necessary arrangements. Since I was not yet engaged in any significant professional activity in Vancouver at that time, I consented for the week or so required for this trip. I declined the monetary compensation offered to me for this service, beyond covering the basic costs involved. The flight to Jakarta through Hong Kong was very comfortable and uneventful; the patient remained stable throughout the journey. In Jakarta, we were put up in a luxurious hotel, shown the city, and entertained and treated with tremendous grace and generosity.

Jakarta, Indonesia's massive capital, sits on the northwest coast of the island of Java. A historic mix of cultures – Javanese, Malay, Chinese, Arab, Indian, and European – has influenced its architecture, language, and cuisine. The old town, Kota Tua, is home to Dutch colonial buildings, Glodok (Jakarta's Chinatown), and the old port of Sunda Kelapa, where traditional wooden schooners dock.

While in Jakarta, I asked for a meeting with the dean of the Faculty of Medicine at the University of Jakarta, which was readily arranged. Upon arrival at the university's School of Medicine, I was warmly received by the dean and two senior department heads. We were soon into a deep conversation on the challenges of medical education, resource constraints, faculty recruitment, and challenges in ensuring equitable access to health care. They had heard of the growing prestige of Aga Khan University and wanted to know more about AKU's innovative training programs, community-based medical education initiatives, its international partnerships and networks, and its reach into developing countries in Asia, the Middle East, and Africa. I outlined the Aga Khan Development Network's vision, mission, and goals, particularly the university's putative role in human resource development on social and health sciences. They were very impressed and looked forward to building beneficial linkages with AKU in research and training. I believe in the months ahead that the university did send delegations to AKU.

Upon my return to Vancouver, I vigorously resumed building my personal and professional life once again. There were several attractive international offers I briefly considered. I recall an offer from the New Jersey University School of Medicine and Public Health, which had an established HIV/AIDS program in Guyana in South America. The university was expanding its academic program to include tuberculosis care, HIV, and tropical diseases and offered a position to head the hospital and training facility. It was an exciting offer, which after some reflection, I declined. I had just returned from a significant undertaking in Africa and, all things considered, decided it was too soon to uproot my life once more so soon.

Fresh Beginnings: Sundry Engagements, Intellectual Enrichment

I set about trying to re-establish my affiliation with the University of British Columbia (UBC) Faculty of Medicine. Robert Woolard, the department head of family practice, with whom I was well acquainted, very kindly encouraged my involvement with the department. He reviewed and discussed my global health work, particularly the efforts to establish the specialty of family medicine in Pakistan and East Africa and the endeavours to upgrade primary care medical practice through outreaches of continuing professional development in some parts of the developing world. His own work supporting the development of family medicine and primary care in developing countries gave him a deep appreciation of the challenges in improving health care in resource-poor countries. After due process, I was soon appointed to the rank of clinical associate professor in the UBC Department of Family Practice. I soon got to know Shafik Dharamsi in the department.

Shafik Dharamsi, PhD, an assistant professor in the department, previously engaged in early childhood development work in East Africa. His academic work and research now revolved around social accountability and community development. His focus in the Faculty of Medicine at UBC was to better prepare future physicians to be mindful and responsive to vulnerable populations' health care needs. He was very involved in interprofessional education, research, and practice of health professionals. Hence, we had a lot to share.

Bob Woolard and Shafik, among others, encouraged me to consider applying for a leadership role in the department since Bob would soon be completing his position as professor and head of the department. However, I balked at considering taking on the head of department position again. UBC's Faculty of Medicine and Department of Family Practice were much more extensive than the young AKU. Besides, the histories, traditions, and priorities were different.

But I did accept Bob's invitation to join a small delegation of the UBC Family Medicine Department on their upcoming visit to Makerere University, Uganda, where a preliminary agreement of cooperation was under consideration between UBC and Makerere. Bob and Shafik were well aware of my long association with Makerere University and our early overtures to establish local networks of cooperation between family medicine departments in the region.

The trip to Kampala evoked nostalgic memories of days and years spent in Africa at various times in my life. It was also a pleasant and stimulating visit. Ideas and common interests in family and community medicine education were shared freely, and tentative faculty exchange agreements were reached. I met Atai, Makerere's head of family medicine, with whom I had struggled in the past to strengthen support and commitment to primary medical care in East Africa. In Uganda, as in Kenya and Tanzania, the progress was slow, the support often tentative as competing claims were placed on universities and the national government's limited resources. Atai expressed the critical need for faculty development and resources, which she was struggling to obtain.

At the conference, I was called upon to share the phase of AKU's early conceptualization and development of postgraduate education in family medicine, the lessons learnt, and prospects for comprehensively linking primary care to secondary care systems. AKU and AKHS had worked strenuously to foster continuity in medical care by connecting primary, secondary, and tertiary care seamlessly. These efforts were ongoing in Pakistan, East Africa, and Afghanistan.

The opportunity to revisit an East African country only months after I departed from Africa stirred mixed emotions. I wistfully recalled the many unaddressed and unique challenges confronting developing countries and the critical need to share knowledge and link best practices between the advanced industrialized countries and those in the developing countries striving to improve their people's quality of life. while disadvantaged by the paucity of human, material and technical resources.

~ ᠑·ᠷ ~

Back in Vancouver, I began to receive invitations to consider positions with clinics and health care organizations. I joined a new facility established to address drug misuse and mental health, a growing public health concern in British Columbia. The ninety-four-bed hospital provides integrated care for adults with severe and problematic substance use disorder and severe mental illness. These integrated care services used a multidisciplinary care model and fostered the rehabilitation of users as productive members of society. My earlier work in community mental health and with the Riverview Psychiatric Hospital in Canada stood me in good stead in this position. I had observed severe constraints in the availability and delivery of mental health care in countries like Pakistan and India and in East Africa. Some of AKU's efforts were directed towards strengthening the proficiencies of frontline physicians and other health care workers in mental health through continuing education, effective referral, and community support. The experience of these attempts facilitated my appointment and involvement with this critical public health enterprise in Canada.

Many patients served by this facility also had concurrent complex medical disorders, such as hepatitis, HIV/AIDS, lung disease, and heart disease, resulting from neglect or delays in seeking appropriate care. With several colleagues, I got involved in programs to improve the early diagnosis, management, and continuing care of these medical disorders, which compounded their disability and significantly impacted their quality of life. Consideration of these problematic patients drew heavily on experience and training from every area of clinical medicine.

About a year later, I accepted a position for training and work as a clinical associate at the Vancouver Cancer Centre, a prominent cancer care facility of the British Columbia Cancer Agency (BCCA). Affiliated with UBC, it served as a specialized teaching unit of the Faculty of Medicine. My earlier interest in cancer care as a generalist physician allowed me to pursue this interest again, this time under the aegis of one of the most advanced cancer diagnosis, treatment, and research facilities in North America.

The General Practice Oncology program offered by the BCCA is designed to offer the opportunity to strengthen cancer care skills and knowledge and provide enhanced care. The program also included knowledge and best practices in screening, treatment, and surveillance, all geared to provide the best support possible to patients with cancer, particularly in remote communities. Upon completing the intensive course, I continued to work at the Vancouver Cancer Centre (VCC) for over four years. My work involved working with some outstanding cancer specialists with particular areas of interest and expertise and assisting with patient care on various standard treatment and research protocols.

Among its multiple programs, the BCCA provided a varied range of support for frontline physicians, including continuing professional development, high-end cancer biology research, multicentre drug trials, and advanced treatments. In this work, I participated in student and physician-in-training education and care of cancer patients under cancer specialists' supervision. I was appointed associate member of the Division of Medical Oncology in the Department of Medicine, University of British Columbia. I remember many memorable encounters with patients at various stages of cancer – from early stages to those requiring terminal care, palliation, and support at the end of their lives.

My excitement also stemmed from the appreciation that cancer patients' care was highly underdeveloped in many low- and middle-income countries. There was a pressing need to advance cancer care at all levels of health care systems in these countries. In this ongoing struggle, I hoped to contribute again in some measure; hence, acquiring additional knowledge was necessary. Cancer is commonly considered a disease of high-income countries; it is now recognized as a global public health crisis. Approximately one in five people will develop cancer before the age of seventy-five, and a majority of cases will arise in low- and middle-income countries, where survival rates are unacceptably low.

I remembered the grim realities of conditions presenting to the AKU/AKHS facilities in Pakistan, where, until the 1990s, there was no organized national or institutional focus on cancer care. Advanced diagnostic equipment was lacking; few standard cancer drugs were available; tried and tested treatment protocols were rarely used by non-specialist physicians and surgeons involved in patient care. Radiation therapy services were severely underdeveloped; even pain relief and palliation of symptoms were inadequate. Support services such as trained cancer nursing, nutritionists, technicians, specialized pharmacy services and administration, information systems, material management, and supporting critical care and surgical services were sorely underdeveloped. Standardized cancer registries were in preliminary stages of development; hence, focusing on high-needs areas was difficult.

My association with the BCCA enabled me to attend several international cancer control conferences in Italy, Korea, Ireland, and Canada. These conferences fostered international collaboration and cooperation in implementing cancer and non-communicable disease control (NCD) strategies. The scientific community recognized that non-communicable diseases, such as diabetes, heart disease, and obesity, share many common determinants with cancer, including lifestyle factors such as smoking and alcohol consumption. Hence, a common public health strategy is crucial to confront the rising burden of these largely preventable conditions.

The International Cancer Control Partnership (ICCP) efforts and partnering organizations such as the UN, the WHO, the International Atomic Energy Agency, and civil society organizations support country cancer control and NCD planning efforts and provide technical assistance and planning advocacy. My recent experience in supporting the development of relevant medical education in South Asia and East Africa has impressed me with the continuing necessity of pursuing productive avenues of linkages.

The BCCA was sympathetic to sharing its knowledge, experience, and resources with some capable organizations in the developing world. However, my approaches to the BCCA leadership for fostering linkages between the agency did not result in tangible direct cooperation. As a provincially funded agency in British Columbia, it is mandated to ensure the complete spectrum care of cancer patients in the province. Financial and human resources limited the agency's outer reach. At individual levels, however, I received encouragement, support, and access to its research and guidelines.

⁓ ა·ㄷ ⁓

I continued to learn and maintain a limited practice in general medicine to the extent possible. I was at a stage where more protracted periods of contemplative mood took hold of me.

> *This is a gift that I have, simple, simple – a foolish extravagant spirit, full of forms, figures, shapes, objects, ideas, apprehensions, motions, revolutions. These are begot in the ventricle of memory, nourished in the womb of pia mater, and delivered upon the mellowing of occasion.*

> *William Shakespeare,* Love's Labour's Lost

I spent more time reflecting on the state and direction that human societies were taking. I also felt a need to re-examine my personal credo – a statement of my convictions – to locate myself in the total scheme of things. I reflected on how circumstances, experiences, and layers of belief shaped my life, perspectives, philosophy, and vision for a more balanced and just world. I accepted that much of what I thought, observed, and held dear was not original or unique but echoed the sentiments and thought and actions of others much wiser and more competent than myself. However, I had accrued a practical guide grounded in my innate sense of curiosity, wonder, experiences, and reflections. The work, the odyssey, and the quest to find meaning and purpose and direction in my life had, to a considerable degree, been shaped by my engagement with the institutions of the Aga Khan Development Network, which in turn was illumined by the wisdom; the humanistic, pluralistic, and ethical imperative; and the foresight, generosity, and wisdom of the Aga Khan, the founder of the institution.

> *… [W]e have not ceased to nurture our ambition to recreated links with the great traditions of learning, exemplary cultural achievements, open, tolerant, emancipating humanism and spiritual inspiration which characterize our common tradition.*

> *The Aga Khan, 1986*

Hence, I keenly followed the network's developments and progress, notably Aga Khan University. I was partly driven by a sense of atavism but also struck by rapid changes in the global human conditions and interactions demanding ever more responsive solutions crafted with care, compassion, and foresight that remained embedded in my mind.

> *The great political and social changes around us are creating opportunities for service that promise to be deeply rewarding to persons with the engaged intelligence to be successful at important but difficult work.*

The Aga Khan, 1994

Itinerant Healer: Enriching Encounters

My personal and professional life was rewarding and now relatively unencumbered. My life was immeasurably enriched by numerous chance intersections or meetings with strangers or occurrences that called upon my skills as a physician during my travels at this time and in early years of my life. If I had maintained a "doctor's casebook," this periodic serendipitous involvement in the medical care of strangers in foreign lands could serve to recall the exact circumstances of these encounters of "peripatetic healing." There were many such fortuitous encounters; I relate one or two that were memorable and gratifying.

On a wide-ranging holiday visit to Southeast Asia, Nilu and I flew into Siem Reap – the province's regional capital of the same name and the gateway to the world-renowned Angkor Wat temple complex, the largest (by land area) religious monument in the world. On arrival, we were met by a friendly tour guide who drove us to our hotel. He introduced himself as Jaya, as I recall. He mentioned that he had been asked to substitute at the last moment for the guide who was assigned to us but had become indisposed. Over the next few days, he guided us on our visits to the splendid Hindu and Buddhist temple complex; the magnificent Tonle Sap Lake, which connects to the Mekong River and forms part of the most varied and productive ecosystem and food source in the country; and other historical landmarks. Tourism is a substantial contributor to the country's economy; a significant number of the population is employed in low-paying menial jobs in the industry.

The Kingdom of Cambodia, home to the Khmer people, was once the largest empire in Southeast Asia, the Khmer Empire. It has a brutal legacy of wars, occupation, the widespread scale of destruction of temples and libraries, forced displacements and labour, purges, and mass atrocities, notably during the barbaric Khmer Rouge regime from 1975 to 1978, remembered for its "killing fields." It is the most land-mined country in the world. The postwar period has led to significant social and economic inequalities between urban and rural development, notably in health, where even safe drinking water is not guaranteed in rural areas.

One evening, at our request, Jaya took us to a renowned old local market to taste the local fish-based cuisine. Over dinner, knowing I was a physician, he shyly asked if I would look at the prescription he had in his pocket for his mother. He was planning to fill the prescription that evening. He had been to one or two local drug stores and found the medications unavailable or exorbitantly expensive. I looked at the crumpled prescription slip he extended to me. I noted that several expensive medications were prescribed. I asked him what his mother's problem was. He began to relate the history of his mother's illness somberly; I learnt that the story's nature was not an uncommon one.

He said his mother had fallen gravely ill a few weeks before, when, on the local practitioners' advice, he and his father had taken her to a hospital in Phnom Penh, Cambodia's capital city hundreds of miles away. The doctors had kept her in the hospital for a few days, done extensive and costly tests, prescribed medications and treatments, and asked that she be brought again in a few weeks for further tests and treatments. He said his father was on his way now by bus to Phnom Penh to sell their small plot of land to some speculators to raise enough funds for the travel and treatment costs. I could see how discouraged he looked. I asked him if I could see his mother before he filled the prescription in his hand. His face brightened a bit.

The following morning, he picked us up from our hotel, and we drove several miles into the countryside. Along the way, I could see many small farm holdings, rundown shops and homes, scattered villages, and occasional health centres and schools. Rural poverty was evident and widespread, in contrast to the tourist-crowded, glitzy Siem Reap with its countless restaurants, nightclubs, and lights. We approached a small rundown house set among a small holding of banana and other local fruit trees. A man approached us on a motorcycle. Jaya introduced him as his brother, who had taken time off from his work at a local bar to come and meet us. They took us inside the tiny, scantily furnished white-walled house, where I saw a curled-up body lying on a bed facing the wall.

A young woman was standing by her side holding a bowl. Jaya indicated that the young woman was his brother's wife, who spent a considerable amount of her time looking after their mother. Jaya and the young woman gently shook the older woman's shoulder and rolled her over onto her back. Softly, he explained to her in the local Khmer language that he had brought a doctor to see her. They helped her sit up supported. The elderly lady looked at Nilu and me and tried to smile. I noticed that her mouth drooped on one side, and she drooled slightly. I smiled at her, approached her, and gently took her hand. It was clear to me that she was paralyzed on one side of her body. With her children's help, I examined her as thoroughly as I could under the conditions prevailing. She was probably in her sixties, paralyzed on one side of her body, due to a major stroke. I went through whatever slips of paper or documents they had, some written in French or local languages, a few words recognizable in English, and pieced the history of events to date. Apparently, she had suffered from high blood pressure for many years and had been prescribed different drugs, most of which were too expensive for the family to afford or not often available at the local drug stores. Then she suffered a major stroke that left her partially paralyzed and dependent upon her children for her care. She had been actively working on their little plot to grow vegetables and fruit for the local markets until a few weeks before.

I took Jaya and his brother aside into a little alcove at the back of the house. I explained to them the nature of her illness and the most likely course of the disability. I reviewed her history, tests, and treatments and the very minimal chances of obtaining tangible benefits from further expensive brain scans, periodic visits to a distant hospital, and costly new drugs recently made available on the market and promoted heavily by drug companies and individual practitioners. All this required the family to liquidate their only material asset – their land and the house. The brothers listened intently and admitted they felt torn by the decision, born of a cultural and filial imperative, to sell their small piece of land. Listening to their account, I felt bound to advise them against taking this irretrievable step that could cost the family their future dearly for an improbable gain in their dear mother's quality of life.

Jaya's sister-in-law joined us. I spent an hour or so explaining and demonstrating steps to them that included simple home-based mobilization and rehabilitation exercises, nutrition, and personal care. I prescribed tried and tested inexpensive first-line drugs, readily available locally, that could control blood pressure and protect and enhance brain function and speed up recovery to the extent possible.

I underlined the importance of blood pressure control, which could be checked at a local health centre.

It was evening by the time Jaya drove us to town, where I entered a pharmacy and selected the medications, which Jaya gratefully took with him to administer regularly to his mother.

The following day, Jaya arrived at our hotel for our last day of sightseeing in Cambodia. He seemed happy as if a load had been lifted off his shoulder. Later in the day, as he drove us to the airport, he said that his father was travelling back home from Phnom Penh that day, and the family jointly had decided not to sell their precious plot and home. He presented a small, beautiful Buddhist figurine to Nilu as an expression of the family's deep appreciation for the guidance and counsel I had provided. He bashfully added that his father had been most effusive on the phone in his expression of gratitude and reminded Jaya that it was providential that, at the last moment, he had been assigned as a substitute guide for us.

Their kindness and heartfelt relief acutely touched me. I felt humbled and profoundly privileged to have been allowed deeply into the family's personal lives and trust. We departed as I mumbled a few platitudes of thanks and gratitude and best wishes.

Another encounter that readily comes to mind occurred while Nilu and I were enjoying a holiday in Morocco, a North African country bordering the Atlantic Ocean and the Mediterranean Sea. It is distinguished by its Berber, Arabian, and European cultural influences. It is the birthplace of Ibn Battuta, a Berber-Moroccan scholar, jurist, and medieval explorer. He widely travelled the Old World, surpassing Zheng He and Marco Polo by thousands of miles. He is the author of perhaps the most famous travelogue in history, the *Rihlah (Travels)*.

Having spent a few interesting days in Casablanca, Agadir, and the maze-like medina and souks of Marrakech, we were on a train to Fez, a historic city. Along this important ancient trade corridor from Marrakech, the Trans-Sahara trade route provided captivating vistas and views of rural settlements on this well-travelled path.

The old-fashioned compartmentalized train was charming and clean. Nilu and I were sitting alone in the first-class compartment, when at a stop, a young local gentleman boarded the train, knocked on our door, and asked if he could sit in our compartment. We were fine with that as we often enjoyed conversing with local people on our travels. This young man, probably in his late thirties, well-dressed in casual Western style, sat on the seat opposite us and, after a few minutes, started a conversation in perfect English by first introducing himself. I recall his name as Bashir. He said he was a tour guide and was on his way to visit his family in Fez, having finished guiding a sizable German tour group. He was a chatty, pleasant fellow, talking about the tours he led, his likes and dislikes, and his family. He was on his way to spend some time with his mother and family in Fez. Quite unabashedly, he started asking about ourselves – what we did, where we were from, how we liked Morocco, and so on. I said I was a physician from Canada involved in teaching internationally. To this, he reacted with some pleasure. He asked if I would mind if he asked my opinion about his nephew, who was in a dire state of health.

He started to relate the story of his eight-year-old nephew, who had had some developmental problems since early childhood. They had consulted specialists in Fez and Rabat, the capital city. The boy had had one or two operations on his abdomen and urinary system. Bashir could not tell me much more about the problem, except that it was a severe financial and emotional drain on his younger brother and his wife and the whole family. The problem exacted a particular toll on his elderly mother. According to him, the boy was partially crippled, was kept at home, and required almost full-time care.

After a few minutes, he asked us where we were staying in Fez, our plans, and who was meeting us at the train station. We were booked into a palatial house with an internal courtyard (called a *riad*) converted into a private hotel in Fez's historic old medina, and we were planning to take a taxi to our hotel. Bashir excitedly said not to worry, that he would arrange for a friend, an experienced tour guide who had a car, to meet us at the station, take us to our hotel, and show us around the grand historical city. Then, slightly abashedly, he asked if I would mind taking a look at his nephew if we could find the time during our stay in Fez, as they were at a loss over what to do with him. They had received conflicting advice from various sources they had consulted.

His openness and friendliness honestly affected us, and also intrigued me by the problem they faced. Bashir phoned his friend, spoke in Arabic, and smiled at us and said everything had been arranged. We would be met by Kerim, a dear friend of his, who would take care of everything. He had to disembark at a suburban stop outside Fez to see his wife and children but would see us later in Fez.

At the architecturally interesting central railway station of Fez, a good-looking clean-shaven man in a light serge jacket came towards us. He introduced himself as Kerim, Bashir's friend and distant cousin. He took us in his car, an old, beaten Fiat, to our hotel deep into the labyrinth of the old medina. Along the way, he pointed out interesting sights. He offered to pick us up later and walk us through the medina. We were glad we had a knowledgeable English-speaking guide as we walked through the narrow-interconnected streets that opened into little squares, markets, great mosques, and tucked-away great homes.

The following day, we spent the morning fascinated by the country's cultural capital and history of the city built in the eighth and ninth centuries by the Idris rulers. The city is also located close to the Atlas Mountains, and the Berber population living in traditional style, which we intended to visit during our stay. The old walled city, centred around the Fez River, is famed for its religious scholarship and mercantile activities. The University of Al-Qarawiyyin, which was founded in 859 is considered to be the oldest continuously functioning institute of higher education in the world. It has also Choura Tannery from the eleventh century, one of the oldest tanneries in the world.

While drinking strong, local Arabic coffee at a tiny outdoor café, Kerim received a phone call. He passed the phone to me and asked if I would speak to Bashir, who was on the line. We chatted for a while, then Bashir asked if we could come to his mother's home for lunch as the family was keen to meet us. I checked with Nilu and accepted the invitation.

The following day, Kerim drove us to a densely populated suburb and took us into a small residence on the second floor of a crowded tenement house. We entered the surprisingly airy, bright living room of the home, where Bashir came to receive me warmly with a traditional Arabic embrace. I noticed an elderly lady who stood up rather painfully from a chair, smiled at me, and took Nilu's hand warmly and took her to a settee covered with colourful throw rugs. A tired-looking young man was standing near Bashir, whom Bashir introduced as his younger brother and the father of young Elian, the boy I had come to see. Bashir's pretty wife was also there, as was a small boy, whom Bashir introduced as his son.

While they served sweet tea and some local savories, I learnt that Bashir's brother, who was a fruit seller at a local market, and his wife were expressing their gratitude that we had taken the time to come to see Elian and for accepting the family's invitation to lunch. I did not see Elian in the room; I asked where he was. Bashir handed me a couple of dog-eared folders containing filed and loose documents, amongst which I saw several X-rays and ultrasound scans, and a few notes mostly written in Arabic. I looked through these, picking up a few familiar French or English words. Bashir, his brother, and his wife took me into a small room where I saw a small boy sitting propped up against some pillows. His dark eyes set in a thin pale face looked expectantly at me. They told me that Elian had difficulty with his spine, bowels, and bladder. He could not go to school, although they tried to give him some basic home-schooling. He had already had two operations, which they did not think had helped much.

I took Elian's small hands, looked him in the eyes, and softly spoke to him. He looked relieved and unthreatened. With the help of his father and mother, I examined him carefully. I particularly checked the spine, the power in his legs, his abdomen, and his genitalia. I recognized his problem, although I had not come across a case as severe as this. Looking through the scanty notes, tests, and examinations, I recognized that Elian suffered from a rare, complex congenital anomaly that involved his muscle, skeletal, urinary, and reproductive systems. The condition, called bladder exstrophy in medical parlance, involves an open, inside-out bladder, abnormality of the reproductive organs, an abdominal wall defect, and occasionally, involvement of internal abdominal organs. I plumbed the hazy depths of faded memories of what I knew of this very uncommon surgical condition, including Professor Haines's lectures on embryology, the study of fetal development, where the body is miraculously shaped and developed by mysterious processes in the weeks and months following conception. Occasionally, nature fails to deliver a perfect product, resulting in the improper or incomplete development of certain organs.

Although this complicated surgical problem was outside my expertise and experience, I realized he needed staged treatment at a specialized university hospital. I carefully weighed my words while gently discussing that prospect with Bashir and his brother. They were not surprised. They had expected Elian's treatment would be prolonged and costly, quite outside their ability to afford such treatment outside the country. I gave as detailed an explanation as I could of the condition that affected the proper development of his bladder, abdominal wall, spinal muscles, and possibly internal organs. I said I would think some more on the problem in the next few days.

The family was nevertheless very grateful for my opinion. We then sat down to lunch, where everyone sat on the floor mats, and several large deliciously aromatic platters, laden with a variety of rice, couscous, olives, naans, spicy vegetables, and meats, were put in the middle. A large tagine was brought out, and everyone ate from the common earthenware pot. Nilu and I were humbled by their ready and natural acceptance of us into their lives, sharing their family meal graciously and warmly.

Over the next couple of days, Kerim and Bashir arranged for us to visit terrains of canyons and ravines of the Atlas Mountain ranges, which are dotted with Berber villages. We were invited into adobe and stone and clay-built homes of one or two local families. Some families lived in their traditional ways, floors covered with carpets and goat hair tents. Kerim insisted we have dinner at his home, where we met his charming wife and children. She suffered from incapacitating symptoms of Meniere's disease, an inner ear disorder which resulted in bouts of severe vertigo, vomiting, and distressing ringing in the ears. After dinner, I went with Kerim to a neighbourhood pharmacy where I was able to find medications that could ease some symptoms of this disturbing disorder. I advised him to obtain a thorough evaluation of her condition by a specialist.

Before our departure, Bashir contacted me to say he was trying to obtain old records of his nephew that he would forward to me. He also informed me that Boston Children's Hospital in the U.S. and a children's hospital in Paris had been suggested to him by doctors in Morocco, but these centres were beyond their financial capacity.

Soon after our return to Canada, I received a few documents, translated into French. I immediately contacted urological specialists at the Hospital for Sick Children in Toronto, as well as British Columbia Children's Hospital in Vancouver, both world-renowned centres of excellence in children's health. I was gratified by prompt responses from both Canadian hospitals, both hospitals I had had some experience working with. I followed up with phone calls and communications directly. The surgeon who contacted me from Toronto was a Lebanese doctor who could read Arabic and French and kindly assured me that he would be happy to treat Elian. In addition, the hospital had agreed to waive most of the costs and fees associated with Elian's treatment, and there were facilities available to house the family for the duration of his treatment. The B.C. Children's Hospital was also generous with its services. I immediately passed on this information to Bashir and worked to connect the Canadian surgeon with the family. Many months later, I learnt that Elian had undergone extensive corrective surgical and rehabilitative treatments and was being cared for by his family and community in Fez.

My innate restlessness soon found me peripatetic in work and recreation, easily finding exciting short-term positions in Canada and abroad. A relative fixture of my work life became annual sojourns in New Zealand. A pleasant few months spent as a locum physician away from Canada's chilly winters enabled a more in-depth cultural, historical, and social exploration of Asia's countries and societies. These jobs often engaged me in care of diverse populations, including indigenous peoples – Maori, the Pacific Islanders, and others of Polynesian descent. Many lived in their traditional cultural milieu, echoing the observed conditions of First Nations people of Canada and the U.S., and Australia's Aboriginals. I was sometimes called upon to teach, supervise, and mentor doctors in training, a task I particularly relished.

The New Zealand archipelago forms the southwestern corner of the Polynesian Triangle, the other two points being the Hawaiian Islands and Easter Island.

My interest in learning about ethnic traditions and cultures harkens back to reflections on the shared human origins but diverse evolution of societies and their interactions today. The lack of understanding and respect for the pluralism of cultures, ethnicities, races, and religions are a source of much fractiousness between nations, people, and cultures. It negatively impacts the quest for a cosmopolitan ethic underpinning human development, of which I consider "health" an emblematic metaphor. Nilu and I set about getting acclimated to a new country by learning about the country's longest inhabitants, the Maori.

The Maori people arrived in New Zealand (Aotearoa in the Maori language) in the early- to mid-1300s from a mythical homeland of Hawaiki. Hundreds of years later, the Maori culture, rich in arts and tradition, is still part of New Zealand's identity. We visited *Maraes,* traditional meeting grounds, and were invited to *Haka,* the community's ceremonial war dance. The Maori still make up about 15 percent of the country's population, a proportion vastly reduced due to devastating internecine wars and conflicts with European settlers and newly introduced diseases. Even today, the people of Polynesian descent suffer an inordinately higher rate of illnesses, fatalities, incarceration, and unemployment. However, determined efforts both by the national government and the Indigenous people themselves show tangible improvement in their lot.

From the arcs of sandy beaches to snow-capped peaks, forests, and parks, New

Zealand is a geological wonder, a paradisial land, ideal for contemplation and the revitalization of body and spirit. I chose smaller towns or rural settings in this beautiful, rugged, hospitable country for my locum work. Long country drives, rolling hills, and volcanic mountains gave a good measure of time to enjoy nature and reflect upon the nature of good living. The startlingly clear star-studded southern skies, best observed late in the night from our rural cottage on open farmlands, infuse a splendid mystical aura to the wonders of nature and life that we blithely ignore in the tumult of the day. I recall reading Rumi's words: *Stop acting so small; you are the universe in ecstatic motion.*

These moments of wonder were also moments of self-reflection. More of Rumi's wise and sobering words came to mind: *Yesterday, I was clever, so I wanted to change the world. Today, I am wise, so I am changing myself.* Refreshed and revitalized, I resolved to let the beauty of what I loved be what I do.

Revisiting Familiar Territories: Remarkable Progress and Developments

On one of these sojourns, I decided to revisit the AKU and AKHS facilities in Pakistan and Tanzania and observe and rejoice in the organizations' progress. The kind and generous invitation extended by the AKU's dean of medicine and the chair of the Department of Family Medicine in Karachi, Waris Kidwai, allowed a one-month-long visit to volunteer my services to the faculty and the department in 2014. During my tenure at AKU, Waris served as RMO in the CHC. He continued to contribute to family medicine's progress as a specialty and service to Pakistan and now oversaw a network of family medicine centres in Karachi and the Sindh province.

The familiar pleasant surroundings and a much-enlarged AKU campus evoked pride and nostalgia. The physical and programmatic expansion was almost explosive; several new initiatives launched in the past years to address the challenges of quality, access, demand, and relevance were evident. Growth continued off-campus, with the addition of diagnostic and treatment centres bringing care to distant regions.

Old friends, colleagues, and acquaintances received me warmly and shared stories of challenges, concerns, and progress vicissitudes. The university and its widespread teaching, service, and research facilities had made tremendous strides in enlarging their reach and scope, which I had the opportunity to visit, observe, and assess. I partook in several meetings, student teaching, and mentoring.

I remember revisiting the Hyderabad Maternity and Child Health Centre. More than thirty years earlier, I was involved in the task force charged with conceptualizing and linking the AKHS-run facility to the academic and clinical expertise of the AKU. It now served as a secondary-level hospital in the network of the AKU's clinical and training facilities in Pakistan. Its much-expanded range of primary and secondary care was satisfying to note; AKU's quality control procedures benchmarked its quality standards. Visiting AKU specialists and faculty enriched the care, teaching, research, and care at the centre. Similar progress was evident in linking and substantially uplifting clinical care at AKHS-operated diagnostic centres in Karachi and the Northern Areas, where decades earlier, I had striven to facilitate medical practitioners' continuing professional development through AKU's CME programs and consultations. The local management leaders I met at these facilities appeared pleased with these developments and supported further integration of the clinical network in teaching and research.

Of the many old colleagues and friends, some memorable meetings stand out in my mind. I remember discussing progress and emerging issues with Camer Vallani, the former provost of AKU, one of the earliest pioneers of AKU's development. I greatly admired Camer for his selfless and untiring services, clear vision, and numerous roles during his active years. Now semi-retired, he continued doggedly to influence AKU's development path in accord with its founding principles. At the same time, he continued his long-cherished but long-postponed research in electrocardiography. He pointed out threats to AKU's mission, which included periodic public security threats that affected the university's ambitious agenda. But he offered thoughtful proposals, born of his profound insights and experiences, which he shared freely with the leadership. I also remember my meetings with Latif Sheik, the pharmacy head, who had done much to standardize drug management protocols within the AKU network.

Amir Gulamhussein, an old friend and a visiting professor of anatomy from the U.K., frequently visited the medical college and contributed his knowledge and experience in strengthening the basic sciences departments of AKU. I had the good fortune to be housed in the AKU guesthouse where he stayed at the time. We had many opportunities to reminisce and survey the landscape of medical education and health care in the institution and the country. Mohamed Khurshid, a cancer specialist and a former dean of the Faculty of Medicine, shared with me his concerns about the underdeveloped state of palliative care at the AKUH and urged me to enlist the Family Medicine Department into an active role in palliative care and pain management at the hospital and ambulatory facilities. I took this up with Waris Kidwai, who felt that while his department was overwhelmed with demands on its staff, he would bring it to the departmental executive committee to consider training and staffing palliative care and cancer patients' pain management.

Both the dean and the hospital CEO encouraged me, unofficially, to provide consultative comments and feedback on my observations on the progress over the last almost thirty years. During my time with AKU in East Africa, I had visited Karachi once or twice and so was somewhat aware of developments in this part of the world. However, the progress, consolidations, standardization, expansion, and linkages in education and advancing health care were quite staggering. Although unapprised of current institutional deliberation, strategic and tactical initiatives, or evolving plans, I did feel it incumbent upon me to submit my longitudinal perspective on the institutional journey equitably – operating in a highly complex and challenging environment over those years.

I wished to underscore the understanding of the university's vision and mission, its promise, and its opportunities, challenges, and concerns. I wrote a report, *"Reflections on an Institutional Odyssey: A Personal Perspective,"* which I later forwarded to the dean and the organization's senior leadership. In my wide-ranging report, I suggested establishing an AKU Centre of Strategic Health Innovations and Research to engage vigorously in the quest for multidisciplinary innovative approaches to specific behavioural, cultural, epidemiological, technological, and affordable solutions to the most prevalent problems affecting the region. I had noted that local centres of excellence dedicated to addressing pressing health problems through the generation and dissemination of contextual and applicable knowledge were sorely lacking in the country and the region. There was also a need to critically evaluate the place, acceptability, and cost-effectiveness of imported devices and medical technologies, often applied uncritically in the developing countries.

My report also underlined some deficiencies at the primary and the secondary levels of programs to confront neglected but much-needed services, including screening and early detection of cancers such as breast and colon cancer, chronic pain management and palliative and terminal care for cancer and other terminally ill patients, mental health and development disorders, and nutritional disorders.

Going forward, it could seek to engage in confronting some of the most difficult universal problems facing medicine and health care in developing countries – ethics, use of scarce resources, patient rights, accountability, the interface between medicine, ethics, and law. An intellectual nexus under a rubric such as the Centre for Medicine, Ethics and Society could be conceptualized towards this end.

A few months later, on a visit to Paris, I met with Shafik Sachedina, the senior-most executive in the Aga Khan Secretariat and the Aga Khan Development Network. We had previously met on a number of occasions, and Shafik had always graciously received me and encouraged and endorsed my role as a voluntary consultant and advisor on a number of programs and projects of the AKDN. We shared views on progress on several fronts in the network.

The following year, I decided to visit Tanzania and to appraise myself on the trajectory of progress within the Aga Khan Hospital and Aga Khan University. I offered short-term services in a voluntary capacity to review and provide input into some areas under development – those areas I had previously been engaged in over five or six years before. I was particularly interested in the developments in post-graduate medical education, in which I had expended most of my time and effort during my formal affiliation with the institutions some years ago. My overtures were warmly acknowledged by Shabuddin Sulaiman, the regional CEO of AKHS East Africa; Amin Kurji, the AKDN's diplomatic representative in Tanzania; and Mushtaq Ahmed, the associate dean for PGME for AKU.

Much had changed in those years: the hospital had attracted several specialists in the much-needed areas of cancer medicine, critical care, kidney dialysis, interventional heart disease management, and surgery. Significant progress was achieved in nursing care, with added competencies in critical care nursing, cardiac care, and cancer chemotherapy services. Graduates from AKU's advanced nursing program brought up-to-date knowledge and skills into the care processes of the AKHD, significantly impacting the quality of medical care. Laboratory services were significantly upgraded, some with the voluntary support of visiting input and support from American and Canadian specialists.

My meetings with Sulaiman updated me on local and regional progress in clinical services development and medical and nursing education. In his expanded role as the regional CEO, he was better positioned to address issues of coordination and sharing of resources and strategy. He outlined the plans for the new phase of the hospital development's imminent construction of a new wing, a complex planning process that had suffered several delays over the years. He appraised me on the progress in upgrading the primary medical centres and the extensive exercise that we had both been deeply involved with. I was pleased to learn that some documents I had worked on to advance and harmonize primary and clinical care served as a template to continue the process of improving care quality in the PMCs.

My meetings with Mushtaq helped me get updated on the progress of the PGME efforts in Tanzania. Mushtaq shared the outline documents on the planned introduction of new PGME programs in internal medicine and surgery. The family medicine residency program was stable. The first few batches of graduates from the program were employed in senior clinical and administrative positions. He asked for my opinion on a request put forward by the Tanzania Ministry of Health to consider a much larger but scaled-down version of government frontline health care practitioners' training.

I called on the ANS program, where Kharunissa Damani, the head of the program, briefed me on progress in advanced nursing studies. I was delighted to learn that the regional ANS program had just introduced a master of nursing degree to upgrade nursing management further.

On my visit to the AKU-IED, I was impressed by significant developments in the field of educational leadership in the country and the high demand for the institute's training places.

I was immensely gratified when many of my former students shared their stories, their challenges, and their plans for the future. To be sure, there were some career and further education questions unresolved. Still, I advised them to be true to their calling and to seek appropriate opportunities within the AKU/AKHS network, national health services, and the private sector, including the local and foreign NGOs involved in health care.

I was invited to give a few lectures and to participate in several planning and review meetings, which I was most happy to do.

Amin Kurji, the AKDN head, was most generous and involved me in meetings with some visiting dignitaries from abroad. He kindly invited me to join a multidisciplinary conference to be held in Arusha to make recommendations on the development of the large AKDN/AKU campus. I was honoured to participate in the conference held on the wooded campus's grounds on the outskirts of Arusha. Organized by the Aga Khan Foundation, participants were from all the major agencies of the AKDN in East Africa. It was an excellent opportunity to reacquaint myself with many heads of AKDN agencies and make some small contribution to the campus's twenty-five-year development plan. It was envisaged that the campus eventually would serve as the main campus of Aga Khan University in East Africa and the planned Faculty of Arts and Science. Dr. Armstrong, the founding dean of the Faculty of Medicine for East Africa – a fellow Canadian from the University of British Columbia – shared developments in the faculty's programs and plans to establish a teaching hospital on the site.

Nilu and I took the opportunity to have a wonderful holiday in the stunning, world-famous Ngorongoro and Serengeti National Parks before flying out to Zanzibar. AKDN had worked for decades in boosting the cultural and economic potential of the island.

At the end of a most satisfying and fulfilling visit, I continued some periodic engagement with the AKDN. One area I was called upon was advising the health care of students, faculty, and families of the newly established Aga Khan Academy in Hyderabad, India. At later times, I consulted on the Health and Wellness Centres (HWC) of the Aga Khan Academies of Maputo, Mozambique, and Dacca, Bangladesh.

We visited India, where I thoroughly reviewed the organization and functioning of the HWC in Hyderabad. This beautiful facility provides a comprehensive education to the most qualified students, mainly focusing on developing local leaders globally.

While in India, I was well received by leaders of Aga Khan Health Services of India and the Prince Aly Khan Hospital in Bombay. This long-established hospital was in the process of significant expansion, adding new physical and programmatic structures. A brief meeting with Sultan Pradhan, a prominent surgical oncologist, whom I had met during his visit to Karachi decades ago and later on my earlier visits to India, was a happy occurrence and an honour. For decades, the Sultan had been involved with AKHS India and given sterling service with his acumen, foresight, and deep commitment to the institution and the people.

As I reflect back to the history, vision, mission, and trajectory of Aga Khan Health Services and Aga Khan University, I recognize with all humility the extraordinary privilege and honour extended to me in my affiliation with these global institutions, which have struggled for decades to "humanize" medicine and make health tangible for millions of people in the developing world.

We are witnessing a massive acceleration in the rate of global change. Today's world is a living environment in which you will have to adapt much faster than your parents did in order to have a positive and constructive impact on the future. Having said this, the means at your disposal to achieve such an impact have multiplied exponentially during the last decade. Never before has there been so much knowledge available about so many different people; never before have we know more about the physical world in which we live; never before therefore have the opportunities been greater to make a better life for more people around the globe.

The Aga Khan, Providence, Rhode Island, U.S., 1996

EPILOGUE

Where is the wisdom we have lost in Knowledge? Where is the knowledge we have lost in information?

T.S. Eliot

The ecology in which human societies dwell – natural and human-made – has altered dramatically in the last few decades in virtually every corner of the world. Burgeoning population growth, rural to urban migrations, population displacements due to wars and conflicts, famine, and economic and political stresses have reshaped the world.

The changing landscape impacts not only human populations but also all inhabitants of the natural world, which is undergoing profound change – and, in many cases, irreversible damage to biodiversity. Species loss is proceeding at an unprecedented rate. Millions of flora and fauna species are extinct or considered at risk, as their natural habitats are lost to encroaching human settlements caused by the clearing of vast tracks of forests, damming, and the diversion and pollution of waterways, lakes, and seas. Destabilized and collapsing ecosystems, changing weather systems, rising sea levels, melting glaciers, increasing greenhouse gases like carbon dioxide and methane lead to global warming and increase the risks of natural disasters – from extreme heat events and forest fires to floods, hurricanes, and heat waves. The planet is at a tipping point, the hottest it has been for the last few centuries. Unmitigated, it could lead to irreversible damage, impacting even critical resources, such as water supply, food production and supply, and national security, and leading to "climate refugees" to add to the problem of economic refugees and political refugees.

Alarm bells of global warming and its consequences were being sounded as far back as four decades ago. Yet, resistance, disinformation, and distortions posed by entrenched and powerful industrial and commercial interests such as the fossil fuel industry, agriculture, and cattle ranching fostered political inertia for decades to address the impending yet predictable disastrous consequences. Global promise, it can be said, has been matched by national wariness. We have more communication, but we also have more confrontation; even as we claim growing connectivity, we seem to experience greater disconnection.

What do the climate and environmental crises have to do with human health, human development, and humanity's future?

Health defined in its broadest interpretation is a composite of biological, psychological, social, economic, and environmental factors. In this age of ready information and access to new thinking, developments, and technologies in areas that affect health and happiness are easily acquired, but in a world overloaded with "information", wisdom is less readily found.

Since the COVID-19 virus hit the world, trillions of dollars have been "found" – in economic stimulus packages, principally in the developed countries, through quantitative easing, massive purchases of government bonds, and other creative means. Yet, a trillion dollars diverted to improving the quality of life of vast numbers of people by enabling optimal health care could transform the experience of most of the tremendous human health challenges facing the world's populations today. One trillion dollars, a vast sum to be sure, is one and a half years of just the U.S. military expenditure. The world's richest 1 percent together own a staggering $165 trillion, more than 45 percent of all global wealth. Piles of money amounting to several trillion dollars are held by private equity and others awaiting lucrative investment opportunities. The world's top fifteen hedge fund managers collectively made over $25 billion in just 2020.

If one were to lose oneself in "blue-sky" dreaming, what might be accomplished with an investment of a trillion dollars in improving the quality of life of people all over the world? For one thing, we could protect humanity from the next pandemic, which could be even worse than the current COVID-19 pandemic. In all probability, we could prevent or cure most diseases plaguing humankind today, particularly those neglected ones.

Since the time I started writing this book, the COVID-19 pandemic has continued to take its toll on human health, health services, economies, and societies in every country on the planet. Grim statistics flash daily on news outlets – worldwide, over two million dead, more than twenty-five million infected, periodic lockdowns and restrictions, too numerous to keep track of, announced daily.

Resentment and backlash are evident and widespread, fissuring societies between those who support and those opposed to measures announced to curtail the virus's spread, resulting in clashes and dissension marked by rebellions and disobedience.

Remarkable medical and scientific promise has been achieved in mitigating the pandemic's effects through newly developed vaccines against the SARS-Cov-2 virus, the causative agent of the COVID-19 disease, a few through collaborative endeavours. However, with glitches in adequate vaccine production and supplies, delivery and hoarding have surfaced, pitting countries and regional blocs against each other, as each country or region vies to protect its population against the pandemic's devastating effects. This phenomenon of "vaccine nationalism" further exposes and aggravates the latent and overt tensions in global relationships at a time when international cooperation and partnerships are most crucial to tame what is a worldwide threat to the well-being of the whole of humanity. Developing countries with the least economic and diplomatic clout appear marginalized in the scramble for precious doses of the vaccines, even as they roll unevenly from production centres. As the director-general of the WHO recently stated, "No one can be safe, until everyone is safe."

The full impact of COVID-19 is still playing out. Hundreds of millions have had their lives disrupted or economically ruined. But the tragedy could have been even worse. A more virulent or mutated strain of the virus recently detected in some parts of the world could be the pathogen's dominant form, just when effective vaccines' arrival created a euphoric mood of renewed freedom. COVID-19 has changed the world, and its tragedy will be felt for years, but we need to raise awareness of the threat of pandemic diseases. It also gives us an inkling of the threat to the world from the climate crisis.

The risks posed by pandemics was known, and some governments maintain a risk register. On top of the U.K.'s register of risks was an influenza pandemic – a 1918-like influenza pandemic. In 2017, its effects on human health, health services, the economy, and populations were war-gamed. We knew what was at stake; now, we have firsthand experience. COVID-19 is caused by a coronavirus and not an influenza virus; this is what caught the response of some governments wrong-footed. And this is not thought to be the last pandemic the world will experience, nor the most devastating.

A substantial investment in anticipatory preparation could protect humanity from the next pandemic. We could transform the human experience of health and disease by preventing, treating, or curing most of the illnesses plaguing humankind today.

In 2018, one disease infected 230 million people and killed about 400,000, mostly children under five, mostly in sub-Saharan Africa. That disease, malaria, has been with us forever. The disease has killed perhaps half of all humans who have ever lived. Malaria is the world's greatest scourge, but it is preventable and curable. Targeted efforts in the last twenty years have halved deaths from malaria. But it still clings on.

Tuberculosis is a bacterial disease that kills almost two million people each year – overwhelmingly in the poor and middle-income countries due to chronic lack of funds and the growth of resistance of the pathogen to our treatments. We can change this. We can also effectively tackle other tropical diseases – such as schistosomiasis, a debilitating parasitic infection, which affects over two hundred million people.

Thinking even bigger, we could probably eliminate all tropical and infectious diseases. Thousands of doctors and scientists are striving to treat and cure the world's biggest killers: cancer, cardiovascular, and neurological disorders, which could be subdued with a large injection of cash and investment.

But if you want to make immense gains in public health on a global scale, and make them sustainable, there is one more serious, ambitious, complex, and expensive thing that needs to be implemented: universal health care. This scenario doesn't seem to something that is talked about by billionaires seeking quick profits, or by governments seeking rapid economic recovery by traditional industries and stimulus.

The World Bank published its first analysis of global health: *World Development Report 1993: Investing in Health*. The report targeted government finance ministers and showed that health expenditure could improve prosperity and individual well-being. To mark the publication's twentieth anniversary, an international *Lancet* commission put together an investment framework to achieve what they called a "grand convergence" in health by 2035. By this, they mean a reduction in deaths from infectious diseases and child and maternal deaths, which could save ten million lives by 2035.

The return on investment in health care is very substantial. By avoiding long periods of poor health, we can generate an economic return that outweighs the health care investments we've put in by a factor of between nine and twenty. It is striking that spending what seems like an impossibly vast sum of money will offer large economic returns.

The document also states that convergence is achievable in less than a generation. Hence, investment in health could pay dividends relatively quickly. The report also claims that universal health care is the most efficient way to achieve convergence in global health. An equitable health care system is necessary to improve maternal and child health, address chronic diseases, improve end-of-life care, and fight epidemics.

Yet, while a trillion dollars isn't enough to change the world health care system, vast improvements could be made in essential health care, including development and deployment of vaccines, improving surveillance and data collection to monitor the progress of eradicating diseases like polio, and addressing people's basic needs – fresh water, food supply, and the living environment. There is a need to support critical bodies such as GAVI, the Vaccine Alliance, an international body that subsidizes the cost of vaccines so that emerging countries can afford them.

At the moment, we have vaccines for fewer than thirty diseases. As well as COVID-19, effective vaccines against HIV, malaria, and TB would be transformational. There are more than 320 emerging infectious diseases, which call for new approaches to vaccine development.

While linked, the health care crisis and climate crisis are bell-weather metaphors for many other unresolved global questions impeding the quest for just humanity and a sustainable future. Amongst these could be counted militarism, human trafficking, forced and indentured labour, and human rights.

It seems outrageous – hubristic even – to suggest we can cure, prevent, or treat all diseases by the end of the century. But the last eighty years have led to previously unthinkable medical advances; the next eight decades can make our current best medicinal practices look like crude science and guesswork. To quote Aristotle: *"Our problem is not that we aim too high and miss, but that we aim too low and hit."*

Ultimately, achieving these big dreams requires unprecedented levels of collaboration and cooperation in global economic, diplomatic, and political arenas and a measure of trust, compassion, and generosity for a more equitable and humane society. Partnerships and alliances can take place at all levels: between national and multinational bodies, between organizations and professionals in similar or complementary areas of work, and between businesses and institutions. They can operate in and span the developed and the developing world.

Hence, to "humanize" health care and medicine, we must think beyond narrow national interests, short-term profits, and stark economic parameters as measures of healthy societies. It would require the progression of human evolution to the next level – characterized by a moral, ethical, and spiritual awakening.

> *To the question of whether I am a pessimist or an optimist, I answer that my knowledge is pessimistic, but my willing and hoping are optimistic.*
>
> *Albert Schweitz*

Appendix

U.N. Millennium Development Goals (MDG)
2000-2015

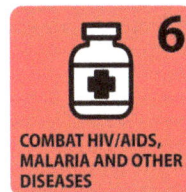

1 ERADICATE EXTREME POVERTY AND HUNGER

2 ACHIEVE UNIVERSAL PRIMARY EDUCATION

3 PROMOTE GENDER EQUALITY AND EMPOWER WOMEN

4 REDUCE CHILD MORTALITY

5 IMPROVE MATERNAL HEALTH

6 COMBAT HIV/AIDS, MALARIA AND OTHER DISEASES

7 ENSURE ENVIRONMENTAL SUSTAINABILITY

8 GLOBAL PARTNERSHIP FOR DEVELOPMENT

2015 Time for Global Action
For People and Planet

UN Sustainable Development Goals (SDG) 2015-2030

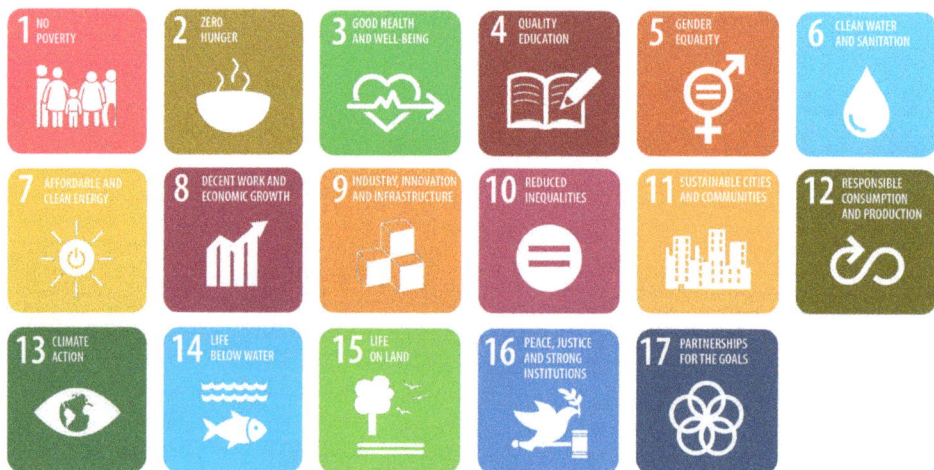

Sustainable Development Goals
17 Goals to Transform Our World

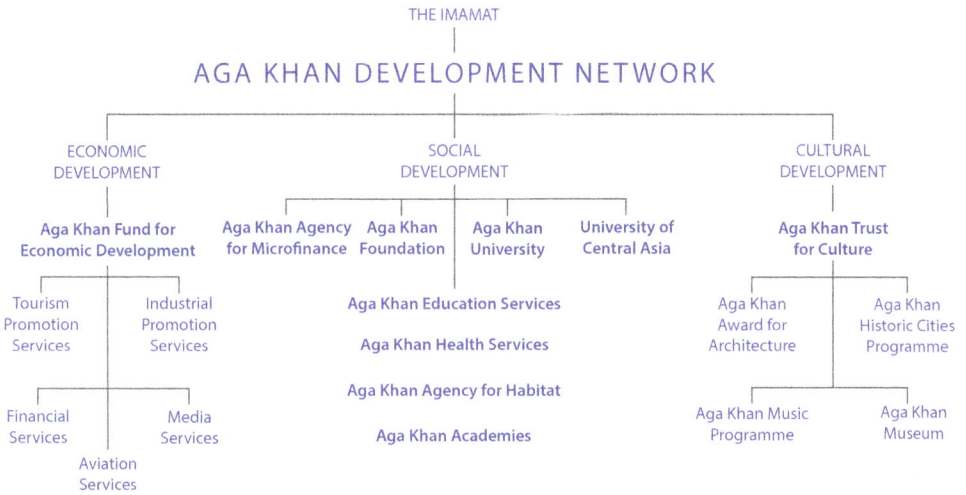

THE IMAMAT

AGA KHAN DEVELOPMENT NETWORK

ECONOMIC DEVELOPMENT

SOCIAL DEVELOPMENT

CULTURAL DEVELOPMENT

Aga Khan Fund for Economic Development

Aga Khan Agency for Microfinance

Aga Khan Foundation

Aga Khan University

University of Central Asia

Aga Khan Trust for Culture

Tourism Promotion Services

Industrial Promotion Services

Aga Khan Education Services

Aga Khan Health Services

Aga Khan Agency for Habitat

Aga Khan Academies

Aga Khan Award for Architecture

Aga Khan Historic Cities Programme

Financial Services

Media Services

Aviation Services

Aga Khan Music Programme

Aga Khan Museum

GLOSSARY

1. Aga Khan: His Highness Prince Karim Aga Khan, Aga Khan IV, is the 49th hereditary Imam of the Shia Ismaili Muslims. He succeeded his grandfather Sir Sultan Mohamed Shah, Aga Khan III in 1957. He is the founder and Chairman of the AKDN.

2. AKDN: A network of private, non-denominational development agencies founded by the Aga Khan, which works primarily in the poorest parts of Asia and Africa. The network focuses on health, education, culture, rural development, institution building, and the promotion of economic development. The AKDN aims to improve living conditions and opportunities for the poor, without regard to their faith, origin, or gender.

3. AKA: Aga Khan Academies

4. AKAH: Aga Khan Agency for Habitat

5. AKAM: Aga Agency for Microfinance

6. AKES: Aga Khan Education Services

7. AKF: Aga Khan Foundation. Established in 1967, the Aga Khan Foundation brings together human, financial, and technical resources to address the challenges faced by the poorest and the most marginalised communities in the world.

8. AKFED: Aga Fund for Economic Development

9. AKHS: Aga Khan Health Services

10. AKTC: Aga Khan Trust for Culture

11. AKU: Aga Khan University

12. AKUSON: Age University School of Nursing

13. AKRSP: Aga Khan Rural Support Program

14. AKUMC: An informal term used to collectively describe the Aga Khan University and its principal teaching hospital, the Aga Khan University Hospital in Karachi.

15. ANS: Advanced Nursing Studies Program

16. AKU-IED: Institute of Education Development

17. UCA: University of Central Asia founded in 2000, by His Highness the Aga Khan. It is a private, not-for-profit, secular university through an International Treaty signed by the Presidents of the Kyrgyz Republic, Tajikistan and Kazakhstan, forming one university, three schools. The university focuses on the social and economic development of mountain societies.

18. Anthropocene Era: A new, present day epoch. An unofficial unit of geological time, used to describe the most recent period in Earth's history when human activity started to have significant impact on the planet's climate and ecosystems.

19. Authoritarianism: A form of government characterised by rejection of political plurality, the use of strong central power to preserve the political status quo and blind submission to authority, that concentrates power in the hands of the leader or a small elite. Power is often exercised arbitrarily.

20. Brucellosis: A bacterial infection that spreads from animals to people. Animals that are most commonly infected include sheep, cattle, goats, and pigs.

21. Cosmopolitan Ethics: Is a way for all people on Earth to engage peacefully and pluralistically. It is rooted in a strong culture of tolerance.

22. Epidemiology: Is the study of the distribution and determinants of health-related states and events (not just diseases). It is also the application of this study to the control of health problems.

23. Filariasis: An infectious tropical disease caused by one of several thread-like parasitic round worms. These are spread by blood-feeding insects such as black flies and mosquitoes. Lymphatic filariasis, commonly known as

elephantiasis, is a painful profoundly disfiguring disease transmitted to humans through mosquitoes. It is a neglected tropical disease (NTD).

24. FRCS: Fellow of the Royal College of Surgeons. A higher qualification in surgery usually used in British systems – England, Scotland, Ireland, Canada.

25. House Physician and House Surgeon: A term used in British health care systems for a junior doctor, equivalent to an "intern."

26. JCI: Joint Commission International, a non-profit organization accredits and certifies health care organizations and programs across the globe. It is recognized as a global leader for health care quality and patient safety.

27. ISO: International Organisation for Standardization is an independent, non-governmental international organization that develops standards to ensure quality, safety, and efficiency of products, services and systems. ISO certification certifies that a management system, service, or documentation procedure has all the requirements for quality assurance.

28. Khyber Pass: Is a mountain pass in Pakistan on the border of Afghanistan. It is one of the most important trade routes and strategic military locations in the world. It forms a bridge between Central and South Asia.

29. Locum (or locum tenens): Is a person who temporarily fulfills the duties of another professional; especially used for a physician.

30. Leprosy: Also known as Hansen's disease is a chronic infectious disease caused by a slow growing bacterium. It mainly affects the skin, the nerves, mucosal surfaces of the upper respiratory tract, and the eyes. It can occur at all ages, and is curable.

31. Malaria: Is a disease caused by a parasite. The parasite is spread to humans through the bite of infected mosquitoes. It is a life-threatening disease and the Africa region carries a disproportionately high portion of global malaria burden. Children under 5 years are the most vulnerable group, and account for most of the deaths from this disease.

32. MUCHS: Muhimbili University College of Health Sciences. Affiliated with the University of Dar-es-Salaam.

33. Neurosurgery: A surgical speciality with the diagnosis and treatment of disorders that affect any portion of the nervous system, including the brain, spinal cord, central and peripheral nervous system.

34. NGO: Non-governmental organizations is a non-profit group that functions independently of any government. Sometimes called civil societies, they are organized on community, national and international levels to serve a social or political goal such as humanitarian causes, philanthropy, or the environment.

35. NTC: Neglected tropical diseases are a diverse group of tropical infections which are common in low-income populations in developing regions of Africa, Asia, and the Americas. They are caused by a variety of pathogens such as viruses, bacteria, protozoa, and parasitic worms. It includes diseases such as dengue, lymphatic filariasis, trachoma, leishmaniasis, cholera, and Ebola.

36. Ophthalmoscope: An instrument used to examine the eye. It can be used to see the back of the eye.

37. Otoscope: Is an instrument to look into the ears. It provides a view of the ear canal and the eardrum.

38. PGME: Postgraduate medical education.

39. Primary Care: The day-to-day health care given by a health care provider. Typically, this provider acts as the first contact and principal point of continuing care within a health care system. Its main purpose is to improve the health of individuals, families and communities.

40. Registrar: A term used in the British system for a physician or surgeon in higher formal specialised training program. Equivalent to "Resident" in the American system.

41. Resident: A physician enrolled in formal speciality training program.

42. RMO: Resident Medical Officer, usually a junior doctor attached to a medical service system in a hospital.

43. Secondary Care: Is the provision of medical care that can't be handled at the primary care level. It usually involves hospital care provided by specialists.

44. Silk Road: Was and is a network of trade routes connecting the East and West, and was central to the economic, cultural political and religious interactions

between these regions from the 2nd century BCE to the 18th century. It played a significant role in the development of civilizations of China, Korea, Japan, the Indian subcontinent, Iran, Europe, the Horn of Africa, and Arabia.

45. Tertiary Care: Care requiring highly specialised equipment and expertise, usually in a teaching hospital.

46. Trachoma: Is a disease of the eye, caused by a bacterial infection. It is a public health problem in forty-four countries, and is responsible for the blindness or visual impairment of about two million people.

47. UNICEF: The United Nations Children's Fund. It works in the world's toughest places to reach the most disadvantaged children and adolescents. It is also the world's largest supplier of vaccines, and supports child health and nutrition, safe water and sanitation.

48. WHO: World Health Organization. Its primary role is to direct international health within the United Nations' system and to lead partners in global health responses. It works in 194 Member States, across six regions, and from 150 offices. It is headquartered in Geneva, Switzerland.

MAPS

Map of Pakistan

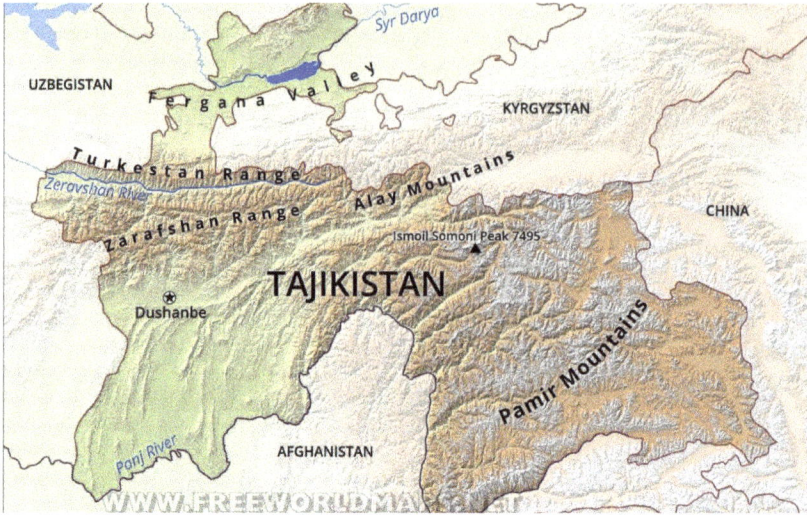

Map of Tajikistan

Map of India

Map of North Africa

Map of East Africa

Map of Uganda

Map of Kenya

Map of Tanzania

CPSIA information can be obtained
at www.ICGtesting.com
Printed in the USA
BVHW020718150921
616061BV00003B/2/J

9 781039 109070